THRIVING IN
TRANSITION

EFFECTIVE LIVING IN
TIMES OF CHANGE

Marcia Perkins-Reed

A TOUCHSTONE BOOK
PUBLISHED BY SIMON & SCHUSTER
New York   London   Toronto   Sydney   Tokyo   Singapore

TOUCHSTONE
Rockefeller Center
1230 Avenue of the Americas
New York, NY 10020

TOUCHSTONE and colophon
are registered trademarks
of Simon & Schuster Inc.

Designed by Irving Perkins Associates

Manufactured in the United States of America

10   9   8   7   6   5   4   3   2   1

Library of Congress Cataloging-in-Publication Data

Perkins-Reed, Marcia A.
Thriving in transition: effective living in times of change/ Marcia Perkins-Reed
p. cm.
"A Touchstone Book"
Includes bibliographical references.
1. Life change events. 2. Adjustment (Psychology) 3. Change (Psychology)
I. Title.
BF637.L53P47 1996   95–25479
158'.1—dc20   CIP

ISBN 0-684-81189-8

ACKNOWLEDGMENTS

The evolutionary process which resulted in this book did not occur in isolation. First, I express my gratitude to my agent, Helen Rees, for her patience and her support of this project. Thanks, too, to Cindy Gitter and Andrew Stuart, my editors at Simon & Schuster, and their staff for their helpful input into the finished product.

I am grateful to those whose work has preceded mine and which opened me to the possibility that transitions need not be painful, but can instead be a training ground. These authors include Charles Garfield, William Bridges, Stephen Covey, Marsha Sinetar, and Al Siebert, among others. I also acknowledge the authors who have translated Eastern philosophy and religion into terms Westerners such as myself can understand, including Stephen Levine, Joseph Goldstein, and Ram Dass. And I appreciate, too, scientists such as Dr. Fred Alan Wolf, Fritjof Capra, and Danah Zohar for helping to make quantum physics understandable to non-scientists.

To the individuals who have participated in my seminars and classes around the United States, to those who gave their time freely to be interviewed for the book, and to those who participated in the focus groups to offer their invaluable insight from the "trenches" of transition, thank you. And I must also acknowledge the many people who have been a part of my life as it has undergone its twists and turns, including my clients, my employers, my co-workers, my friends, my spouses, and my family. You have all—albeit unknowingly—taught me about transition, and how to thrive in it.

And finally, I offer a special thanks to my life partner and husband, Jay, for supporting me in so many ways as he allows me to freely express my creative self. The light of your love means more to me than I can begin to say.

CONTENTS

INTRODUCTION

Chances are, if you have picked up this book, you are facing a major change in your life. It may concern your job, your marriage, your health, loss of a loved one, or just the general state of flux in which we all find ourselves as our lives accelerate relentlessly. You have a vague sense of discontentment, of being lost among the crowd. You try to cope, but previously effective approaches no longer resolve the problem. You wonder if anything can.

This book is for you, and the thousands like you, who realize that you are treading that tentative ground between what I will be referring to as the Old Zero—a linear, sequential, orderly life pattern—and the emerging New Zero—a fluid, dynamic, discontinuous life map. In the Old Zero environment, our experience told us that life transitions occurred infrequently, and that the best way to face them was to "keep up a good front," or to "stay with it," thereby denying our inner experiences. We learned to blame others—*anyone* else—so that we didn't have to take responsibility for what was happening to us. We analyzed, manipulated, and controlled what we could until some sense of stability returned.

Constant change is now the norm. Whether we accept it or not, transition is occurring all around us—and within us. Our old strategies no longer suffice. Why? Because we face an entirely new kind of change today, and it requires new tools to manage it. The tools we need are the traits of the Thriver, described in the following pages. The Thriver approach has emerged through closely examining my own experience with change, researching the transition process, and studying those who manage change well.

My personal transitions have been many. I have moved at least two dozen times in my thirty-something years. My father died when I was at the impressionable age of twelve, and a friend was nearly killed by a drunk driver eight years later, just after we had spent an evening together. Two divorces, a new marriage at this writing, three career changes, and at least a dozen job changes have colored my history. I became a lawyer, started my own practice, and then sold the practice and my home two years later to embark on a yearlong nationwide seminar tour via motor home—following my heart and inner guidance. I have weathered over three years of recovery work and numerous other changes. And I have learned some approaches to facing change—simultaneous and sequential, voluntary and involuntary—which are so ingrained in me that I now actually *welcome* transition, and *enjoy* going through it.

Since the release of my last book, *When 9 to 5 Isn't Enough: A Guide to Finding Fulfillment at Work,* I have spoken at hundreds of conferences and worked with dozens of individual clients, coaching and discussing effective strategies for career transition in today's climate. However, I began to notice that people were also experiencing broader transitions than just those relating to their careers. "What you say is well and good," they would tell me, "but what about my situation? I've moved, become a parent, and am trying to become integrated into a new job and community, all in the space of the past year. I'm feeling overwhelmed!"

Others were facing difficult adjustments such as single life following a divorce or the death of a spouse. And still others were confronting their losing battle with an addiction to a substance or process and the significant life changes that accompany recovery from those addictions.

I set out to discover the strategies used by people who deal well with multiple, simultaneous changes—people I call

Thrivers (see Chapter 3). I compared my own transition strategies with those used by the Thrivers I read about and those I knew. I explored the fields of psychology, spirituality, physics, and organizational development to begin formulating an approach that would work not just in the job or career change arena, but during any time of major life change—and even when several transitions are occurring simultaneously. I began to teach courses and workshops on how to thrive in transition, sharing the Thriver Profile and a road map of the transition process. My students and seminar participants welcomed the ideas, and kept encouraging me to share the material with a wider audience.

But I was reluctant to put pen to paper without further exploration. So I began seeking people who had either faced one or more major crises in their life and come out a stronger person for it, or who seemed to be healthy, happy, and maintain a sense of balance and perspective despite numerous shifts and changes in their lives. I searched magazines, books, newspapers, and the extensive base of people with whom I have worked or become acquainted during my past ten years in business. Of those, I chose sixteen people (eight men and eight women) to interview in depth about their experiences in transition. The interviews lasted about an hour each. In addition, I chose representative stories of celebrities to factor into the equation. And finally, I conducted four focus groups to explore the differences (if any) between male and female styles of facing transition, as well as any variations between strategies for facing voluntary change and managing a crisis-type transition.

The Thriver Profile, then, as presented in the following pages, is the synthesis of this research. I have used parallels from quantum physics, psychology, and Eastern philosophy to further illuminate the concepts discussed. Thrivers have developed ways of being that enable them to remain unruffled by change. They share six clusters of character traits, which can be learned by anyone who makes a commitment to doing so. They have also developed the ability to use transitions as a training ground for their own evolution, welcoming each change as the vehicle through which new aspects of their character are revealed.

Thrivers understand the six phases of transition—Discontentment, Crisis, Sorting-out, Vision, Action, and Evaluation—and use them in facing everyday shifts. Though they may feel uncomfortable emotions, or find themselves in uncharted territory, they embrace these experiences and move through them with grace. Each transition they undergo builds on those which preceded it, increasing their inner strength and self-confidence.

HOW TO USE THIS BOOK

You may already be a Thriver, seeking even further development of your skills in managing change. I hope that you will find yourself reflected in the stories and concepts presented here.

Or you may be a would-be Thriver, hoping to glean the secrets to successful transitioning from the pages of this book. For you, a note of caution. As you read these pages, it will be tempting to read the principles and the examples given, and to simply try to "do what they did" to deal with your transition. While that may work in a handful of cases, this book is not intended to be a recipe which, if imitated exactly, will guarantee that you emerge a Thriver. Thriving is not about imitating behaviors; it is about accessing inner resources and marshaling them to face increasingly complex life changes. It contemplates that each individual will develop an inner stability that is not altered or threatened by external circumstances.

Remember: if your old ways of coping still worked, you wouldn't be reading this book! To confront transitions today requires a new kind of openness. This way of being has no hard and fast rules, but is fluid and changing like the waves of the sea. Yet it has a feeling about it that is recognizable only by consulting our own inner compass. It is an entirely unique experience for each of us, and yet there is a universality that I hope I have conveyed that allows everyone to find their own answers to their deep personal dilemmas.

This book is divided into four parts. In Part One, we set the context for change: what brought us to where we are today, how we have attempted to adapt, and the ten traits of those who do not adapt well to change, whom I call Copers. Then, in Part Two, we will become acquainted with the Thriver Profile—the six clusters of traits which characterize people who thrive during transition. In Part Two we will also explore the road map of the transition process—an entirely new Dynamic Model of Transition which describes transition in *today's* world.

Part Three explores each of the six clusters of the Thriver Profile in detail, offering real-life examples from the subjects interviewed for the book. Part Four then applies the Thriver approach to specific transitions such as career change, divorce, grief following a loved one's death, and addiction recovery. It also addresses "complex transition," in which several changes occur simultaneously.

Finally, I include two appendices for your use. Appendix A is a resource list of books and contacts which provide more detailed situation-specific information, as well as some of the sources on which I have relied in compiling the Thriver approach. Appendix B offers a series of exercises which will help you develop the Thriver traits for yourself.

It is my heartfelt desire that this book illuminate the dark, confused places in you that long to move beyond just surviving, into a happy, vibrant, energizing life, in which you embrace, rather than resist, the transitions your life brings.

MARCIA PERKINS-REED
Portland, Oregon
Fall 1995

PART ONE

A CONTEXT FOR CHANGE

1

FINDING
A NEW ZERO

❧

*The jolting changes we are now experiencing
are not chaotic or random but, in fact, they
form a sharp, clearly discernible pattern. . . .
Moreover, these changes are cumulative—
they add up to a giant transformation in the
way we live, work, play, and think.*

—Alvin Toffler
The Third Wave

Change is engulfing us. Every day new species of lifestyle
emerge as we become increasingly mobile, as technological developments challenge us, as business becomes global, and as
families take on new forms. What used to take days now takes
fractions of a second. And we feel powerless to face the on-
slaught, let alone stop it.

We have been taught that life transitions occur infrequently,
requiring a sort of temporary adjustment but leading, inevitably, to renewed calm. Transition was just a "blip" on the
computer screen of our life; momentary, transient. What characterized the majority of our lives was the familiar family unit,
a stable community, a steady job, and a circle of friends that ac-
companied us throughout our lives.

Reading this scenario today, it hearkens back to another era. It does not typify the lifestyle of the near-twenty-first-century individual. Now change happens quickly and constantly. It does not come and go, but persists. It is always there, causing stress in every moment, yet unnoticed by most of us because it has become so much a part of our experience. There are times when we face crisis, such as the death of a loved one, a life-threatening illness, or an unanticipated job layoff. And there are other times—many of them—when we simply feel restless and discontented, sensing the need for something more. We want a different job. We crave more time with our family. We wish for better health. We long for spiritual connectedness—a sense of community.

The stability which used to follow crisis or change has vanished.

Peter, a successful forty-five-year-old investment advisor, knows the stress of transition firsthand. Having successfully re-covered from a logging accident at twenty-eight in which his back was broken, after which he spent months in bed recuper-ating, he found himself facing another kind of change. After eleven years of marriage, he felt discontented. He recalls:

> It probably took me two years to admit to myself, through a lot of counseling, that it wasn't the marriage I wanted, and that was really hard. It was especially uncomfortable thinking about separation, because my parents had divorced when I was twelve, so it took all that counseling for me to admit that divorce was even an option. I had a hard time acknowledging that I would do that to my daughter, or that I would face my truth about what I wanted out of a relationship, which wasn't what I was getting in the marriage.

Peter and his wife did divorce, but that was just the begin-ning of his time of transition. When his former wife accepted a job in a town five hours away from the couple's home, Peter as-sumed primary custody of their ten-year-old daughter Jenny. To assure Jenny as much stability as possible, he purchased the couple's house from his former wife, allowing Jenny to stay in her familiar school, neighborhood, and home. But Peter was accustomed to working sixty to eighty hours a week, including most evenings. Clearly, his new role as a single parent would require changes in his routine. So he decreased his workload to forty-five hours a week, but the strain proved greater than he anticipated: He contracted a serious case of the flu which left him bedridden for nearly a month.

> That was a real turning point for me, sort of like a low point. Economically all of a sudden I didn't make any money, and because of the way my income works, if I don't work it affects me for a couple of months afterwards. So basically I didn't make any money for four or five months. But that's when I realized I had to totally change how I approached my work, and how I thought about my time investment versus my level of income. As it turned out, between the year I'd worked eighty hours a week and the year after I'd been ill, I earned almost exactly the same amount of money, but in the second year I did it in 30 percent less time. I felt good about that.

Within just a few short months, Peter had experienced transition in three major life areas: his marriage, his role as a parent, and his work. His system overloaded. As the stress spilled over into his physical health, he had to make drastic changes in his approach to work and his lifestyle. His stable, familiar past was a distant memory.

Peter's situation is not unusual. Over the past several years, in my workshops throughout the country, I have heard thousands of individuals express frustration with the pace and intensity of their transitions. They struggled to deal with not just one change at a time, but multiple transitions occurring simultaneously. As they began to make career changes, they concurrently confronted marital distress, financial uncertainty, or identity crisis. They sought answers to such fundamental questions as "Who am I, and what do I want?" At times, I was not certain how to help them. My subsequent research and personal experience have shown that we *can* learn to live happily, even in the midst of such challenges, by learning the Thriver approach to transition.

OUR OUTMODED VIEW OF TRANSITION: THE OLD ZERO

For decades, the foundations of our society—from family to work life, religion to politics—have been fairly stable. Changing jobs, spouses, or the city or country in which we lived was relatively rare. Instead, we spent most of our life in the same company, the same community, with the same friends and an extended family group. Life-changing events such as the death of a loved one or the social stigma of a divorce or job termination substantially interrupted our otherwise calm existence. And when they did occur, we sought to bring them to a quick conclusion so that we could once again return to our comfortable, relatively static lifestyle. I call this slower moving, stability-seeking paradigm the *Old Zero.*

Zero represents our baseline: the point of departure from which a system begins. Whether we are discussing the temperature, a mathematical construct, or our own belief system, we begin at zero. The rest of the system flows from there.

In the Old Zero world view which dominated from the 1950s through the early 1980s, transition represented an event, a momentary interruption in an otherwise stable life experience. The Old Zero is illustrated in Diagram 1-1.

Diagram 1-1
THE OLD ZERO

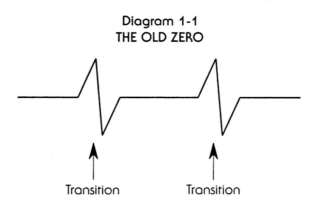

Transition   Transition

The Old Zero's observations about yesterday's external environment were substantially accurate. Stability and predictability were the norm until recently. In the Old Zero, as with the laws of Newtonian physics, objects and situations in our lives were viewed as existing separately from us. We acknowledged no fundamental connection between ourselves and our planet, or between the economy and events in other countries and ours; we functioned more or less independently. We saw ourselves as dynamic, and events as static.

But the Old Zero was not fully valid even when it prevailed. It assumed that when we emerged from a transition phase in our lives, we would be the same people we were when we entered it. However, by definition, transition ensures that it will transform us in some way.

A transition is a shift from one situation or state of being to another, whether gradual or abrupt.

In other words, transition is not a brief interruption, after which one's experience continues on the same level as before. Rather, transition is a passage *from one state to another.* The woman who has just been told that her husband was killed in an accident is not the same person who emerges one or two years later, having dealt with the grief and integrated his death into her experience. While she still has some of the same friends, and may still live in the same community, she is not the same person internally. She may be reluctant to go to the places she and her husband went to together for fear of stirring up uncomfortable feelings. Or she may find that she is rediscovering creative interests and aspects of herself that she had relinquished while they were married.

Today, the Zero point has changed. Shifts have begun to occur in technology and business that reverberate on a global scale and intensify our sense that we are experiencing more change than ever:

• *New computer technologies have speeded up the pace of our lives dramatically.* Such developments as artificial intelligence, the coming information superhighway (with its anticipated revolution in our shopping, banking, recreational, and personal habits), and virtual reality are products of the ever-increasing speed with which computers can process information. They threaten to overwhelm us, while challenging us to keep up. A recent poll of U.S. adults reflects the public's ambivalence about these changes: Although 63 percent believe computers have made life easier, 42 percent say the advance of technology is leaving them behind.[1]

• *We have become alienated from our natural rhythms.* Nearly 60 percent of us have used a computer at some time, either at work or at home.[2] As the computer invades our culture, it changes the way we perceive time. Whereas it is possible to experience clock time, the computer functions in nanoseconds, which we cannot experience. As Jeremy Rifkin so aptly observes in *Time Wars,* "Never before has time been organized at a speed beyond the realm of consciousness." Not only can we not experience computer time, but because it is an artificially created time system, it increases our separation from the natural rhythms of life. This alienation has contributed to the recent explosion in exploration of Eastern mysticism, holistic medicine, Native American practices, and going "back to nature," as individuals seek to rediscover a sense of connectedness.

• *We are working more than ever before.* It was predicted in the 1970s that by 1990, a thirty-hour workweek would be the norm. A crisis of leisure time was anticipated. But recent studies show that far from decreasing our worktime, we are working more than ever before. Between 1969 and 1989, the annual time worked by an average American rose by 158 hours, adding almost one month of work annually, while vacation and sick time shrank by 15 percent. Especially hard hit were women, whose work time rose 287 hours.[3] We seek a respite from a lifestyle that presses in on us from all sides, making stress and exhaustion more commonplace than we would like.

• *As the pace of life quickens, we place a higher and higher premium on efficiency.* Management strategies that emphasize quantity above quality dominated until very recently, when the Total Quality Movement began. This "quantity over quality" focus has been called the "new time" by Jeremy Rifkin: "The new time substituted quantity for quality and automatism for the rhythmic pulse of the natural world. . . . To become 'regular as clockwork' became the highest values [*sic*] of the new industrial age."[4]

We may wonder why the pursuit of quantity and efficiency has prevailed for so long. A study conducted by psychologists Robert Knapp and John Garbutt of seventy-three male undergraduates reveals the rewards of pursuing quantity over quality. They found that the highest achievers on standardized tests were those who placed a high value on the notion of speed. The correlation between achievement and valuation of time was determined by having the students read a series of phrases and then list, in order of preference, the expressions that evoked the most and least satisfying images of time. "The high achievers see time as an obstacle to overcome, and an enemy to defeat. They equate faster and faster learning with victory over time; to win is to beat the clock."[5] Although going to battle with time may result in a temporary victory—in the academic arena or in the global marketplace—its consequences in the form of violence, alienation, and a kind of "time poverty" for family and personal needs are hard to ignore.

To compound the speeding up of our lives, we are also making changes more frequently than we did in the past. Serial monogamy, multiple geographic moves, and frequent job changes in an individual's life are no longer looked upon as unusual, as they would have been under the Old Zero. We see evidence of increasing mobility in virtually every area of our individual lives:

• **Career Changes:** According to the U.S. Department of Labor, most people currently in the workforce will be employed in three to six careers during their lifetimes, each lasting approximately ten years. This number increases steadily as the duration of each career shrinks, with the new generation of workers anticipating some six to ten careers before their working lives are over.

• **Relationship Changes:** Relationships are also in flux. The divorce rate in the U.S. is now over 50 percent (much higher in some areas). Alternative forms of relationships and family units are emerging, such as those formed when two divorced people remarry and merge their respective offspring to form a blended family unit.

• **Workplace Composition:** The number of single workers has risen dramatically, leading to a pursuit for more meaningful interaction—a "surrogate family" for many—in the workplace. Nearly two-thirds of the new jobs in the next decade will be filled by women and minority workers, challenging employers to manage and capitalize on diversity in their organizations.

• **Geographic Mobility:** According to 1990 census data, nearly half of all Americans were not living in the same house— or even the same community—just ten years before, in the previous census.

THE NEW ZERO

In the face of such facts, we begin to realize that *the Old Zero model of transition is obsolete.* Transition is not an isolated event which is followed by calm; rather, it is a constant, discontinuous reality in our everyday experience. Moreover, we are beginning to discover that we are not separate from the events of our lives, but co-creators of them, just as in physics the scientist's expectations and beliefs inadvertently influence the phenomena he or she observes in experiments (more on that later).

Replacing the Old Zero model is a new archetype which I will be referring to as the *New Zero.* In this system, the norm is an accelerated pace of life which results in frequent—and sometimes simultaneous—transitions. The New Zero is illustrated in Diagram 1-2.

The New Zero requires that we develop the ability to flow with the changes that confront us rather than resisting them, and to accept that change is the norm and not the exception. It calls upon us to balance the pursuit of mechanized routines and efficiency—which served us well in the Industrial Age—with more organic life rhythms that emphasize quality, rather than quantity.

Diagram 1-2
THE NEW ZERO

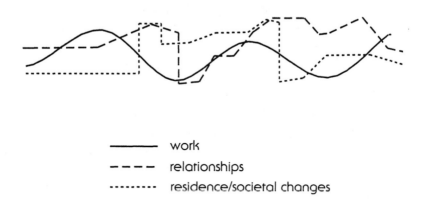

—————— work

– – – – relationships

· · · · · · · · · residence/societal changes

This approach to change is at once novel and ancient in its origins. The Eastern mystics have long understood the importance of viewing circumstances as transient. According to the Buddhist Doctrine of Impermanence, suffering comes "whenever we resist the flow of life and try to cling to fixed forms . . . whether they are things, events, people, or ideas."[6] The *I Ching*, a holy book of the Chinese, "is based on the conviction that, while everything changes all the time, change itself is unchanging and conforms to certain ascertainable metaphysical laws."[7] The principles of Taoism, too, embrace the notion of constant cyclic change: "If one refrains from acting contrary to nature or . . . 'going against the grain of things', one is in harmony with the *Tao* and thus one's actions will be successful."[8] These ancient teachings aptly describe the need in our current culture to once again honor the natural cycles of life, including change and transition. The pursuit of harmony, rather than mastery, should be our objective. By combining the insights of these great thinkers with the perspectives of modern technology and psychology, we can devise a strategy which will sustain us even in the midst of chaotic change.

In the New Zero, each transition overlaps with others of varying intensities. Just as we complete one transition (as Peter suc-

cessfully resolved his divorce), one or more new transitions begin—or are already in process (e.g., Peter's sudden single parent-
hood, combined with his health challenge and work changes).

**We now recognize this transformation from the Old Zero
to the New Zero as a "paradigm shift" which is occurring
in virtually all areas of our lives.**

The term "paradigm" was coined by science historian
Thomas Kuhn to describe a pattern or framework of thought.
A paradigm is simply a shared set of assumptions and beliefs
about the world and how it works. These beliefs help us explain our experiences and understand why things work the way
they do. When we have a "paradigm shift," we begin looking at
the world differently, which can allow us to find new solutions
to troubling old problems.

From the old linear, hierarchical, predictable paradigm, we
have begun to move into a world described as cyclical, fluid,
team-driven, flexible, and globally minded. This is the paradigm of the New Zero, which has ushered in the phenomenon
of what I will be referring to as *Quantum Transformation*. In
this environment, we are fundamentally transformed both in-
dividually and at a global level by our transition-laden lifestyle.
(See the diagram on the opposite page.)

As these trends challenge the very foundations on which our
society has been based, we begin to see that transition is an ongoing process. It will not cease, as long as we are alive, so we
must develop skills to be happy and healthy *during* transition,
not just after it is resolved. We have not been trained in how to
stay healthy—to thrive—during such challenging times. They
draw us to the very edge of our resources, forcing us to look
beyond what we have known, and develop new models for
dealing with our world.

Our old ideas, the rules of the Old Zero, die hard. And indeed when we are in the midst of one paradigm—even in its
late stages—it is extremely difficult to see the possibility of a
new one. For example, when we have just felt the blow of a
loved one's death, it is hard to imagine ever feeling happy

OLD ZERO	NEW ZERO
stability	fluidity
predictability	unpredictability
isolated transitions	multiple, simultaneous transitions
linear paradigm	cyclical paradigm
rigid hierarchies	flexible networks
moderate pace	accelerated pace
long-term employment	frequent job/career changes
delayed results	instantaneous results
lifetime marriage	serial monogamy
strong community ties	frequent geographic mobility
one family model	many family models
conformity	diversity
closed systems	open systems
regional/national emphasis	global/international emphasis
external structures	internal authenticity
dependency	self-responsibility

again. Some of us cling relentlessly to the Old Zero in a kind of denial, hoping it can still apply to us. Others have embraced the New Zero and are moving fully into it. And then there are the fence-hangers, halfway in the old and halfway in the new, not ready to accept the New Zero as the current norm.

The question is no longer whether we will experience frequent transition: we will! The question is, will we use it as an opportunity to learn and continually improve ourselves, or will we keep manipulating our circumstances in a desperate attempt to maintain our comfortable (if outmoded) quest for security?

Welcoming the New Zero as the baseline which applies to our experiences of transition today—and tomorrow—is the critical foundation we need to manage successfully the changes of our lives. As Jeremy Rifkin observes, "With everything changing so fast it is necessary to construct a temporal cosmology in which change is honored as the only timeless truth."[9] It is clear that things are different now, and that they will only become more different in the future. I will leave it to other authors to expound on how society should be different, or on whether we can stop or slow the waves of change. For our purposes, I will assume that change is a constant and that it will continue. With that as our New Zero, how can we successfully integrate constant change into our lives? How can we face not only crisis, but voluntary change in a healthy, enjoyable way, rather than viewing it as an unpleasant interruption of an otherwise happy life? In short, how can we learn to *thrive*—not just cope, or survive—as our lives undergo their constant process of change?

NOTES

1. Associated Press poll 2/94, as quoted in *The Oregonian*, February 22, 1994.
2. *Ibid.*
3. Schor, Juliet, *The Overworked American*, Basic Books 1992.
4. Rifkin, Jeremy, *Time Wars*, Holt & Co. 1987, pp. 86–7.
5. *Ibid.*, pp. 59–60.
6. Capra, Fritjof, *The Tao of Physics*, Shambhala 1991, p. 95.
7. Schumacher, E. F., *Small Is Beautiful*, Harper & Row 1973, p. 210.
8. Capra, p. 117.
9. Rifkin, p. 156.

2

COPING

MANAGING TRANSITION
IN THE OLD ZERO

❧

A skeptic often harbors an idealist within
who has suffered the pain of disillusionment
one too many times.

—Deepak Chopra
Unconditional Life

As Ellen began another week at her job selling database software to area hospitals, she noticed a gnawing inside. She had become quite successful in her six years on the job, and had recently been promoted to sales manager. But it wasn't enough. Ellen knew she needed greater variety in her job than she had. Could she find it within MedicManagement? She vowed to begin, in earnest, exploring her options.

When Ellen arrived at the office, she found her boss had left an E-mail message to meet with her at ten. "Good," Ellen thought, "this will give me an opportunity to start probing other possibilities within the company." But the meeting didn't give her a chance to do so. Instead, her boss told Ellen that although her performance was excellent and she would get a glowing reference from MedicManagement, recent market changes required them to make some layoffs. Today was to be Ellen's last day of work.

If you were Ellen, how would you respond? Would you consider this a disaster? An opportunity? Or a little bit of both? Your response will depend on whether you are a *Coper,* who relies on ineffective or outmoded strategies for coping with life changes, or a *Thriver,* who develops creative, innovative strategies to face change and grows in the process.

COPER CHARACTERISTICS

When faced with the prospect of any kind of major transition, we first respond physically. Shallow breathing, constricted arteries, heightened senses, and changes in our brain waves are augmented by secretion of various hormones in the classic "fight or flight" response. These reactions can even occur when facing a nonphysical change or stress, such as witnessing a violent act in a movie or computing a math problem. They are our way of "preparing for the worst," and sometimes cause us to resist what is necessary for our growth.

Complementing our physical responses is a wide range of psychological responses to transition. Coping is one of the ways we attempt to "adapt," or "make a fit," between ourselves and an impending change. In situations where only one major change occurs in our environment at any given time (the Old Zero), adaptation is relatively straightforward. We have a built-in "impending change sensor," which scans our environment to detect anything new or out of the ordinary, and lets us know that a situation which may require adaptation is coming. We then modify our behavior to respond.

Coping, however, is counterproductive in most cases because it is a defensive, reactive strategy, not a proactive one. While the common usage of the term "to cope" refers to an attempt to overcome problems and difficulties, its primary definition is to "maintain a contest or combat."

Coping puts us at war with change, rather than helping us to live peacefully with it.

We find ourselves combating transition instead of effectively managing it. We develop headaches, stomachaches, accidents, and excuses in an effort to avoid inevitable change. Coping makes us sick and tired, and offers us no lasting solutions. Clearly, coping is not the most empowering way to approach transition. However, we must understand what coping is, and to what extent we rely on it, before we can adequately modify our own patterns.

Coping, as we use the term here, is one of the adaptation strategies psychologists call "immature" or "maladaptive." One of the longest studies of adaptation ever undertaken, the Grant Study, overseen by George Vaillant, followed over 100 college men for more than forty years to assess their adaptability to life experiences. Vaillant identified some eighteen different adaptive mechanisms used at various times by his subjects. These strategies, drawn in part from the writings of Sigmund and Anna Freud, ranged from "psychotic mechanisms" such as delusional projection on one side of the scale, to "mature mechanisms," such as altruism and humor, on the other. They chose strategies that markedly impacted numerous aspects of their lives. Those subjects who used the mature mechanisms were found to be much better adjusted and much happier; made more money in careers that were more satisfying; and had better social lives and fewer mental and physical illness than those using immature mechanisms such as fantasy, projection, passive-aggressive behavior, and the like.[1]

Our ability to choose one of the mature mechanisms for dealing with change may vary depending on the amount of stimulation we face at any given time. When the amount of stimulation is within the range that we can effectively deal with—our "adaptive range," as Alvin Toffler calls it—we retain our sense of control over our destiny. If the amount of stimulation or change in our environment exceeds our adaptive range, however, we find ourselves unable to adapt effectively.

Individuals who make coping their *modus operandi* for life I call "Copers." They have chosen immature or maladaptive strategies for so long that they have become a habit. Their adaptive range has become so narrow that Copers don't believe they have any other choice but to react as they have in the past.

Let's look briefly at the **ten traits shared by Copers.** You will notice that they base their entire existence and philosophy of life on the assumptions of the Old Zero, which anchors them in the past and handicaps them in dealing with change today.

Need for Control

Copers need to believe they are in charge of their lives. In times of transition, they try to achieve resolution as quickly as possible, hoping that their stability and tranquility will return. And although psychologists have found that it is important to feel some sense of control in our lives to be healthy, Copers are overcontrolling. They complicate their lives to the point that it takes all of their energy to keep everything and everyone in line. They may create crisis after crisis—at work, at home, and in their personal life—so that they have an object for their crusade for control. Yet instead of utilizing the crisis as an opportunity for self-exploration and growth, Copers deal strictly with the external aspects of the situation. If a loved one dies, they make the funeral arrangements, send thank-you cards for donations and gifts, handle the deceased's estate and other affairs—and deny any feelings of sadness, loss, or grief. In my courses on transforming codependency into co-creation in the workplace, many participants identify with this "crisis manufacturing" process. They frequently comment that "If there isn't a crisis in my life, I get bored. I don't know what to do!" Millions of dollars and hundreds of employee hours are spent each day on crises that were manufactured by the Copers within the organization. This obsession with control, as it becomes more and more impossible to satisfy, can easily channel itself into addictive or compulsive behavior, as they desperately attempt to cope with the stress which results from their need to be in charge.

During transition, it is normal to feel disoriented, as basic segments of one's life are being rewritten. Yet Copers have a difficult time simply "being with" this disorientation, letting it run its course. To restore a sense of security, Copers may start a new diet just as they lose their job, or they may change to a radically new hairstyle simultaneously with the break-up of their marriage. These seemingly positive actions must be carefully scrutinized, for at this early stage they may constitute denial, distraction, or an attempt to smooth over their uncomfortable feelings.

To retain their sense of control, Copers try to shorten their transition by forcing external circumstances to move more quickly. Yet they may also feel a sense of emptiness, restlessness, and profound lack of meaning if they don't give themselves a "rest period" now and then (described later as the Sorting-out Phase of transition). This period, if allowed, would give them an opportunity to notice how they feel about each of the aspects of their life, and to consider any needed changes. They could then take appropriate action—which may include broaching a new career area or interest—to get themselves back on track with their inner passion and purpose.

Manipulation of externals is a Coper response to an unmanageable internal experience.

In other words, "If I can't manage my inner feelings, I'll find something in the outside world that I can change, and do it. Surely that will make these uncomfortable feelings go away." But it doesn't work—at least not for long. As one woman puts it:

> My relationship ended in December. I was dumped. I dealt with the rejection in my typical pattern: to fill every second of my time with something that doesn't allow me to feel or think about it. It's a very strong anger that drives it. I need[ed] to change jobs, so I applied my anger to this purpose. I was working my regular forty-hour job, then took a second job, and then signed up for classes. I have dropped down from forty hours on the second job to twenty-four hours due to class schedules. When physically I reach the end of my rope, I will deal with my failed relationship. In the meantime, I will get a lot done. I always do this. Somehow I can't just sit and think—I must act. I'm getting older and this method of dealing with crisis is getting rougher to handle. I can and will change it when I physically must.

There is a point in the transition process where a new body image, new hairstyle, or new job title may be appropriate experimentation, a trying on of a new role. But that can only occur after we have navigated the earlier stages of our transition: facing our crisis or discontentment, and being willing to experience a Sorting-out Phase (see Chapter 4), with its confusion and disorientation. The woman quoted above has not allowed herself to do this. Until she does, her efforts at manipulating her external circumstances will only postpone her growth and divert her energies from her current commitments.

Another danger in relentlessly trying to control external circumstances is that many life changes will not be easily or quickly resolved. For example, when Sara's marriage became intolerable, she moved out and immediately consulted an attorney. She asked the attorney to proceed as quickly as possible to file the necessary divorce papers (her objective being, of course, a quick resolution of this relationship transition). The attorney did so, but her husband was uncooperative. He hired an attorney to file documents opposing her petition, but refused to communicate with her and delayed the proceedings unnecessarily. Sara had two choices: she could be miserable throughout the delays and the legal process, experiencing depression and/or physical illness, and essentially put her life on hold until it was brought to conclusion. Or she could begin to explore her feelings, sufficiently grieve over the loss of her marriage, bring new people into her life for support and shared communication, and remain relatively unruffled by the external events that are happening to her. A Coper would choose the first path. When life presents them with an opportunity for self-exploration, Copers are too busy orchestrating the events and people in their lives to notice.

Mistrust and Suspicion

Copers mistrust everything. Overly skeptical, they believe that life and other people are fundamentally "against" them, and that they must constantly be on the defensive to avoid being taken advantage of.

Cindy was a person whose suspicion paralyzed her in her career path. As an engineer in a high tech firm, she believed that "If AB Company's new system is that much better than ours, they probably pirated the technology." She took every personnel move personally: "They must be trying to force me out." Cindy stayed in her job long after it ceased being a challenge for her, preferring stability to the uncertainty of considering a change. She was convinced that anything else would be so radically different from her present situation that she would have to prove herself all over again. It was simply easier to stay in the job she was familiar with than to open her mind to a more fulfilling opportunity that may exist elsewhere.

The suspicious nature of Copers can make them reluctant to take risks, whether in their personal or professional life. They have no innate trust in their internal resources, or in their ability to emerge successfully from voluntary (i.e., self-initiated) change. As a result, they often stay "stuck" in relationships and jobs that no longer meet their needs.

Left unchecked, suspicion, based as it is in fear, can ultimately manifest itself in the form of panic attacks, agoraphobia (fear of open spaces), or other neuroses. In most Copers, however, it simply constricts their life experience to a narrow range within which they feel safe. The unfortunate consequence is that they never tap the wonder and beauty of themselves or other people, nor many of life's adventures which they are unwilling to encounter because of their fear.

Disconnection from Spirituality

Another component of the Coper profile is their problematic relationship to religion and spirituality. Most Copers, even those that attend a church or synagogue, are fundamentally disconnected from their innate sense of spirituality. They may go through the motions of worship by celebrating religious rituals or attending services regularly, but they fail to draw any sense of personal meaning from these outward manifestations of spiritual activity. When a crisis or major life transition occurs, they lack the spiritual roots from which to draw support.

Spirituality, in this context, refers not just to religious affiliation, but to a belief in something bigger than themselves; an example of this is the "Higher Power" concept used in twelve-step groups. Whether conceptualized as a traditional God, nature, or an invisible but ever-present force for good, most Copers are reluctant to embrace such an idea—until they really need it.

Copers believe the parameters of life lie only in what they can see, a viewpoint that inevitably leads to disbelief in a greater spiritual dimension beyond the material world. Accordingly, they have a tendency to try to exert control over other people and things. If they do talk to God, they often try to tell Him what to do. In *A Return to Love,* Marianne Williamson explains the basis for this characteristic:

> The issue underlying our need to tell God what to do is our lack of trust. We're afraid to leave things in God's hands because we don't know what He'll do with them. We're afraid He'll lose our file.[2]

To move beyond mere coping, we must learn to develop a sense of surrender to and connectedness with a Higher Power. To Copers, this prospect can be frightening. They are afraid that God will call on them to do something they don't want to do. Marianne Williamson further describes it:

> Some people have said, "But I'm afraid to surrender my career to God. I'm a musician—what if He wants me to be an accountant?" My answer to that is, why would He? Wouldn't He rather have someone who understands numbers do that job?[3]

This reluctance (or refusal) to believe in God, and to trust God's action in their lives, may stem from a disillusioning experience in the Copers' past in which they feel God has let them down; or perhaps they had no spiritual training in their upbringing, so spirituality never became an important part of their everyday life. As adults, they felt no need to explore it.

Whatever the reason, Copers have not pursued spirituality as a key dimension of their lives (which, as we will see, is an important aspect of the Thriver Profile). Instead of believing in something larger than themselves that they can turn to in times of crisis, they have become overly self-reliant and self-sufficient; they have to make their own way. While these traits are not negative in themselves, they frequently evolve into ego-centered behavior and a belief in one's indispensability ("No one else can do it like I can"). This in turn leads to a false sense of fulfillment in their jobs and relationships—until the day comes when they lose their job, their spouse, or their health and must confront the fact that life will go on—even without their performing their former roles. This can be devastating to their psyche. And without a solid spiritual foundation, the process of rebuilding their life can be a lengthy, tortuous one.

No Sense of Purpose

Developing a sense of mission or purpose eludes Copers. Either they have not yet confronted difficult questions such as "Why am I here?", or they have asked the question and found the answers lacking. Our sense of purpose often (but not always) emerges through our spiritual beliefs, as a "calling" for our lives. Since Copers are disconnected from their spirituality, the issue of life purpose has little significance for them. It is as though they are adrift on the rough waters of change, but they have no guiding force or principles to steer them through the turbulent swells.

No entrepreneur would expect to launch a successful business today without a mission statement. Yet Copers try to manage their lives that way. By going from one day to the next and doing only what is in front of them, they never identify with a higher purpose or consider the reason for their life activities. They lack what Stephen Covey calls a "personal mission statement": a personally authored "constitution" for their life which expresses the vision and values that are most important to them.[4]

The majority of my career counseling clients are perplexed about their purpose in life. And without that sense of purpose, any career decisions they make will lack cohesiveness. A sense of mission or purpose provides the template by which we determine which activities and people to allow into our lives, and which to decline. If we understand, for example, that our life purpose is to bring beauty into the world, we will study and work in areas such as home decorating, flower arranging, painting, or other activities which help us develop our creative self-expression. We are unlikely to participate in anything which has no intrinsic aesthetic value, such as computer programming or statistics, unless we see a way in which those activities can serve our purpose.

Living without a sense of purpose, Copers rarely (if ever) experience the satisfaction of achieving an important dream or aspiration. Though they may set goals and carry out the activities to achieve those goals, they either fall short of finishing them or feel empty upon completion, because there is no higher purpose for their accomplishments. Copers live at the surface level of their lives, failing to probe the deeper meaning of their experiences. Until they transcend this limited view, they cannot fully experience the transformation which awaits them in the transitions they experience.

Victim Thinking and Blaming

Another trait shared among Copers is their tendency to blame other people and circumstances for their situation in life. When something happens, it's "their" fault; "they" did it to me; "I'm going to get those so-and-so's."

Unlike Thrivers, Copers allow the circumstances of their lives to limit them. Consider the story of Brian Tracy, who, through his own determination and curiosity to discover the secrets of wealth, emerged from a background of poverty to become an independently wealthy motivational speaker. His disadvantaged beginning in life became a catalyst, a driving force which stimulated him to find a way to become wealthy and successful.

When presented with such stories, Copers will insist that these individuals were "lucky," that the hand of fortune was kind to them, or that some other "stroke of luck" caused these people to become rich, to regain their health after a tragic accident, or to achieve success in their field without the traditional education or training. To the Coper, these people are in a different category—out of reach and hence fair game for criticism, jealousy, and ridicule.

By separating themselves from the ranks of the affluent, healthy, and successful, Copers can justify their life choices and buttress their beliefs about life by showing how "it never happens to me." The Coper "wins" in the sense that his or her beliefs are proven to be true—but at what price? Playing the victim and blaming external forces for their lot in life prevents them from maximizing their capabilities. They never have the opportunity to tap their true potential and see what they could create if they set their mind and energy in a positive direction.

Psychologists refer to individuals who adopt the victim/blaming orientation as having an "external locus of control." That is, these people believe that the forces controlling what they do, how they react, and how they feel are outside of themselves. If they have planned a camping trip and it rains all weekend, they believe the only choice is to be upset by the bad weather. External events—such as their favorite team losing a game or their car being damaged while parked on the street—control their feelings.

Copers are reactive, rather than proactive, in their own lives. They think that life happens to them—that they are not involved in creating their own experience. At the whim of their life experiences, feeling no sense of control or initiative, Copers have far more difficulty dealing effectively with major transitions because they believe circumstances determine how they must feel.

The following questions will help you determine whether or not you have an external locus of control:

1. Do you blame your upbringing for the quality of your emotional life today?
2. When your plans for the day are changed by external circumstances, do you become upset by the change?
3. Do you expect your boss or your company to provide you with fulfillment and challenge in your work?
4. When you spend time with friends, do you let their opinions, moods, or statements influence how you feel?
5. Do you usually let your spouse or partner decide what activities to do, where to go, and how the time is spent when you are together?
6. Does a substantial portion of your conversation center on "things" (the weather, the cost of living, activities, and what other people think about those things), as opposed

to internal subjects such as feelings, your relationship with the person you are talking to, or what matters most to you and to them?

If you answered "yes" to several of these questions, you will benefit from building a more internal locus of control. We will explore ways to do this in the next chapter.

Since Copers look outside themselves for the cause of their experience, they repeat the same patterns over and over. They may marry several spouses with very similar personalities that effectively complement their victim stance.

I do not mean to suggest that anyone would do this consciously. Usually the only way to recognize this unintentional, subconscious process is to examine the area of life that is causing us unhappiness. By becoming aware of our patterns, we can then make an informed choice to change, if we want to. It is a Thriver trait to examine our lives, to become aware of our patterns, to accept our part in creating the situation, and to change.

Disconnection from Feelings (Especially Negative Ones)

Copers have not developed a vocabulary of the heart. Raised in families where strong emotions were not acceptable, they have no outlet when they feel angry, sad, guilty, or hurt. They are detached from their emotions, often unaware of what they are feeling at any moment. As a result, they rarely experience a full range of emotions when they are in the midst of the disturbing changes of transition. "Oh, I'm fine," they tell everyone, while holding their true emotions in check. They limit themselves to the so-called positive emotions of love, happiness, joy, and excitement, repressing their negative feelings and hoping that they will simply disappear from lack of attention.

As a result, Copers' awareness of themselves is limited. According to the "Johari Window" model (see Diagram 2-1), we have four "panes" in our self-awareness. First is the Open pane—what we know about ourselves that others also see. This is the part of ourselves that we show the world. Second, we have a Blind segment—those things about us that others see but we don't. If we manifest strong emotions through facial expressions, tones of voice, or other mannerisms of which we are unaware, they fall within this second pane. This pane is disproportionately large in the case of the Coper. Third is the Hidden pane, the private segment which contains things we know about but try to keep concealed from the world—our "deep, dark secrets." And fourth is our Hidden Potential, the parts of us which have yet to evolve. These are the parts which often emerge during transition.

Diagram 2-1

JOHARI WINDOW[5]	
Open	Blind
Hidden (Private)	Hidden Potential

Copers' incomplete self-awareness results in their getting "stuck" in loops of repetitive, counterproductive behavior, the causes of which they are entirely unaware. Faced with transition, their first instinct is to react as they did in the past. So if the last time they began having relationship problems they withdrew emotionally and refused to confront the issues, that will be their first coping mechanism when those issues recur. Or, if they are more confrontational by nature, they will react angrily, blame the other person for being wrong, or stomp out of the room. These two examples of ineffective responses to conflict and potential transition are "knee-jerk" reactions. They may temporarily ease the pain, but allow the real issues to go underground. They rarely result in permanent resolution of the matter, nor do they facilitate growth in the individual.

For most of us, it takes a number of cycles of this kind of behavior before we realize we are in a rut. We begin to notice that the same dynamics occur with *every* boss we have, or *every* intimate relationship—not just one person. We are then moving toward the Thriver Profile, preparing to examine our behavior, become aware of our feelings, and make a conscious choice to change. Until we begin the process, however, we are helplessly trapped in an endless unfulfilling cycle.

Times of transition are fraught with emotion. It is natural to feel pain from the loss of a job, marriage, health, neighborhood, or other trappings of our pre-transition life. There may be a vague sense of uneasiness, frustration, irritability, or unusual tension. At first, it's nothing specific, just a more acute emotional state than usual. Copers try to go on with their daily routine, hoping it will pass. Then they notice that they forgot what someone told them only yesterday, or they miss an important deadline at work. They wonder what is wrong with them.

If they refuse to face their feelings directly, they may experience unexpected outbursts or unexplained depression. Their denial of their feelings also causes them to carry emotional baggage into their new situation, inhibiting them from living up to their highest ideal. The core of their being becomes clouded by resentment, unforgiven hurts, perceived wrongs, and unacknowledged losses. Copers erect walls around their hearts to keep them from being hurt or wronged again. Unfortunately, these walls also prevent them from fully experiencing their lives, let alone thriving during times of transition.

Rigid Thinking

Copers hold fast to their pre-conceived models of the world. As they search for the One Right Answer to the challenges of their lives, their rigid thinking blinds them to other, more creative options.

You know people with this kind of thinking. Their style of prejudicial, parochial thinking forces everything they encounter into one of a limited number of predefined categories. There is no middle ground in this kind of a system; everything is black or white. There are no shades of gray. Unfortunately, there is also no room for inventing a new way, for finding a new answer, or for changing one's personal paradigm about life.

Systems of thinking that become rigid are destined to decay and die, much like a plant that becomes brown and stiff as it loses its life. Vitality and fresh ideas can no longer enter the system. Shutting out new input and failing to keep learning and growing can lead to increasing discomfort for the aging Coper. As the mind clings to its rigid (and soon outdated) models of the world, the physical body stiffens in response, often resulting in mental and emotional depletion.

Copers have not developed the ability to cultivate new interests, activities, and relationships. As a result, they tend to age less successfully and less happily than Thrivers. Their rigid thinking alienates them from others and hardens them into people who are disturbed by change, rather than thriving in it. And their entire lifestyle can take on a stiff, lifeless tone, as though they are just going through the motions of living.

Negative Attitudes

To Copers, the proverbial glass is always half empty. They think the worst in every situation, and allow their own beliefs to do them in. Recently, in Germany, a coal mine disaster occurred:

> A small group of miners were trapped underground after a massive cave-in. They realized that the air in the mine shaft would last only a limited number of hours. As it turned out, just one of the group was wearing a wristwatch, and he began to announce the time while the men anxiously awaited rescue. To sustain hope in the others, he did not announce the right time, however; he called out one hour whenever two hours had passed. Six days later, a rescue team found the trapped miners; astonishingly, they were all still alive with one exception—the man who wore the watch.[6]

The man with the watch was less hopeful about the group's chances for rescue and survival because he knew the real time. His beliefs caused him to lose hope before the others—with tragic consequences.

This true story illustrates the tremendous impact of our beliefs on our experience. Copers' negative beliefs about life— even if based in fact—become self-fulfilling prophecies. The Pygmalion Effect, in which students who are thought to be less talented or intelligent than the rest of the class become that way in response to their teachers' treatment, is an unfortunate result of holding such beliefs, whether about ourselves or others.

Successful appliance and furniture retailer Tom Peterson knows the devastating effects of this phenomenon:

> I was a relatively average student—C's, D's, [an] occasional B. And when I got into my senior year of high school I decided I really wanted to be a chemist, so I really beared [sic] down in chemistry and physics, and I got straight A's. I took my SAT test, and when the counselor gave me my results, she said, "Tom, you rank in the 1st percentile of all graduating seniors—that's the *bottom* 1 percent. I really thought you were a better student than that. You shouldn't go to college, you just don't have those kind of skills. Get a job laying asphalt, working on a road department someplace."

Peterson was heartbroken, particularly in light of his father's insistence that he get an education since his father hadn't had that opportunity. Peterson found an ally at a Minnesota college who allowed him to enter college even with his low SAT score. But the stigma of that designation—"the bottom 1 percent"— thwarted his efforts. He got D's and F's in every course, and quit. It was only a few years later, when he tried college again in an extension course and asked to take the SAT over again that he learned that his initial results had been distorted: the pencil he had been given to take the test was not electrographic, so the electrographic machine could not read any of his answers and scored his test as though he had answered every question wrong. In fact, he was in the 70th percentile!

Because Peterson is a Thriver, he did not let the label established by the distorted test permanently stand in his way. Copers, on the other hand, will allow this to happen. They internalize the labels placed on them by others and develop a belief that they can only be as good as their labels. Rather than challenging these aspects of their self-concept, they allow themselves to remain stuck in unfulfilling situations, with their beliefs "justifying" why they can't be proactive in improving their lives. They are held captive by their own perceived limitations.

No Healthy Support Systems

Copers are often loners. If they do have a group of core friends, they consist of others who share their fundamentally negative beliefs about life. They reinforce each other's pessimism and sabotage any efforts at proactive change. You know the type—they're clustered in the office coffee room, devouring the latest gossip or rumors about their co-workers, the company, or the boss, or moaning about how terrible their lives are because of their spouse, their chronic aches and pains, or their background.

This attribute was examined in the Grant Study referred to earlier. Working from the premise that mental health and the capacity to love are in some way linked, the 100 men were ranked as either "friendly" or "lonely." Ranking was based primarily on whether the individual had achieved a relatively stable marriage and made a few sustaining friendships, and on the researcher's subjective experience of each man. Thirteen of the men in the study were classified as Lonely, twenty-seven as Friendly, and the balance in between. The Lonely men had by far the poorest adolescent social adjustment. Half were distant from their own children. Their mothers tended to dominate their adult life, and they had much higher incidences of physical and psychiatric care than the Friendly men.

Interestingly, 85 percent of them failed to take their full allotted vacations, and the same percentage exhibited immature defensive styles. But the most striking difference between the Lonely and the Friendly men was that the Lonely men were more frightened. They expressed a fear of sex; were afraid to trust others; and, lacking faith in their athletic ability, shunned competitive sports.[7]

It is the feeling of separation as much as the fact of being a loner which contributes to the Coper Personality. Alienation, or a feeling of separation, has been shown to increase the strain we experience when faced with stress. Psychologist Suzanne Kobasa assessed the stress from recent life events of 157 general practice lawyers, and found that although the stressful events alone did not determine whether or not the individual suffered resultant illness, the personality characteristic of alienation and the use of regressive coping techniques were important determinants.[8] So if we feel a sense of separation, we are more likely to become ill during or following a transition than if we have a support system on which we can rely.

Lack of a healthy support system can be especially devastating when we are faced with a major crisis, such as the death of a loved one. Grief specialists have found that when a loved one dies, those who have an established network of friends, family, and other support on which they can rely integrate the loss most easily, without risk of "complicating" their grief process.

Lack of Balance/Achievement Orientation

Copers tend to be out of balance in their lives. They place an unwarranted emphasis on external "things"—the house, the car, the schedule, the job—and less attention on their relationships, their hopes, desires and passions, and their innate creative abilities. They pursue achievement rather than balance, becoming workaholics or withdrawing into other kinds of escape: alcohol, drugs, compulsive shopping, sex, or gambling. They have taught themselves to ignore how they are really feeling.

It is not uncommon for the Coper's identity to be entirely enmeshed in their work. They believe they are what they do. And when confronted with a conflict between work and family loyalty (e.g., an important client meeting conflicts with a daughter's school play), they will usually choose the work-related commitment. Since they draw their sense of self from the work they do, any opportunity to further cement their personal value through achieving at work will be pursued. It is not until they face a major life crisis that they may reconsider their priorities (if even then).

This trait of disproportionate achievement orientation is not without consequences in the personal lives of Copers. In *Pathfinders,* Gail Sheehy describes an exercise she conducted with over 100 young women successful in finance. Each of them had achieved success in her field and was earning $30,000 or more annually. Sheehy had them graph their ups and downs at five-year intervals throughout their life in three key areas: (a) achievements, (b) personal relationships, and (c) overall life satisfaction. Then, she asked them to determine whether their overall satisfaction line correlated more closely with their achievements or their relationships. These professional women were astonished to learn that their overall satisfaction was significantly more closely related to their relationships than to their achievements, although their primary focus up to that point in their lives had been their work. (Sixty percent of the participants were childless, and half of them were unmarried, despite being in the thirty-something age range.) As one participant stated, "Unless you step back and look at what you're giving up to be a high achiever, a malaise might come over you from years of neglecting needs you denied you were dragging around."[9]

On our deathbeds, very few of us will say, "I wish I'd spent more time at the office." We are more likely to feel that what we missed was time with our families, time pursuing interests that have meaning for us, and time for ourselves. While we should not have to wait until we are confronted with crisis to realize what really matters in our lives, many of us do. Copers proceed through life, doing solely what's required of them in their jobs and other commitments. They remain oblivious to the fact that they have few good relationships in their lives, and that those they do have are faltering due to lack of attention.

The Coper approach is exemplified in the following scenario, from *Lifebalance* by Linda and Richard Eyre:

> Imagine a busy professional man, driving home from the airport after a week-long convention out of town. It's Saturday afternoon, and he's anxious to see his family. The two or three weeks prior to the convention had been so hectic that he was getting home after dark every night and after the kids were in bed. He turns onto his street and sees a small girl playing in his front yard. A friend of his daughter's, he guesses. She looks a little older than his daughter—maybe a new family has moved into the neighborhood. He wonders where Sammy is. She must be around, or this little friend wouldn't be here. It is not until he pulls into the driveway and the girl runs toward the car that he realizes it *is* Samantha. How can she have grown that much? He feels a pang of joy as she reaches up to hug him—and then a wave of guilt. His own daughter. For a minute he didn't recognize his own daughter.[10]

This Coper has a skewed sense of priorities. If most people are asked to assess the relative importance of work versus family and to compare their stated priorities with the time and energy they devote to each, there will often be an inverse relationship. That is, most people will say their family is more important than their work, yet they spend more time and energy on their work. When faced with a major life shift, such as job loss or financial reversal, a profound disorientation occurs. Rather than face this disorientation head-on, Copers will look for the most expeditious route to a new job or a new money-making strategy so that their sense of stability is restored. This strategy can be like trying to hold one's finger over a water leak in a thin plastic bag: it may plug that leak, but the water will just come out somewhere else. The next overlapping transition will occur, and their energy is drained in this endless cycle of crisis management. The lifeboat is sinking fast, and they are in it—unless they rethink their strategy.

Copers fail to understand the importance of the relationships in their life, nor do they devote time to cultivating them. They are too busy scaling the career ladder, monitoring their investments, creating crises, doing *anything* to stay busy and avoid genuine interaction. Perhaps they lack the skills to communicate honestly and openly with the people in their lives, or they may be suppressing painful memories of childhood experiences, fearful of repeating them in their own family. Unwilling or unable to develop genuine relationships with their co-workers, family, or friends, they keep everyone busy with time-pressured projects that thwart well-meaning attempts to improve interpersonal communication.

But no matter what the reason, Copers place more priority on the "things" in their life than on the people in their life. Lured by the financial payoffs of the "American dream," they choose the often short-lived rewards of achievement over the lasting values of quality of life, balance in their emotions and priorities, genuineness and openness.

In summary, Copers share the following characteristics:

COPER CHARACTERISTICS	
1	Need for control
2	Mistrust and suspicion
3	Disconnection from spirituality
4	No sense of purpose
5	Victim thinking and blaming
6	Disconnection from feelings
7	Rigid thinking
8	Negative attitudes
9	No healthy support systems
10	Lack of balance/achievement orientation

Now let's return to Ellen, whom we met at the beginning of this chapter. How would she react to her situation if she were a Coper?

Feeling the need to control, Ellen would probably go out the very next day and update her résumé, read the help-wanted ads in the newspaper, and assess her network of contacts. She would try to find another job immediately, and if anyone asked her what had happened with MedicManagement, she might reply, "Oh, they just found a good opportunity to dump me. They've been out to get me for some time now." Ellen might apply for unemployment benefits, and if turned down, she would blame the system for failing to help her.

Ellen would not stop to reassess her life purpose or to reexamine what kind of work she really wants to do. Reacting to her understandable pain at being rejected by the company and losing her monthly income, she would focus her energy on blaming the company for "doing it to her." She wouldn't allow herself to cry or to express her pain, and would be unlikely to seek counseling. Her conversations with her friends would be oriented toward gaining sympathy for her plight. Ellen would also be unlikely to look outside her existing field for work, because her suspicious nature and rigid thinking would make that seem too frightening.

She would be pessimistic about her chances of finding a new job quickly, citing "the job market" or "the industry" or "the time of year" as the reason (not considering that her own negative attitudes, which she most likely conveys in each interview, are a bigger stumbling block for her). Finally, Ellen would not reawaken any of her hobbies or creative pursuits, nor take advantage of the time off to rest and recharge her emotional and mental battery. Rather, she would push relentlessly toward that next job, anxious to avoid feeling "in between," and "without a role" whenever anyone asks her what she does for a living.

Do you see yourself in Ellen? If so, don't despair. You are among the majority of people today who become overwhelmed when faced with transition, and who have not yet learned the tools for effectively living during such times. In the next chapter, we'll begin to look at the Thriver Profile, which provides a workable and very satisfying alternative to the Coper approach we have discussed here.

NOTES

1. Vaillant, George, *Adaptation to Life,* Little, Brown 1977, pp. 80, 87.
2. Williamson, Marianne, *A Return to Love,* HarperPerennial 1992, p. 213.
3. *Ibid.,* p. 181.
4. Covey, Stephen, *The 7 Habits of Highly Effective People,* Simon & Schuster 1989, p. 128.
5. Luft, Jay, "The Johari Window: A Graphic Model of Awareness in Interpersonal Behavior," *Human Relations Training News,* Vol. 5, No. 1., (1961) pp. 6–7.
6. Chopra, Deepak, *Unconditional Life,* Bantam 1991, p. 67.
7. Vaillant, *Op. cit.,* pp. 303–9.
8. Kobasa, Suzanne, "Commitment and Coping in Stress Resistance Among Lawyers," *Journal of Personality and Social Psychology,* Vol. 42(4), pp. 707–717 (1982).
9. Sheehy, Gail, *Pathfinders,* William Morrow 1981, pp. 132–5.
10. Eyre, Linda and Richard, *LifeBalance,* Ballantine 1987, p. 1.

PART TWO

THRIVING

3

THE THRIVER
PROFILE

❧

*The important question of our time is
whether we can make change our friend and
not our enemy.*

—Bill Clinton

Imagine yourself walking along a path through the woods.
Beside the path, some grass and weeds are growing, mostly
brown or dull green in color. As you round a bend, you notice
something quite remarkable: Suddenly the flora have changed.
Now you see bright green vegetation and brilliantly colored
flowers. "How strange," you say to yourself, "that the plants in
one area can be seemingly teetering between life and death,
when those living very near them are vibrant with life. What ac-
counts for the difference?"

We might ask ourselves the same question as we observe the
ways in which people respond to transition. Why do some
struggle, resist, and become miserable during such times, while
others seem to enjoy the process, grow, and actually thrive? Is
the environment a factor? Perhaps in our example above, the
plants in the second patch have more sunlight, more water, or
better soil in which to grow. Certainly environment plays a role.

When we are in a low-stress environment, doing things we enjoy with people we like, the level of stimulation is within our adaptive range and it is easy for us to thrive. And there are times—even for Copers—when this occurs. But often, we are faced with changes in our surroundings that challenge our ability to adapt. Yet people thrive even under those conditions. What is their secret?

I asked horticulturist Ray McNeilan what enables some plants to adapt to drought or even flood conditions while others die. Do they change their chemistry? He replied:

> No, not their chemistry, although there are some instances of chemical change. It's more their *ability to change their structure.* Some plants put out a different kind of root system when they're growing in water that is more effective in drawing oxygen.

Moss and lichens can grow on rocks, not because they were necessarily designed to do so, but because they have adapted to their location. Their root system anchors them to the slippery surface on which they live.

In the human dimension, Thrivers have developed a similar ability. Most of them have faced hardship—sometimes devastating hardship—and, using their difficult experiences as a catalyst, have "grown a new root system," if you will. They have learned to adapt to changing circumstances, even constant change, with ease. And more than that, they have actually begun to seek out change, to initiate it in their own lives *before* a crisis occurs.

To put Thriving into the current cultural context, it is helpful to think of it as the individual equivalent of the corporate concept of Total Quality Management ("TQM"). An important component of TQM is continuous improvement in what one does or in the product one makes. In Japanese, this is called *kaizen*. "*Kaizen* is all about the ability to make very small improvements in processes and products every day."[1]

Thrivers approach their personal as well as professional life in this way. Applying a kind of *continuous self-improvement,* they daily scan their internal and external environment, asking themselves questions such as these:

- How can I improve myself as a person today?
- Is there anything in me that is preventing my personal relationships from being as open and mutually satisfying as they can be?
- Is this job still fulfilling my need for creative self-expression, or is there another type of work—even if radically different—that would meet more of my changing needs?
- Is the way I am spending my time reflecting my authentic priorities?

By constantly challenging themselves to a higher standard of excellence, without driving themselves compulsively, Thrivers learn the skills of implementing and responding to change, both internally and externally. These well-honed skills enable them to face crisis with relative ease. Thrivers "roll with the punches," navigating gracefully through numerous assaults on their serenity.

WHAT IS A THRIVER?

To "thrive" is to grow vigorously; to flourish. The plant analogy is fitting because it provides us with a clear picture of the most natural kind of thriving. Our goal, if we desire to improve our ability to deal with transition, is to see ourselves like that thriving plant, blooming brightly and bursting with life. As we develop the Thriver Traits (described below) within ourselves, we will both manage change better and feel more alive and vibrant.

The people I call Thrivers share many of the same traits identified by psychologists and others who have studied excellence in human beings. Charles Garfield has spent more than twenty years studying "peak performers," whose six key traits he defines as: having a sense of mission, purposeful activity directed toward achieving mission-related goals, self-management through self-mastery, team-building and team playing, mental agility in making course corrections, and anticipating and adapting to major change while maintaining momentum and balance.[2]

Abraham Maslow coined the term "peak experience" to describe blissful states of oneness which characterized "self-actualizing" individuals—those reaching the highest human potentials. Self-actualizing people have, by definition, gratified their basic needs for belonging, affection, respect, and self-esteem. They are actively pursuing a higher set of needs, which Maslow calls "B-needs" or "metaneeds," such as truth, beauty, wholeness, aliveness, justice, order, and simplicity. Also characteristic of self-actualized individuals is a devotion to some task, call, vocation, or work outside themselves.[3]

Marsha Sinetar has carried Maslow's work into the mainstream of current consciousness. In *Developing a 21st-Century Mind,* she describes people she calls "creative adaptors," also known as "personal entrepreneurs." These unique individuals "manage, organize, strategically plan and execute the pressures of day-to-day living in ways that meet, rather than thwart, their own personal needs, values and goals."[4] They are intuitive yet objective, can resolve paradox and create a vision, hold positive mental energies and remain non-dualistic while living in a dualistic society.

The findings of Maslow, Garfield, Sinetar, George Vaillant, and others concerning individuals' *overall* patterns of adapting and living parallel the results of my own and other research on the specific issue of managing life transitions. And Suzanne Kobasa, in studying layoff-generated stress, coined the term "hardiness" to describe the people who rose above the masses—in this case, those who endured the Bell Telephone divestiture of the mid-1970s. Those who found challenge in their circumstances, felt some sense of control, and were committed to and intensively involved in what they were doing were defined as "hardy."[5] The "hardy" subjects experienced less illness (which frequently follows stressful life changes) than other individuals subjected to the same events.

What we each need to do today, if we are to thrive in the current climate of change, is to develop a kind of *"change hardiness"*—an ability, developed through modeling and practice, to traverse the shifting terrain of our lives with ease, as though we had been doing it all of our lives. It is less a prescribed set of behaviors than an orientation to our lives. People who become change hardy in the New Zero do so because they have released their stranglehold on external stability. Thrivers don't expect that the rules about their work, their relationships, or their life that worked yesterday will continue to work tomorrow. They are constantly reinventing themselves and everything in their lives, using the *kaizen* principle and developing stability using their internal abilities and resources.

THE THRIVER PROFILE

Thrivers share six clusters of traits which, whether innate or learned, enable them to remain healthy and happy during transitions of any kind. I call this group of trait clusters the *Thriver Profile*. Each cluster identifies a key set of characteristics that may lead to varying behaviors, depending on the person and the circumstances. However, these characteristics were prominent among all of the Thrivers I have studied.

Following is a brief outline of the traits. In Part Three, we will elaborate on each cluster in a separate chapter. The order in which the clusters are presented is not one of priority, as no one cluster is more important than the rest. However, as we will see later, each cluster is especially useful at a different phase of the transition process.

Cluster 1: Attentiveness

The great Zen master's first lesson to the student who wanted enlightenment was "Attention!" And when asked what the second lesson was, he replied, "Attention! Attention!"

Paying attention to what happens in both their internal and external environment is a fundamental attribute of Thrivers.

The *Attentiveness Cluster* consists of four traits. The first, *self-awareness,* enables Thrivers to give heed to their inner messages and to strive to learn more about themselves. Their goal is to widen their awareness of the Blind and Hidden Potential

Diagram 3-1
ATTENTIVENESS CLUSTER

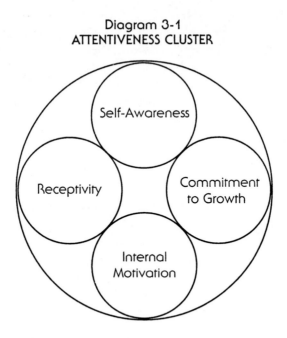

panes of the Johari Window discussed in Chapter 2. They have learned, often through bitter experience, that if they deny the messages of their emotions, their body, or their intuition, they will build up a psychic residue which will demand resolution later on—probably at an inconvenient time or in an undesirable manner.

The second component of attentiveness is *commitment to growth*. Pursuing their personal growth and expanding themselves in new ways are priorities for Thrivers. They are always reading, taking seminars and classes, talking to interesting people, and learning new things. Continuous learning, a part of the commitment to growth, is a part of their lifestyle.

Unlike Copers, Thrivers have *internal motivation*. Their locus of control operates from the inside out. If the weather or the sports page results are not to their liking, they refuse to let those facts determine how they will experience their day. Instead, they will choose to be positive, happy, optimistic—even sad or depressed, if those are their genuine feelings—regardless of external circumstances. This gives them a healthy sense of control in their lives, without having to manipulate people and situations like the Coper would.

Finally, Thrivers share a *receptivity to new ideas*. They are on the other end of the continuum from the rigid thinkers of the world. When presented with a new concept, Thrivers are likely to respond, "Oh, isn't that interesting?" or "Really . . . tell me more about that." They dismiss stereotypes as overly limiting and quickly outmoded, and they have a fluid thought process that makes them joyful playmates in the game of life. They are open to novel thoughts, weighing them against their existing mindset and integrating those that are helpful. This way, they continue evolving and thinking creatively throughout their lives.

Cluster 2: Groundedness

Diagram 3-2
GROUNDEDNESS CLUSTER

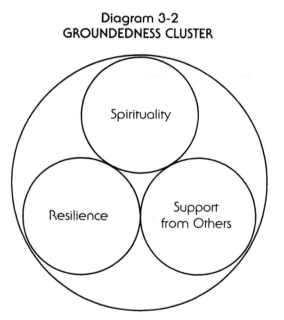

The *Groundedness Cluster* can be conceptualized as a three-legged stool. When all three legs of the stool are strong, the individual has a firm foundation for dealing with anything life hands out, even a serious crisis such as the death of a spouse or a freak accident.

The first leg of the groundedness stool is *spirituality*. All of the Thrivers I have studied have some form of spiritual belief system which gives them a sense of life beyond what is visible in the physical world. Their spiritual practices—whether they be traditional church affiliation, walks in the woods, or burning incense at a certain time and place—provide them with a multitude of personal benefits. They have a sense of community with their Higher Power and with their fellow humans. These practices serve as rituals of celebration and commemoration of special events, which in turn give life a welcome rhythm.

Thrivers exhibit a breadth of self which comes from acknowledging the physical, mental, emotional, and spiritual aspects of their being.

The second leg of the stool is *support from others*. Thrivers have cultivated a support system for themselves. They maintain relationships with their extended family, growing together through the changes of their lives. Many of them have lifelong or other long-term friends with whom they share their ups and downs. They place a higher priority on their relationships with others than they do on achievement, though paradoxically, they are often highly successful in their careers.

Rounding out the Groundedness Cluster is *resilience*. Thrivers have developed the ability to bounce back from adversity. Most of them have experienced severe challenges to their health, security, and self-esteem, but they have learned from their trials and rarely allow themselves to be knocked down very far before they pick themselves up and get back into the game. This inner resilience, combined with the support from close friends and family and belief in God, render them unassailable when life throws them a curve.

Cluster 3: Trust and Emotional Balance

Thrivers' ability to *trust* both in life and in themselves is the opposite of the mistrust, suspicion, and blame found in Cop-

Diagram 3-3
TRUST CLUSTER

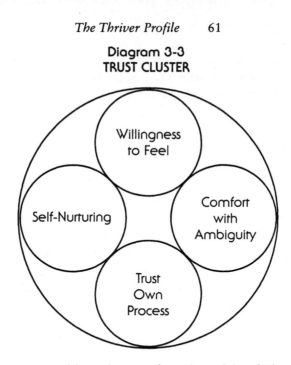

ers. Thrivers are able to let go of rigid models of "how things should be" and have confidence in the way things actually are. Their guiding principle is "My life is perfect, just as it is and just as it is not. Everything that is happening to me is just as it should be." They are emotionally balanced in their approach to transition and are willing to confront not only the excitement of new choices, but also the discomfort, loss, and disorientation that come with some phases of the transition process.

There are four doorways into this kind of trust. First is the *willingness to feel.* Human beings are designed to feel a wide range of emotions, from sadness and pain to ecstasy and bliss, as well as everything in between. Thrivers relish each emotion, knowing that "to feel is to be alive." Unlike Copers, they do not shun the "negative" emotions of anger, guilt, and fear.

Thrivers use these strong feelings as messengers to show them what issues they need to explore so that they can move ahead in their lives.

Additionally, Thrivers communicate their feelings when they occur, through talking, journaling, counseling, or whatever means are appropriate. They have learned to talk honestly about themselves without judgment. They "own," or take responsibility for, their feelings and experiences, rather than placing the blame on others.

The second doorway, *comfort with ambiguity*, is particularly critical in the New Zero environment. Anyone who has been through a corporate downsizing or other structural change knows the feeling of being "in between": the restructuring is sure to occur, but management is still working out the details. In these situations, Thrivers have learned how to continue to be productive, to attend to their own career development, and to integrate the new policies, practices, and working relationships when they come. Thrivers do not let uncertainty or this awkward "in-between" stage disturb their positive outlook or their effectiveness.

Through enhanced self-awareness and practice, Thrivers have learned the third doorway, *trust in their own process.* That is, they allow themselves to experience their feelings, and they trust that each of the elements which disrupted the way things were will be resolved in the proper time and manner. As we will see, this trust, combined with the receptivity characteristic of the Attentiveness Cluster, often produces surprising results. Jobs perfectly suited to the Thriver's background and preferences are created just for them, or the disharmony they were feeling with a friend or family member resolves itself in an amazing way. These results further reinforce trust, opening the Thriver to even greater outcomes the next time.

The final doorway to trust is the *ability to be self-nurturing.* In the hustle and bustle of today's busy lifestyles, many of us find ourselves relegated to the bottom of our own priority list. Thrivers know that if they don't allow self-nurturing a place in their daily life, they will deplete their energy and have less to give to their commitments. Thus, they schedule some "selfish" time each day. This habit fosters a dedication to people first, things second.

Thrivers determine what nurtures them—massage, yoga, exercise, golf, meditation, or nature—and regularly spend time engaged in those activities.

In doing so, Thrivers develop a trust that if they take care of themselves first, the other commitments in their lives will be taken care of, too.

Cluster 4: Proactive Purpose

Diagram 3-4
PROACTIVE PURPOSE CLUSTER

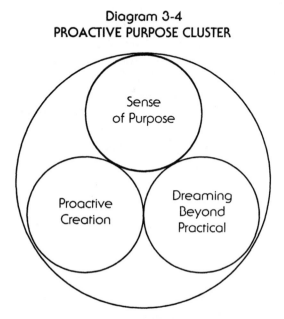

Thrivers have confronted pivotal life issues such as "Why am I here?" and "How can I make my life more fulfilling, more the way I want it to be?" They use the answers to these questions as the guiding force in their lives which provides cohesiveness to their goals and lifestyle choices.

First, they have a clear *sense of purpose.* To the Thriver, life purpose is the reason for being. Without it, life wouldn't make sense. Through a variety of means, including deep introspection and personal or group exploration, they have arrived at a realization of the purpose for their life. That purpose informs every aspect of their lives and fuels the fire of their dreams.

Thrivers realize large aspirations by *dreaming beyond what appears practical.* They refuse to limit themselves to "what's been done before." Constantly testing their own limits, relying on their faith in the Divine, they translate their purpose into wonderfully creative ventures.

Thrivers dare to dream big, and their dreams tend to come true.

As we will learn, they develop, over the course of time, a skill in *visioning* their future which leads to greater and greater likelihood of success. Whether they are starting their own business or traveling around the world, making their first million dollars or having their first child after they were told they were infertile, Thrivers challenge the odds—and win.

The proactive aspect of this cluster is *proactive creation:* the ability to bring one's vision into reality. Thrivers recognize that far from being a victim of their circumstances, they are co-creating their lives. From the vision planted within them, in whatever area it may lie, they use the *Principles* of *Proactive Creation* (described in Chapter 8) to systematically manifest the kind of life they desire. The results? A high level of fulfillment, and a sense that nothing is impossible.

Cluster 5: Optimistic Confidence

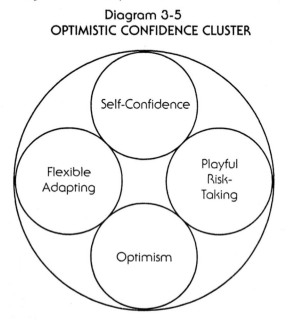

Diagram 3-5
OPTIMISTIC CONFIDENCE CLUSTER

Self-Confidence

Flexible
Adapting

Playful
Risk-
Taking

Optimism

A fifth trait of Thrivers is an unflappable *optimistic confidence*—in themselves and in their ability to respond to what happens to them—"response-ability." Without this sense of optimism, they would, like the Coper, remain stuck within the narrow confines of a range of experiences that feels safe, never venturing into the higher levels of satisfaction that lie outside their comfort zone.

Optimistic confidence arises from four platforms. First, all Thrivers share a strong *self-confidence*. This self-assurance is, in most cases, developed over time, although some Thrivers feel they have always possessed this quality.

Thrivers are hesitant to doubt themselves, even in a new, unfamiliar situation.

Building on successes of the past and drawing on resources they know they have, they approach any challenge with assurance.

The second platform of optimistic confidence is *playful risk-taking*. Thrivers view life as a game to be played, not a problem to be solved. They take what others would call risks when called for, but when asked why they did it are likely to respond, "It didn't feel like a risk; it was something I had to do." They know that nothing is forever, and that if their chosen activity does not turn out as they expected, they can change their minds again. This frees the Thriver to explore new options without a heavy attachment to the expected result. The Game of Life becomes fun to play, and the welcomed bonus of success and prosperity often accompany the willingness to risk.

The key to this cluster is *optimism*, the ability to expect the best possible outcome from an event. When faced with what some would call disaster, Thrivers know that good will emerge from the situation, even if it takes some time to see it. They have an innate belief that there are no accidents in life, which enables them to find meaning in every occurrence.

The final aspect of optimistic confidence is *flexible adapting*. Like the plant that changes its structure to fit its environment, Thrivers are adept at modifying their habits as well as their thought patterns to integrate the changes around them. Because they are not firmly invested in rigid beliefs about how things should be, nor in any particular outcome of their choices, Thrivers are dynamic individuals who continue to experience new levels of personal challenge and success throughout their lives.

Cluster 6: Holistic/Systems Thinking

Diagram 3-6
SYSTEMS THINKING CLUSTER

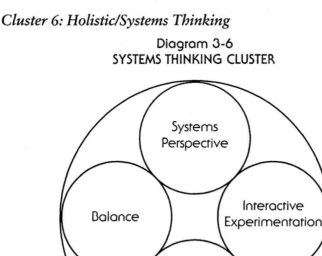

The final cluster of the Thriver Profile, *holistic* or *systems thinking,* springs from the Thriver's ability to see the "big picture." They recognize that life, like the cosmos, with its ceaseless cycles, is one large system, ever evolving into a higher order. As participants in and co-creators of that system, Thrivers keep the *systems perspective* in mind, by which they think in wholes rather than segments, even in mundane, day-to-day decisions. They understand that each element is necessary for the system to be healthy, and that many aspects of their life may be impacted by a single transition.

An integral part of this perspective is a constant engagement in *interactive experimentation.* That is, they see their life experiences as a scientist would view the laboratory: as an environment in which lessons are learned and discoveries are made. Rather than limiting themselves with labels like "success" and "failure," Thrivers recognize that each situation they face requires a choice, which will lead to a consequence. They can either learn from that consequence, or they can label it, which often leads to restrictions and frustrated expectations.

However, if they learn from their experiences, their next choice will probably be more likely to create the result they desire. By observing their own process, Thrivers learn to anticipate transition and to circumvent many crises altogether. Using their sense of detachment and whole thinking, they avoid short-sighted action which may have far-reaching results.

Critical to the systems thinker is a *sense of humor.* Since life is a game to Thrivers, they learn to laugh at themselves and the humorous situations of life. They look on the bright side, and use humor to illuminate difficult circumstances. Thrivers understand the physical benefits of laughter in loosening up tight emotions, lightening up the energy of a challenging moment, balancing their more serious side, and opening the passageway to the spirit. Through skillful use of this gift, Thrivers develop a joie de vivre unparalleled in non-Thrivers. They enjoy their life, and their joy rubs off on all who come into contact with them.

The final component of systems thinking is *balance.* Thrivers vigilantly monitor the correlation between their stated purpose, values, and priorities and their investment of time and energy. They exercise regularly, manage time carefully, and take "time-outs" daily, weekly, and annually to rejuvenate themselves, develop creative pursuits, and maintain their health at all levels. Thrivers know when to say no. They set reasonable limits on their expenditures of time and energy, and follow through to maintain those boundaries so that they can remain centered, focused, and aligned with their purpose.

In summary, Thrivers share the following six clusters of traits, which enable them to successfully encounter transition, and even initiate it when appropriate:

THE THRIVER PROFILE	
Cluster 1	Attentiveness
Cluster 2	Groundedness
Cluster 3	Trust and Emotional Balance
Cluster 4	Proactive Purpose
Cluster 5	Optimistic Confidence
Cluster 6	Holistic/Systems Thinking

Ellen—Another Look

From this description of the Thriver Profile, we begin to sense how Thrivers respond to transition. Perhaps you have even thought of a person or two you know who are Thrivers. And more importantly, we have begun to see the possibilities for reacting to our own challenges in new ways.

To understand the Thriver more clearly, let's return to Ellen, who was laid off without notice from MedicManagement at the beginning of Chapter 2. We've seen how she might have reacted as a Coper. Now let's find out how she actually *did* react as a Thriver.

Ellen's dissatisfaction with her job as sales manager had become evident through a personal growth program she took shortly before her layoff (*self-awareness*). She knew the job was not meeting all of her newly articulated needs, and as indicated, she was ready to explore alternative options at Medic-Management when she was laid off (*commitment to growth; internal motivation*). After her layoff, she did qualify for unemployment benefits, so, as she put it, "the layoff allowed me six months of informational interviewing, experimenting, trying out different ideas, just doing a lot of research" (*receptivity*).

She continued to practice yoga (*spirituality*) and exercise regularly during her layoff, and talked to friends and colleagues about her situation (*support from others*). Though she felt emotional and wanted to cry at first—and did for about a week— (*willingness to feel*), she knew she didn't like what she was doing, and had already thought about changing jobs. Having accepted the gift of six months of exploration, she decided to experiment (*playful risk-taking; interactive experimentation*):

> I was going to allow myself to do anything I wanted to do, within reason, and within a method that I can support myself. And also it needed to have some growth potential. So I looked at all kinds of things—I talked to people about selling art, selling clothes at Sak's, I had all kinds of wild ideas. And I thought that was very cathartic, because oftentimes people have these fantasies about what they want to do, extend a hobby into a career, and you do that and you fall flat on your face because you got too committed on a path. Whereas this allowed me to mentally, like making spaghetti, throw it all onto the wall and see what sticks. And then the things that do stick you start picking on and saying: does this really make sense? how does it fit into my needs?

Ellen had a nursing background and an interest in computers, and had sold database systems to hospitals. Her vision became one of wedding those two elements into some kind of a job that would meet all of her basic needs: independence, variety, and working with people. She was convinced that it existed in the marketplace (*optimistic confidence*). Through her networking, she ultimately found her "ideal job"—a position as a systems analyst with a metropolitan hospital. Her function is to assist patients and caregivers who use computers as a tool but do not have all of the technical knowledge that might otherwise be expected of them. Essentially, Ellen helps these individuals manage the technological changes of computerization as smoothly as possible. She negotiates with the software vendor (using her previous experience as a database salesperson), trains, and performs a whole host of other activities. And she tries to keep her work within an eight-hour day, rather than the twelve-hour days she was working at her previous job (*balance*). Says Ellen: "I feel like a little kid. It's such a fun thing to do all day."

Are You a Coper or a Thriver?

For each of the statements listed below, indicate a "1" for "not true of me at all," "2" for "sometimes true of me," and "3" for "frequently or mostly true of me."

___1. I often suspect ulterior motives behind other people's acts and decisions.

___2. I know myself well, including my strengths and weaknesses, beliefs, values, and priorities.

___3. I am a loner, and have very few friends.

___4. I believe in a Power greater than myself, or regularly practice a religion.

___5. I haven't thought much about my purpose in life.

___6. I choose how I will feel about my circumstances, rather than letting them determine my mood.

___7. I find it most effective to expect the worst so that I'm not disappointed.

___8. I have a strong network of family, friends, and professionals from which I draw support.

___9. I know how to manipulate people and circumstances to get them to do what I want.

___10. I am not afraid to feel my whole range of emotions, whether comfortable or not.

___11. In my list of priorities in life, work and/or financial status ranks higher than my family.

___12. I take good care of myself, including eating a healthy diet, exercising regularly, monitoring my stress level, and getting enough sleep.

___13. Spirituality is not an important part of my life.

___14. I enjoy taking risks—and regularly do so.

___15. I rarely feel angry, depressed, frustrated, or sad.

___16. I organize my life around a strong sense of purpose, and actively initiate necessary changes and set ambitious goals to carry out my purpose as I understand it.

___17. I believe that most things are either right or wrong, good or bad—nothing is in between.

___18. Before I act on a choice, I think about the ramifications of my actions on other people and on other parts of my life.

___19. The things that have happened to me are usually someone else's fault.

___20. I am able to bounce back when things don't go my way, and to trust that eventually I will come out of the situation a better person.

___21. The people I spend time with often complain and gossip about others.

___22. I am not bothered by uncertain or ambiguous times in my life; I use them to grow.

___23. I often work evenings and weekends, and rarely take vacations.

___24. I actively seek out new experiences, and am committed to ongoing personal growth.

___25. If the weather isn't suitable for my plans, I often become depressed.

___26. I believe I can do anything that I put my mind to.

COPER   THRIVER

_____   _____

Now, add your total score on the left column (the *odd* numbered items). This is your "Coper Quotient." Next, add your total score on the right column (the *even* numbered items). This is your "Thriver Quotient." If your score is between 26 and 39 on either column, you have a strong tendency toward that approach to transition. If you have a low Coper Quotient, you will normally have a high Thriver Quotient. If you are equally balanced between both, you find yourself engaging in ineffective strategies in approaching change more often than you need to in the New Zero. You can increase your Thriver quotient by doing some of the exercises contained in the balance of the book.

Being a Thriver makes each day of our lives an adventure. The Thriver orientation buoys us against the tides of change, assuring us that we can face whatever is ahead. But what about the process of transition itself? Is there a cycle of predictable events that occur within a transition that, once understood, can help us relax even more into the process? Indeed there is, and that is the subject of our next chapter.

NOTES

1. Barker, Joel, *Paradigms: The Business of Discovering the Future,* Harper Business 1992, p.80.
2. Garfield, Charles, *Peak Performers: The New Heroes of American Business,* Avon Books 1986, pp. 31–2.
3. Maslow, Abraham, *The Farther Reaches of Human Nature,* Viking 1971.
4. Sinetar, Marsha, *Developing a 21st-Century Mind,* Ballantine 1992, p. 11.
5. Kobasa, Suzanne, "Personality and Resistance to Illness," *American Journal of Community Psychology* Vol. 7(4), pp. 413–423 (1979); "Hardiness and Health: A Prospective Study," *Journal of Personality and Social Psychology* Vol. 42(1), pp. 168–77 (1982).

4

A ROAD MAP FOR TRANSITION

❧

Now that we are all participants, like it or not, in the age of computers, peak performers recognize that change occurs against a background that is itself in motion.

—Charles Garfield
Peak Performers

I have asked dozens of groups throughout the United States what words come to mind when I say the word "transition." Common responses include these descriptors:

- frightening
- uncertain
- bad
- unsettling
- out of control
- chaotic
- burdensome
- unexpected
- full of loss
- challenging

Yet others describe transition this way:

- exciting
- full of self-discovery
- good
- helpful
- a metamorphosis
- the best thing that ever happened to me
- an opportunity
- mind-expanding
- growth-producing
- a sense of freedom

Transition is all of these, and more. Called a "little death" by psychologist Dr. Robert Tannenbaum, transition marks a rite of passage each time it occurs. A part of ourselves is left behind each time we change jobs, move, leave a friend or intimate relationship, or face the loss of our health or a loved one. It is at times like these that we long for a template by which we can measure our experiences. "Is this normal? Am I doing it right? What will happen next? What is the best decision for me to make?"

Our thinking mind wants answers. It prefers to have the entire scheme of events laid out in advance. But transition doesn't offer us that luxury. It is full of uncertainty, strong emotions which we may not be accustomed to feeling, and important decisions which must be made. And like the shifting images in a kaleidoscope, the background is also changing. Compounding our struggle to deal with personal transitions are transformations in our workplace, our society, and our planet.

QUANTUM TRANSFORMATION:
LEAPING TO A HIGHER ORDER

Transition, in short, feels chaotic. Swirling around us are changing relationships, new possibilities, unfamiliar desires and needs. We wonder where it is all heading. This process of transition—whether of a sudden, crisis-driven nature or a more gradual, voluntary change—can be understood more clearly by borrowing some concepts from physics concerning how nature, and the particles that comprise it, behave.

When Isaac Newton developed his principles of physics, they eventually became the norm and replaced the accepted view of the world. And while a majority of physicists continue to adhere to the Newtonian school of thought, which views evolution and change as a linear process, a revolution has occurred in that field akin to the reformation which must occur in our view of transitions. According to Newtonian physics, all particles will follow the same path and reach the same ultimate state, when starting from a given set of initial conditions. There is no room for chance, and no so-called "quantum leaping," i.e., unexpected sudden moves to another orbit. Newtonian physicists believe that particles have properties totally independent of the observer, and thus can be observed objectively. If we applied the Newtonian paradigm to transitions, we would say that our circumstances and the people in our lives have no connection to our own mindsets, beliefs, and attitudes. We are not responsible for what happens to us and are totally at the mercy of our origin and our circumstances.

In the "new physics" of quantum theory, however, as in the New Zero, entirely different principles govern. Three key postulates have been drawn from three paradoxes which physicists discovered as they were attempting to explain the world of matter and energy.[1] They form the basis of Quantum Transformation, our term for the kind of change that occurs in the New Zero.

Postulate 1: Change occurs discontinuously, and its source is unpredictable. This principle comes from physicists' observations that the particles they examined moved, but did not follow familiar laws of mechanics. Rather than moving gradually from one place to another, they would suddenly jump to an unexpected point. This kind of discontinuous shifting parallels our experience with transition in the New Zero. We never know when or where the next new technological development or corporate downsizing will occur, let alone where the desires of our mind for new forms of creative expression will lead us. And as Peter Senge has pointed out in *The Fifth Discipline,* we face many situations which involve "dynamic complexity," in which "cause and effect are subtle, and where the effects over time of interventions are not obvious."[2] That is, the action we take in an attempt to change our situation may have different consequences in the short term than in the long term.

Postulate 2: We create (or at least heavily influence) our own reality. Quantum physicists have discovered that scientists conducting an experiment can dramatically influence the outcome of that experiment by their mere presence. This concept is called the "observer effect." In the human dimension, psychologists have demonstrated that teachers' perceptions and expectations of their students will correlate closely with the academic performance of those students.

This is why some people who grow up in poverty perpetuate that way of living to their death, but others coming from the same background rise above their circumstances to become highly successful. It is as though these latter individuals have removed their "poverty-colored glasses," and have learned to perceive the world in a new way, one that offers the potential for wealth and success.

Individuals—whether Copers or Thrivers—have a strong influence on the "experiment" of their lives. Some believe that they create their life experiences; others see themselves as victims. But regardless of which perspective we hold, it is increasingly clear that our perceptions, beliefs, and expectations are extremely important in shaping our lives in the New Zero.

Postulate 3: There is an order in the New Zero; it simply isn't the order we expected. The new order involves us in its creation, and it includes phenomena which cannot be easily explained, if at all. The classic experiment which brought physicists to this principle is the "double slit experiment." In this procedure, a stream of particles is directed toward a screen. A second screen, placed between the stream's source and the original screen, contains two long, parallel slits. Each particle must pass through one slit or the other to reach the final screen, where it leaves its imprint or dark spot. But if the experimenter closes down one of the slits, more particles will reach places on the final screen than if both are left open. It appears that the particles actually change their structure and become waves when they pass through the slits, and waves can interfere with each other's path of travel on the way to the final screen. So does the experiment examine particles or waves? With one slit open, it is particles, but with two slits, it is waves. The nature of the stream varies, depending on how the experiment is set up.[3] The truth is that the stream is at the same time waves *and* particles, but the "Uncertainty Principle" of physics tells us we can only perceive or measure one of the aspects at a time.

Human beings, too, are complex and multifaceted. When they are confronted with a new situation, such as making their first presentation to their department, they may call on any number of personal strengths, skills, abilities, and aptitudes to successfully complete the task. Or instead, they may summon a host of excuses why they cannot do what they are called upon to do. Both the positive abilities and the negative (or limiting) excuses are equally and always present; it is up to the individual to choose which dynamic will govern in the current scenario. The choice is further influenced by whether or not the person wants to give the presentation, whether the reward is sufficient to justify the effort, and the like.

In the new kind of order which governs transitions in the New Zero, result B does not always follow, logically and predictably, from act A. Replacing the linear system of "cause and effect" in the new order are *"quantum correlations,"* or *"nonlocal events,"* according to quantum physicist Dr. Fred Alan Wolf. In these synchronistic occurrences, two or more events may take place in separate spaces, or even at separate times, but may nevertheless be linked. To use the often cited example, when a butterfly flaps its wings in China, it may impact the weather in the U.S. And something a person in New York does on a Sunday afternoon may in some way impact another person in Los Angeles the following Tuesday. This is due to the connectedness of our minds through what Carl Jung called the "collective unconscious." This principle is at work in the "hundredth monkey syndrome," in which an idea or invention appears spontaneously at several places in the world at once, despite there being no apparent physical connection among the people claiming to have thought of it.

Thinking with these principles in mind requires a major shift in our approach to making choices during a transition. The Western culture's Old Zero way of thinking conceptualizes an arrow going directly from situation A to new choice B without so much as a pause, let alone a setback or unexpected turn of events:

$$A \longrightarrow B$$

The shape of a transition diagram in the New Zero is more of a spiral than a straight line. Synchronistic, New Zero thinking requires that we think in terms of wholes; that we look for nonlinear relationships between seemingly unrelated events; and that we think in terms of curves rather than straight lines. In our example of the request to do a presentation, we may desire the promotion, and receive the request to make the presentation.

At this point, fear of speaking enters the equation, as does our perception of our speaking ability. We then decide whether to give or not to give the presentation, perhaps looping through the analysis process several more times, debating the respective merits and importance of the promotion versus our fear and perceived ability. Ultimately, we may proceed with the assigned task, but not until we have considered all the elements of this somewhat complex scenario and (perhaps unconsciously) weighed the impacts of our choices on each of them.

Disorder in nature—and in our decision-making process— often precedes the emergence of a new order. Like the particles of physics, there is always some movement percolating beneath the surface of our lives, for we are dynamic beings. But in the period leading up to a transition, a "foreign element" enters our mental system, something that doesn't "fit" with the way things have been. It may be a chance remark, an uncharacteristic reaction, anything out of the ordinary.

The moment that element enters our mental environment, it sets off a chain of events which lead to a transition. We do not know its type, or what we will do in response to it, but we do know that a change is beginning. And from that initial element which injects disequilibrium into our experience, one thing is certain: as a result of the disorder, which destroys or alters the old structure of our lives, a new, higher order will emerge.

Although it may be of some comfort to us when facing transition that there is a "deeper orderliness" at work, the collapse of the old layer of order is usually not a pleasant experience. In fact, a great deal of pain, sense of loss, and letting go often need to occur for us to move fully into the new order. Knowing this key principle will assist us in passing through the period of pain, confusion, and grief.

The purpose of transition is to facilitate our growth, and in some cases, to give birth to an entirely new level of being.

Growth is painful, but like the ecstasy which the new mother experiences after the excruciating pains of labor, there is a celebration—and a transformation—on the other side of our life-change experience.

What I am encouraging us to do is to see the transition events in our lives as more than an inconvenience, as something besides an arbitrary act of fate which interrupts our well-planned lives. We must transform our eyes. Are we on this planet merely to get an education, take a job to pay our bills, raise children, retire, and die? Or is there in fact a deeper meaning behind these familiar experiences, one with a cosmic significance?

If we view our life as our training ground, the purpose of which is to perfect our skills in being truly human, then the purpose of transitions themselves is transformation. What happens to us is not nearly as important as how we feel and act during the process. We cannot predict what tragedy or ecstasy we will encounter during our lifetime, nor will there necessarily be any logic to when these events befall us. But if we commit ourselves to grow from our life experiences, whatever they may be, we cannot help but profit from our transitions.

Perhaps the job change does not work out the way we had hoped, or moving to another state ends up being more unpleasant than the situation we left. Does that mean the transition was a failure? Not if we have begun to follow the inner voice of our dreams and our passions. And we may also find that, in the process of the apparently "unsuccessful" transition, we discover new inner strength or creative abilities of which we were previously unaware.

THE DYNAMIC MODEL OF TRANSITION

Just as quantum physics has subsumed Newtonian physics, a new *Dynamic Model of Transition* is replacing the linear, sequential stage models which predominated during the 1970s and 1980s. Psychologists in the Old Zero relied on stage models, which view transitions as following a predictable sequence of clearly defined occurrences, to explain how human beings develop through their lives. In 1976, Gail Sheehy, in her best-selling work, *Passages,* outlined progressive, predictable stages linked to chronological age through which, she claimed, each of us pass as we mature. The monumental success of Sheehy's book and its successors, *Pathfinders* and *New Passages,* underscores our craving for predictability, and for an orderly sequence of clearly defined transitions. Not surprisingly, stage theories continue to abound throughout psychological research literature.

The most popular transition model is that of William Bridges. He posits a three-stage progression (the range in recent theories is from three to seven stages) which begins with an ending of what was, continues through a "neutral zone" characterized by confusion and disorientation, and concludes with a new beginning. While the Bridges model may be useful, it fails to include key aspects of the process that occur before the ending and after the new beginning. Remember that the very nature of transition today is that of a *constant state,* not an isolated event. Therefore, it is a cyclical, rather than a linear, process. As one loop is completed, another has begun, intertwining with the first and building on its momentum. The Bridges model and others which consist of a linear sequence of events typify the Old Zero. The New Zero, on the other hand, is characterized by cycles and wholes, fluidity and diversity.

Stage theories, as sociologist Orville Brim, Jr. states, are "a little like horoscopes. They are vague enough so that everyone can see something of themselves in them. That's why they're so popular."[4] While these theories may accommodate our desire for certainty, as well as our need to believe that we are not alone in our experience, unfortunately they do not apply to transition in the New Zero. In today's world of multiple simultaneous transitions, such theories oversimplify our experience to such an extent that they become meaningless. They rob us of the fullness that transition has to offer.

The basic premise of the Dynamic Model is this:

Transition, while not without predictable components, is a unique, individual process.

Unlike the stage theories, which resemble Newtonian physics in assuming that certain kinds of life changes will be experienced in the same way by each person going through them, the Dynamic Model recognizes the uniqueness of each individual's experience of change. The primary purpose of a life transition is to assist the experiencer in evolving as an individual, whether through gradual, steady growth, or by means of a "quantum leap," in which one suddenly surges from one way of being to another. During the transition itself, life may appear to be chaotic. Emotions, thoughts, perceptions, and events may seem disjointed and confusing. But there *is* order in the process. A new level of experience is emerging, which will only become apparent as one moves through the transition process.

The Dynamic Model of Transition recognizes six phases which typically occur within any life change. The six phases are shown in Diagram 4-1.

While the phases of transition often occur in the sequence depicted in Diagram 4-1, they do not always follow that order. A new vision may appear in the midst of a crisis, but its implementation may not occur until after the Sorting-out Phase. To avoid this temptation to impose a linear model on any particular transition, it may be helpful to think of each of the six phases as *tasks of transition*. While the order may vary, each of

Diagram 4-1

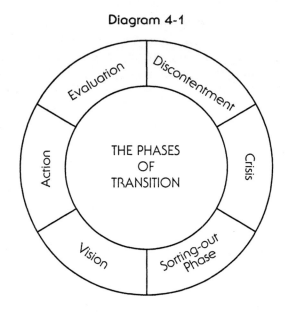

these tasks, or phases, must be completed during any successful transition. Let's look at each phase in more depth.

Discontentment Phase: The precursor to most voluntary (or self-initiated) transitions is a sense of dissatisfaction with the current state of affairs. Our job is not as enjoyable as it once was. We feel unhappy with our body image and wish to lose weight. We notice the debt piling up and know something needs to change. While initially vague and unclear as to its source, the *Discontentment Phase* manifests itself in symptoms such as being bored with what used to interest us, or no longer feeling the same sense of satisfaction with our work, or with a relationship. Psychologists' term for this feeling, "internally generated disequilibrium," aptly depicts the way it feels. Something is off center, unsettled.

The word "discontent" comes from a Latin root which literally means "cannot hold in" or "cannot contain." In other words, when we feel discontented, we can no longer contain our former way of being; we must create a space for something new to occur.

If we ignore the signs that a new phase of life is approaching, we risk an explosion of our life force, which usually results in a crisis.

Crises become less and less frequent in our lives as we develop our skill in using the Thriver Traits, particularly the attentiveness cluster discussed in the previous chapter.

It is only by undergoing the "initiation" of discontentment that we can enter a higher order, for in physics it is recognized that "nonequilibrium [generated by discontentment] is the source of order. Nonequilibrium brings 'order out of chaos.'"[5] As we notice our discontentment, we align ourselves with it in order to become open to the message it has for us. A personal transformation has begun.

Attorney Mike Long, who recently transitioned out of the traditional practice of law to join an organization which assists attorneys with transition and stress-related issues, describes his period of discontentment this way:

> After graduating from law school I passed the California Bar. [Then] I took the Oregon Bar and was later hired as an associate in a small Portland firm. I worked very hard to learn how to be a lawyer and to prove myself.
> The firm provided me with a variety of assignments and experiences. I soon discovered that I wasn't really interested in corporate and business law or even civil litigation. I constantly felt that I was engaged in a charade. I was sure that sooner or later the partners were going to see through me and discover my incompetence and inability to practice law. During my first evaluation, the senior partner told me that I needed to read the Corporations Code from beginning to end. I remember thinking I would rather undergo an organ transplant.

As time went on, Mike noticed his productivity slipping as depression set in:

> I began working longer hours and getting less done. I found that aspects of litigation conflicted with my value and belief system. I was given some projects and cases that I felt completely

incompetent to handle. My own pride, insecurity and survival skills prohibited me from admitting this to any of the partners. At home I was unable to explain my dissatisfaction to my wife. I rejected her concerns and suggestions that I was depressed. I argued vehemently that I had no energy or interests when I got home because I was working so hard. In reality, I was becoming increasingly depressed and could not see it.

Discontentment can range from relatively mild dissatisfaction, as in the wish that something were different, to outright depression or suicidal thoughts. Mike's inner sense of the incongruity between his passion and his work went unchecked until depression set in and began to impact his marriage and his self-esteem. A downward cycle had begun that, if not heeded early, was destined to lead to a crisis.

Crisis or Decision Phase: Some transitions begin with a *Crisis Phase,* such as the sudden death of a spouse or child, an automobile accident, the onset of an illness, or the end of a relationship. These are referred to as "unavoidable" crises. Other changes appear to begin with a crisis event, but in fact were preceded by warnings that were ignored. Examples of these "avoidable" crises are the divorce that follows months or years of our spouse's expressing his/her unhappiness in the relationship, or a heart attack after years of smoking, eating a high-fat diet, and perpetuating a sedentary lifestyle. If we had listened to the earlier signs which told us we needed to pay attention—to our spouse, our body, or our lifestyle—it would not have reached the crisis point.

But for many of us, it is only when the condition reaches a crisis that we become willing to make the necessary changes. There is something painful that we can avoid, or something pleasurable that we can experience, by avoiding the change as long as possible. In other cases, we make a decision to change prior to a full-fledged crisis occurring (sometimes following a period of discontentment), and our transition is underway.

If our crisis is an avoidable one, its onset is *not* the time to berate ourselves or to wish we had made the needed adjustment earlier. But it *is* the time to notice our patterns. Do we always wait until a crisis arises to deal with important issues in our lives? Is that the way we want it? If not, we can realize that we do have a choice, and through practice, we can learn to take earlier action to avert avoidable crises and, when we notice we are discontented, move directly to the Sorting-out Phase of transition and let it guide us into Action.

Crisis—particularly the avoidable type—is experienced more intensely by Copers. They sense it as a threat to their well-being. It may occur unexpectedly, as the death of a loved one often does. Or it may follow a period of discontentment in the process of making what began as a voluntary transition, as it did with Mike Long:

> After being with the firm for less than a year, I hit bottom. I knew I could not continue my charade. I had begun to realize and admit that the zealous advocate role did not fit my personality and values. In the past I had always been so determined, goal-oriented and clear about what my next step would be. I had reached a point where I felt absolutely lost, alone and without a clue of what to do or where to turn.

Because Mike did not act on his inner feelings, the partners in his firm ultimately resolved his dilemma for him. Two of the partners called him in one afternoon for a meeting, citing the drop-off in his productivity and noting that they sensed he was unhappy with the firm. Accordingly, they decided to terminate his employment and asked that he complete his work within two weeks and leave the firm. Though painful for Mike, it did remove him from a situation in which he was obviously unhappy, and opened the door to an appropriate new opportunity.

To thrive during crisis, we must develop our sense of groundedness. Our spiritual practices, our support network, and our inner resilience provide crucial help during these difficult times.

In a voluntary transition—i.e., one that is self-initiated for the purpose of self-improvement—the Crisis Phase is experienced as a *decision* point following increased awareness of the need for change. For example, the decision to lose weight only occurs after someone notices the lethargy, unattractiveness, or poorly fitting clothes which result from excess pounds. At this point, one is truly ready to pursue change. Reaching this point is significant, for researcher James Prochaska has found that only 20 percent of any given population is truly ready to change at any one time.[6] After making the decision, the individual is ready for the next step: considering options to accomplish the desired result, such as dieting, exercising, or seeking counseling to resolve larger lifestyle or personal issues.

Sorting-out Phase: Every transition includes a period of sorting out, in which we feel confused, as though we have lost our bearings. We may fear that something is wrong with us for feeling this way, yet it is an important period. The *Sorting-out Phase* is a time for our inner development, in which we reflect on our values, our purpose, and our options. It is like the apparently dormant wintertime in a plant's life, when the only growth occurring is internal and often invisible to the casual observer. Because it is an uncomfortable time, marked by confusion and disorientation, many people attempt to avoid it. And the fact that Western cultural norms allow no space for such periods of inner exploration makes the Sorting-out Phase perhaps the most difficult period of any transition. Our challenge is to find ways to perform the critical inner work of exploring our feelings and dreams, while continuing to carry on with our daily responsibilities.

The Sorting-out Phase is where our sense of disorder, or "entropy," is at its peak. We experience feelings which are new to us, for we are entering a new period of our lives. We have lost our moorings—and often with them, our sense of self. If we have placed undue emphasis on our role as an engineer at ABC Widgets, or as the wife of Mr. James or the mother of Sean and Susie, then a job layoff or divorce will stun us as we stagger to rediscover who we are apart from the role we have assumed for so long.

We are challenged to delve deeper into ourselves, to spend time in solitude, and to determine what our soul is calling us to do next. While we are in this phase, we may feel unmotivated to carry out our usual daily activities. We may fear that our vision and sense of direction will never return. Feeling like we may drown in the sea of emotions that is washing over us, we try to find words for our experiences, to make sense of the illogical discomfort that has invaded us. "Will I ever *not* miss him?" we may wonder, following a loved one's death or an unwanted divorce or break-up. "What kind of work will *really* satisfy me?" may be our query after leaving an intolerable job situation. Or: "How should I spend the time I have left to live?" following a terminal medical diagnosis.

Three primary activities comprise the Sorting-out Phase:

Activity No. 1: **We allow ourselves to feel our feelings.** Every transition brings with it feelings of loss of the old situation or behavior, as well as uncomfortable emotions such as fear, sadness, and apprehension. We must let ourselves experience these feelings, and express them in an appropriate way. We may wish to keep a journal, talk with our spouse or close friend, or seek outside help when needed. (More suggestions for expressing our feelings are given in Chapter 7.)

Activity No. 2: **We complete unfinished business concerning the situation we are leaving.** We may use rituals of various kinds for this purpose, or we may conduct a memorial service or other ceremony, write a letter, or do the mental or spiritual work of forgiving someone who has wronged us. We may find that other situations from the past that are similar to our current experience are again brought to mind if we have not made peace with them. Processing these past events, too, is part of the Sorting-out Phase.

Activity No. 3: **We explore the options for our next step.** We may do informational interviewing to select a new job or career area. Or perhaps we challenge ourselves with a new activity— bungee jumping, rock climbing, or motorcycle riding—to help us stretch our boundaries and access parts of ourselves that are yearning to be expressed. After a period of exploration, the available options narrow to one or two that attract particular interest. Then, visioning is about to begin.

Mike Long went through a Sorting-out Phase when he realized he had hit rock bottom in his job. Feeling lost and unsure what to do next, he turned to outside resources to provide assistance during this confusing time. He consulted with a career counselor who coached him in the art of informational interviews and networking. "More importantly, [the counselor] was able to instill hope in me that I could identify what I wanted to do and make a successful transition to this new career area." Sometimes this kind of emotional support is the greatest gift we can receive during the Sorting-out Phase, since our own sense of self ebbs in the midst of the transition. Mike conducted over fifty informational interviews during his exploration process, and worked as a counselor at a reduced wage so that he could explore that field. In addition, he contemplated the termination of his job and the circumstances surrounding it. He realized that the situation and the decision had not only been painful for him, but for the firm as well. He allowed himself to feel his pain and the associated shame at not being "good enough," and to learn from it.

It requires trust to successfully navigate the Sorting-out Phase. By being undaunted by the ambiguity which characterizes this unsettling period, nurturing ourselves, and trusting that the outcome will be positive, we become ready to move into the exciting phase of visioning.

Vision Phase: Like the first rays of the new dawn, a vision of the next phase in our path begins to appear. Whether it is the job that we can't stop thinking about, or the nagging belief that we *can* return to full health despite what the doctors say, the vision is the embodiment of how we want the next period of our life to look. Prior to this phase, there are an infinite number of possibilities of what could come next (which is why the Sorting-out Phase feels confusing and overwhelming). But as we near the *Vision Phase,* we "reduce the wave packet," to borrow a term from physics, so that the multiple possibilities merge into one direction. This in turn creates a positive momentum which has been described as the "hand of Providence" urging the vision into manifestation. A creative reawakening occurs as we rediscover our newly shifted foundations and begin to move forward in the new direction.

Thrivers are proactive in creating the next phase of their life, whether it be learning to live without their deceased spouse, embarking on a new career, or deciding where to move. Their sense of purpose and ambition, combined with their skills of proactive creation, help them use each transition to carry them to a new, more fulfilling level of possibility.

Through his trial run in the counseling field, Mike Long discovered that his passion lay there. He began to see himself working in the field of social work, somehow combining his legal and counseling skills toward a more fulfilling end. And from that point on, the action he needed to take became clear.

Action Phase: Thrivers do not hesitate to take action on their dreams when the time is right. The *Action Phase* begins once their vision is clear; they find a step—however small—to begin moving toward it, and they take it. With optimism and a flexible sense of adventure, combined with a willingness to take risks to build their self-confidence, Thrivers act on the momentum their vision has generated. One step leads to the next, often in unexpected directions, but always toward a greater good and enhanced fulfillment.

Mike Long's action step after he discovered his interest in social work was to return to school to get his master's degree in social work. This in turn set off what he describes as an "acute crisis in my marriage," which was eventually resolved through therapy. The ultimate outcome of Mike's situation is his current job, which involves assisting attorneys with stress, burnout, substance abuse, and transition issues.

Evaluation Phase: The final task of transition, which leads directly into the next cycle of discontentment, is the *Evaluation Phase*. If we merely take action and do not periodically ask ourselves whether the action we have taken is fulfilling our vision, we can easily be distracted or lured away from our chosen course. Thrivers periodically examine their goals and vision in every area of their life, analyzing how they feel about their decisions to change and whether further change is necessary. They aren't afraid to experiment, to laugh at themselves, and to monitor their investments of time and energy to ensure an ongoing balance.

Through this constant monitoring and periodic reevaluation, the discontentment which leads to the next transition can be easily accessed and dealt with before a crisis erupts. As the observer of our own transitions, we begin to have an increasingly greater influence on their direction. We and our experience become a "self-referential loop" (see Chapter 10 for further discussion) providing constant feedback about where change is needed, and whether we are progressing in the direction of our desires.

Dr. Fred Alan Wolf points out that virtually every scientist who has made a revolutionary discovery, as well as the majority of individuals who make major changes in their lives, have a period of "recanting" when they wish (temporarily) that they had never made the move. This is not unusual, but typically follows the excitement of the new idea. Typically, the recanting period passes and they settle comfortably (for the time being) into creating and building this new dimension of their experience.

Reflecting on his transition, Mike Long had these comments:

> Each stop along the journey, however, has brought personal growth and increased satisfaction. For many years I tried to do what others expected me to do or what I thought was the "smart" or the "right" thing to do. I ultimately began to enjoy satisfaction in my career and greater happiness and enjoyment in my life when I began to follow my heart.

Each of the phases of transition we have just described is associated primarily with one of the trait clusters of the Thriver. In the next six chapters, we will examine each phase of transition in conjunction with the cluster of traits which corresponds with that phase. Diagram 4-2 illustrates the relationship between the phases of transition and the Thriver traits.

Is There a "Midlife Crisis"?

Some psychologists have suggested that transitions accelerate around midlife and create a type of "midlife crisis." My research suggests that the notion that we experience one particularly traumatic crisis at midlife is a product of the Old Zero,

Diagram 4-2
THRIVER TRAITS

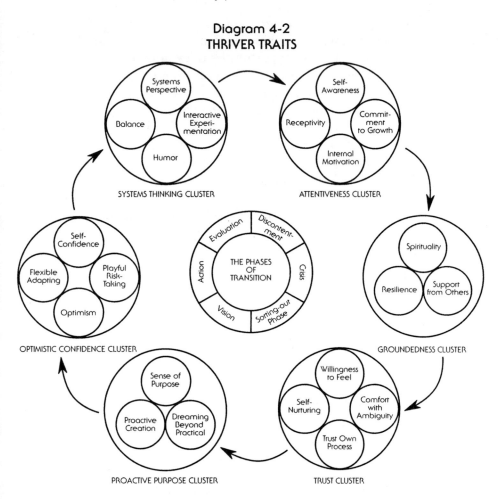

when linear career paths and stable relationships were the rule. In the New Zero, we undergo both major and more minor life transitions throughout our life. Returning to college at age forty, fifty, or sixty is no longer unusual, nor is having two or more spouses during one's life.

Our age is not as accurate a predictor of a major life transition as are the events which have preceded it, and the extent to which we have been open to our feelings about those events. If we have muddled through the changes of our life with tunnel vision, failing to allow ourselves a Sorting-out Phase, or refusing to be proactive in designing a vision of a fulfilling life and carrying it out, we can be assured that a crisis is not far ahead. Life offers us countless opportunities to explore our depths and to expand our boundaries. If we accept the invitations it provides, we will thrive; if we ignore or refuse them, we will face crisis and unhappiness until we change our ways.

While it is true that some transitions are more traumatic for some people than others, there is no universal formula for determining at what age or in what situation a given person's "quantum leap" opportunity will occur. Hopefully, as we develop the tools of the Thriver and increase our understanding of the transition process, we will have a lifeline to hold on to as we move into a new dimension.

The Gifts of Transition

Transition includes both pain and joy, confusion and newfound clarity. And since in the New Zero our life course is less predictable, it is common to wonder what outcomes will make a transition worthwhile. Those who have experienced major transitions are eager to share the many gifts it brings. Most of the Thrivers I interviewed mentioned that they learned one or more lessons from their transitions. From the importance of adjusting one's priorities to finding new aspects of oneself, development of empathy to learning to look inside oneself for the answers, many of the most significant lessons in life come from navigating a key transition.

A transition has resolved itself when its lessons are clear, and the external events—as well as the inner turmoil—have calmed down, resulting in a new level of comfort with the person who is emerging. Following transition, we should feel good about what has happened, about the steps taken or the progress made. A sense of peace and internal happiness is common. Now, the series of events can be viewed with a detachment, describing in a more or less objective manner what has occurred and the impact it has had. Oftentimes, a particularly pivotal transition may also result in a sharing of our newfound knowledge with others through forming an organization (e.g., Mothers Against Drunk Driving), supporting a cause, or starting a business which carries forth the vision inspired by the transition.

Whatever the nature of the transition, it is sure to bring a growth and change—often at a deep level. Indeed, one's transitions weave together to form a beautiful tapestry of one's life. Without them, life lacks the color and depth, which results from moving successfully through change.

NOTES

1. I am indebted to Dr. Fred Alan Wolf for his insights on quantum physics, both in interview and through his books: *Taking the Quantum Leap,* Harper & Row 1981; *StarWave,* Macmillan 1984; and *The Dreaming Universe,* Simon & Schuster 1994.
2. Senge, Peter, *The Fifth Discipline,* Doubleday 1990, p. 71.
3. Wolf, Fred Alan, *Taking the Quantum Leap,* Introduction.
4. "The Prime of Our Lives," *Psychology Today* May 1987, p. 68.
5. Prigogine, Ilya and Isabelle Stengers, *Order Out of Chaos,* Bantam 1984, p. 286.
6. Prochaska, James, *Changing for Good,* William Morrow 1994, p. 15.

PART THREE

TRAITS OF
THRIVERS

5

PAYING ATTENTION
TO OUR
DISCONTENTMENT

❧

*Life comforts the disturbed and disturbs the
comfortable.*

—Dan Millman
*No Ordinary
Moments*

For some reason unknown to me, I feel like something is missing in my life. I have a good job, a boyfriend who cares about
me, and am pursuing my college education—a long-time goal. I
just don't feel content. I know my life has a purpose, but I can't
seem to identify what it is. Maybe I should take some courses in
subjects I haven't yet explored. Or maybe I just need to get more
centered within myself and know that the answers will come.

These musings, which reflect my feelings midway through college, are not unlike those of any Thriver who is on his or her
path of awakening. The discontentment reflected here involved
major life issues—career path and life purpose. But it may also
emerge regarding more "minor" concerns such as a feeling that
we are not spending enough time with our children, or a desire
to add another hobby or activity into our already busy lifestyle.

Managing transitions effectively—of whatever type—requires that we become ever more attentive to the first indication that change is coming.

With many of the individuals I interviewed, the Discontentment Phase first becomes noticeable through physical symptoms. It may be an overall tension, a knot in the pit of their stomach, a headache, a cold that won't go away, or a compulsion to eat or drink more than usual. It may also manifest itself in mental unrest. Some people notice that they ask themselves a lot of questions about what's happening in an area of their lives, or they experience an amorphous, intuitive sensation that something new is ahead. By learning to recognize these unique sensations of impending change, we can stop resisting it and begin to welcome it. When the Discontentment Phase comes, we must clear the way for a new aspect of ourselves to emerge. Attentiveness is the key to confronting and working through these vague feelings of discontentment which occur as transition begins.

The cluster of traits which comprises attentiveness includes four aspects:

- self-awareness
- commitment to growth
- internal motivation
- receptivity to new ideas

SELF-AWARENESS

The Buddhist concept of "mindfulness" provides a meaningful parallel for what is meant by attentiveness in general, and self-awareness in particular. Contrary to the Western emphasis on the future—how to plan for it, achieve future goals, and avoid calamity—Eastern teachings encourage us to focus on the present, and to "be here now." The essence of this kind of attentiveness is "to directly participate in each moment as it occurs with as much awareness and understanding as possible."[1]

When we are aware, in this sense, we do not simply see

things that happen and interpret them according to our preordained ideas. Rather, we notice our feelings, the occurrences in our lives, and our more subtle perceptions of other people and how they respond to us and purposely do *not* automatically try to evaluate those phenomena through the filters of past experience and judgment. Our observations take on a childlike quality as we look at things as though we are seeing them for the first time.

As we open our eyes and our minds, we in fact begin to see aspects to the situation or relationship which we could not see before.

We realize how our mental filters actually prevent us from seeing what has been there all along. As Stephen Levine explains in *A Gradual Awakening*:

> We have stiff, unchanging conceptual labels in a world full of change which, of course, causes a split between the concept and the reality, and a resulting tension. We don't really see reality. We see only the shadows that it casts and those shadows are our concepts, our definitions, our ideas of the world.[2]

Until we expand our perception and allow our labels to dissolve, we only see the world as we want to see it. Our subjective definition of the world may directly contradict its objective reality. True awareness, as contemplated by Eastern thought, is unbounded by labels, free from interference by the mind. It simply observes, without attempting to judge or react.

It was during my own spiritual crisis in college that these concepts began to have meaning for me. As I sensed that my childhood beliefs no longer fit the person I was becoming, I began searching for an alternative belief system that corresponded to the self that I had become. Many uncomfortable feelings arose during this process. I decided simply to allow those feelings to be, to notice them and the new ideas I encountered without judging them as good or bad, right or wrong.

I soon began to reap a number of benefits from this kind of attentiveness. I became much more open to playing the game

of life, becoming flexible and rewriting the rules when necessary to accommodate new experiences along the way. By letting
my emotions be my teachers, but simultaneously detaching myself from the powerful hold they would otherwise have on me,
I found a new freedom. This process allowed me to see things
in a much more objective way, and to access creative ideas and
insights that were previously closed to me. As Dhiravamsa, an
Eastern mystic, describes it:

> Buddhism teaches the Middle Way, which is the way of bal-
> ance. This cannot be created, but it will come to you with the
> right understanding, through awareness. Without awareness, the
> balance is lost and we swing to extremes of thought and action.
> Enlightened people are those who have constant awareness in
> life, who are free from psychological sleep, whatever they are do-
> ing.[3]

Thrivers are psychologically awake. Through vigilant attentiveness to their own emotional states and life situations, they
can detect the first twinge of dissatisfaction. They notice it, examine it, and ask it what it has to teach them. Then, after some
time for reflection and exploring their options, they take appropriate action. But their self-awareness, active in every moment of their lives, allows them to avert many of the crises
which Copers may face as the result of inattention to their true
feelings.

Psychologists tell us that in certain situations, self-deception
and denial are natural reflexes which we use to protect ourselves from the truth. Copers in particular use the technique of
denial to shield themselves from painful knowledge about
themselves. This is the only way they can maintain a positive
self-image. But in the long run, accumulated denial results in
destructive emotional and physical consequences.

Many people deny their physical symptoms until they develop to the point of requiring hospitalization. Jay, for example, had spent years doing aerobics on a regular basis, both to
control his diabetes and to stay in shape. Because he had been
doing high impact aerobics, however, his body had taken a
beating and he felt he needed a rest:

I quit [aerobics] for a year. And at the end of that year I had a heart attack. So symptoms leading up to that were shoulder pains, but only when I had really exerted myself, when I'd climbed a flight of stairs. I usually climbed the same flight of stairs five or six times a day, and every time I'd get up to the top, I'd feel short of breath, and I'd have this pain. After I'd gone ten feet on the flat floor, my pain went away, and I thought, "I've got to get back to the aerobics. My condition is simply that I'm not exercising like I used to." That was my rationale—that was my avoiding the fact that I was really having some pain, and that I did need to see a doctor. So I had indicators, and certainly didn't pay attention to them.

A few weeks later, he was staying with a friend, and practicing with a sailing crew for a race from Victoria, British Columbia to Maui.

I had exactly that same feeling in my shoulder when I was standing at the sink doing the dishes. And it was at 8:30 in the morning. And I thought, "Wait a minute. There are no stairs around here. I did not just walk stairs." And that scared me. I thought, "How can this be when I know in fact that the reason for this is that I need to get back to exercising?" Well, it blew that whole belief that I had. And of course I went into denial again, and said that this will pass.

Jay said goodbye to his friend, got in his car, and began the three-hour drive back to Portland. Experiencing severe pain most of the way, he kept a vigilant eye on his symptoms to be sure he was still fit to drive.

I was saying to myself that I'm having all this pain, but I can't stop. It would be foolish for me to pull off to the side of the road here, isolate myself, and be in this pain and not have some movement, not have some forward movement to get myself to where I can get some help. One of the things I decided to do was to try to get stopped by the police, so I started speeding, and was speeding down I-5 going south at 85 and 90 miles an hour, and didn't see one cop!

Ultimately, Jay made it to the University of Oregon Health Sciences Center, where he had planned to get a refill on the special food he was eating as a participant in a study of diabetes. When he arrived, the attending physicians quickly recognized his symptoms and checked him in for evaluation in the intensive care unit. Jay's open-heart surgery occurred several days later, and required five bypasses. His denial of the pain leading up to it could easily have led to a fatal heart attack had he not finally acknowledged the seriousness of the pain and gone to the hospital for treatment.

Another form of denial is the "perfectionist syndrome." Actress Markie Post consciously adopted this pattern in childhood. "It was an almost idyllic childhood," says Post, "but I have terrible memories of the early years, when my older brother was very sick."[4] Born with a deformed trachea requiring several operations, her brother had a long convalescence. Post helped with his care.

> I knew how worried my parents were, so I made the decision that I would be extra good and not add to their burden. But because I also had resentments, like any kid whose parents' attention is focused elsewhere, I figured I must be a very bad person deep inside.

This negative self-image haunted Post through her high school years, into her drama training in college, and even into her brief first marriage and the beginnings of her acting career. When she was cast as Lee Majors's sidekick on *The Fall Guy* in 1982, her friends considered the role her "big break," but Post immediately plummeted into what she calls a "delayed identity crisis." She had always felt she had to wear a cheerful mask, and as a result had no one with whom to share her deep depression.

> Once again I was trying to be good, despite all my resentful undercurrents. I wanted to show my negative side, but my Miss Perfect self-image didn't allow it.
>
> I used to think there was this ugly soul hidden away. When I finally got down there and looked around, I discovered it wasn't

so bad. And once I could drop the artifice of trying to be perfect, I could accept my dark side as part of human nature too. I could finally stop beating myself up all the time.

Post found that her Discontentment Phase generated deep introspection, which led to the discovery of feelings and patterns of which she was previously unaware and, ultimately, to the ability to be more genuinely expressive in her life. And indeed, attentiveness offers us that gift. To the extent that we fully accept ourselves, we actually begin to have a fuller experience of the world.

Self-awareness requires the kind of "bare attention" that allows us to welcome each feeling, each event, and each aspect of ourselves so that we can fully accept and experience the changes in our lives.

> Bare attention also brings the mind to a state of rest. An untrained mind is often reactive, clinging to what is pleasant and condemning what is unpleasant, grasping what is liked, pushing away what is disliked, reacting with greed and hatred. A tiring imbalance of mind. As bare attention is cultivated more and more we learn to experience our thoughts and feelings, situations and other people, without the tension of attachment or aversion. We begin to have a full and total experience of what it is that's happening, with a restful and balanced mind.[5]

Meditation

What many Thrivers do to enhance this sense of awareness is to spend time at the beginning of each day sitting quietly, noticing their body, and visualizing their upcoming day. They see it unfolding in the highest and best ways, some of which they know they are not yet aware. And they notice whether they are feeling discontented or satisfied, happy or sad, expectant or full of dread, or whether any "floating" sensations of loss, guilt, or other emotions exist. They simply sit with these feelings, allowing the emotions to teach them what they need to know.

Journaling

Writing spontaneously about whatever comes to mind can be helpful in accessing feelings that we had not realized were there. During the Discontentment Phase, as we reflect on our journal entries, we can ask ourselves if there is a trend to our discontentment. Does it center around work issues? A troublesome relationship? How we are feeling about our physical health? Or is it a more general lack of meaning or purpose which may have its root in a spiritual void? Our answers to these questions will determine the appropriate next step.

Weekly Planning and Renewal

At the beginning of the week, Thrivers also do weekly planning and renewal. They spend time resting, renewing their inner resources, and ensuring that their priorities for the week are in place on their calendar and in their mind before they encounter the daily distractions which divert their attention elsewhere. In Chapter 8, when we discuss proactive purpose, we will explore in more detail how Thrivers create their world the way they want it to be.

COMMITMENT TO GROWTH

Thrivers never tire of learning. Often well-educated, their schooling does not end with college. They keep up with (or ahead of) the latest developments in their field, and often continue their life education through personal growth seminars, self-help books, and classes offered through local colleges, churches, and non-profit organizations. Virtually all of the individuals I interviewed view themselves as someone who is constantly improving him or herself, and fully 25 percent had enrolled in one or more intensive, several-day-long personal growth programs.

Continuous Self-Improvement

Mediocrity is not sufficient for the Thriver; only excellence will do. In companies operating by the principles of Total Quality Management, employees are encouraged to suggest ways of continually improving the company's products or services. Each day, an improvement of just .001 percent will accumulate over time to enable the company to maintain its competitive edge. Likewise, Thrivers are always looking for ways to increase their level of fulfillment, balance, and overall life satisfaction. This continuous self-improvement, or *kaizen,* also has a cumulative effect over time, resulting in dramatic improvement and growth in their personal lives. In essence, a kind of positive momentum is created by adopting this strategy, and is furthered still more by its continuation. In fact, many Thrivers find themselves on what feels like an "accelerated path of learning" that allows them to experience more life in less time, without undue stress.

What often stimulates Thrivers to investigate new directions for their learning is a sense of internal pain or lack of fulfillment. At age thirty-five, Alan noticed a kind of "psychic pain of not being very fulfilled at where I was at and how things were working." This psychic pain led him to therapy, which in turn led to his discovering the extent of dysfunction in his family of origin. He had recently met the woman who would become his future wife, and just as they were getting to know each other, he had a serious bicycle accident, leaving him with a broken neck, and had to wear a back brace for several months. Just after Alan came home from the hospital, his wife-to-be informed him that she was pregnant. They then decided to keep the baby and to get married. To try to manage these major life transitions, Alan enrolled in an intensive weekend-long program called "On Course":

> I wanted to be better at this thing called marriage. I had a terrible model for marriage—my parents were not very good at it and they eventually divorced. And I thought, "There's got to be a better way to do this." And so that really launched my commitment. It was a huge thing to take on; . . . it was almost like three

horizons. I didn't know what I was going to find, and I sort of put them all up there and said this is where I'm going to go, . . . I'm putting this into my life because I want to be good at it. That's why I took On Course—I figured I needed to get some levels of commitment going in my life because all of this stuff was coming at me real fast.

Alan had gone to dozens of trainings sessions and seminars, and had become disinterested because most of them focused on methodology, external things to do, and tools which could make one's life more effective. Though such workshops had a place in his early awakening, Alan was ready for something deeper. When he encountered On Course, he sensed that it was different from the other seminars he had experienced; it was an inner journey. By the end of the weekend you would have "set out on a journey rather than having some kind of completed, money-back guarantee sort of format. It was actually an initiation . . ."

Alan found that to be true. And the clarity which came from participating in that workshop helped buoy him through the difficult times that followed. The pregnancy was not an easy one. Alan's wife spent the majority of it bedridden, while Alan nursed his broken neck and tried to perform his job as a sales manager from home. Unresolved issues from Alan's childhood arose early in their marriage, further complicating the relationship. Without Alan's internal commitment to work through these changes and continue to learn and grow, both the marriage and Alan's work and health would have suffered great damage. He recalls many dark nights during the first two years of his marriage where something would happen and he felt his response was inadequate:

> It wasn't effective for me to stay there and be in that behavior for the rest of our marriage or [my son's] childhood, so I knew I had to change. And looking at some of those hurdles, I couldn't tell you that I knew I would make it through successfully. I just simply started putting a foot in front of the other, and I have found that when that stuff happens, there's some assistance that I identify as the hand of Providence. "A commitment to move forward gets you some assistance that you wouldn't otherwise get" is a principle that I've come to identify in this process.

Alan has discovered that by continuously challenging himself to go deeper within himself, he is able to deal more effectively with not only the existing situations and commitments in his life, but also with new experiences that confront him.

The *Cycle of Continuous Self-Improvement,* which Alan's experiences illustrate, can be diagrammed as follows:

Diagram 5-1
THE CYCLE OF CONTINUOUS SELF-IMPROVEMENT

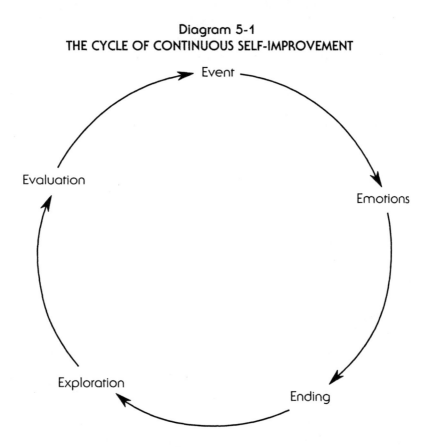

Beginning with an *Event* (which can consist of an internal event such as the "psychic pain" which Alan experienced, or an external event such as facing marriage, pursuing a new job, or receiving a medical diagnosis), some *Emotions* arise. As we feel these emotions, we realize that a part of our life is *Ending.* This may be an old way of viewing the world, a relationship, or a perspective on our job or our health that no longer applies.

Along with the Ending, comes *Exploration* of opportunities for learning and growth that will be helpful in dealing with the Event and the Emotions, as well as the Ending. Ultimately, one or more of these options is pursued, followed by *Evaluation* of the results, leading in turn to another Event, and beginning the cycle again.

This cycle, which is a scaled-down version of the phases of the transition cycle, can occur dozens of times in the course of a day (with varying degrees of intensity depending on the severity of the event), or just several times a month. Thrivers have so keenly cultivated their skill in passing through the Cycle of Continuous Self-Improvement that it has become almost automatic for them. And when they find themselves unsure about what to do next, this model can help them get back on their chosen course.

In addition, Thrivers' commitment to Continuous Self-Improvement leads them to a point of decision when they sense that an area of their life needs to change. This decision point serves as the equivalent of the Crisis Phase of the transition and often ushers in a Sorting-out Phase during which they sort through their options for making the desired change.

INTERNAL MOTIVATION

Jonas grew up in a community which was very competitive, not only in sports but also in school. All of his early experiences were competitive in some way. Adopting his parents' beliefs in hard work, doing things for oneself, and improving oneself and the community, he applied himself to his schoolwork and learned early on to be independent. But the kind of competition which he began to exhibit was not entirely external:

> I grew up in that environment, but what I got from it personally was to compete with myself. I've heard a lot of people talk about that, but in my case it was really true. What my parents taught me was to always try to do the best that I could do. They were very hard working folks and they gave me a great example. What my coaches and teachers taught me was to be true to my-

self—in other words if I prepared and did a good job, the competition would take care of itself. I didn't compete against other kids, even though I played team sports. *I really competed against myself,* and I think that's carried over. I'm very internally motivated.

Jonas's internal motivation is characteristic of Thrivers. Rather than letting events outside of themselves determine how they will feel and behave, Thrivers choose their frame of mind on a moment-by-moment basis. Many Thrivers describe themselves as having always been internally driven. For others, internal motivation develops as the result of a key life transition.

Alan, whom we met previously, found that during the first stage of his adulthood, his desire to improve himself was linked to a desire to please his internal father figure. Having been given the childhood message that he was smart but didn't apply himself (so he would never get ahead), he adopted the typical firstborn personality profile: He became a super-achiever, was driven to obtain his goals and was determined to be the best at what he did. He excelled in his field, and became the top national salesman at the bicycle company for which he worked. Then he realized, through therapy and introspection, that he was still trying to impress his father, who had passed away years ago:

So he really wasn't somebody I needed to impress any longer. Then I made a switch and had a change of understanding about all this. I got off the treadmill of enslavement to my own need to be a perfectionist. That has been a really slow process and I've had to give myself time to let that occur.

Nationally known motivational speaker Terry McBride learned internal motivation through a different kind of transition. From a construction accident at age twenty-three, Terry embarked on a grueling series of thirty major surgeries on his spine and abdomen over the course of the next eleven years, during which, at times, he was not expected to live. Doctors told him that the best he could hope for was to live as a cripple in a dysfunctional body. For the first few surgeries, he put his fate in the hands of the doctors who were operating on him, hoping their expertise and wisdom would lead to his becoming well and whole. But each time another surgery wasn't success-ful, or failed to remove all of the infection that threatened to overtake his body, he became more and more discouraged, as did his family and others supporting him through this difficult process.

Since it seemed the medical profession was failing him, Terry began reading self-help books about healing and exploring al-ternative medicine, trying desperately to find something that would make him well.

> What I began to study was choice. At first I began to look out-side of myself. So I'd [explore alternative healing methods]. And what I began to discover was that what they told me I needed to do to get well would be purely based on what they had studied. If I talked to somebody who was into deep tissue massage, and I'd tell my story, at the end of conversation what they would say was, "You know what's going on is your deep tissues are holding memories from the past." If I went to somebody that was an as-trologer, at the end they'd say, "When's your birthday?"
>
> And so what I began to see was that in all these other healing disciplines, people got well, but everybody had a different model. But in each of those disciplines there was a subtle little thing that says you can choose a new reality.

If Terry had been cocky before his surgeries, he became downright confident as they ground onward. What saved him, and what has resulted in his becoming totally whole and func-tional today, he says, is refusing to accept the reality that the doctors insisted he accept. His refusal reached a peak when his doctors sent him to the hospital psychiatrist for evaluation. When the psychiatrist acknowledged that Terry must be angry about having to spend the rest of his life in a wheelchair, having to go to the bathroom in a bag, and facing possible impotency, Terry replied, "Stop. I do not want to talk with you about this." The doctor said, "I know you don't." So Terry clarified what he meant: "No, no. I'm not going to talk to you about this. I am not going to face your reality." And then the doctor said, "Son, you're looking at the world through rose-colored glasses.

You're in denial." Terry replied, "No, doctor, I am at choice."

Terry acknowledges that the doctors were not negative people; it's just that they saw him as diseased. They wanted Terry to learn to live with his disease. Terry refused to do so. From that moment on, his healing progressed to the point that he can now live a normal life as a successful speaker and husband. He is currently writing his autobiography in an aptly titled book, *The Hell I Can't!*, to help others claim their power to choose what their experience means, rather than being a victim of their circumstances.

Dr. Frank Colistro, a psychologist who works with individuals in career change, also notes the importance of internal motivation in successfully navigating transitions:

> There are a lot of successful people who make transitions very easily and I never see them because they're not going to pay money to come to somebody like me to tell me how great they're doing. And typically, those people are very *internally oriented*. They always are evaluating themselves and asking themselves first when it comes to life-satisfaction questions.
>
> So they're the kind of people who will quit a job because they aren't happy, even if it means they're going to be losing money or seniority or status. They're the people who will exit relationships because they know they're unsatisfying, and they'll have a sense about when trying more isn't going to really result in much, because the other person just isn't willing to put out. (emphasis added)

An important shift which often precedes the development of an internally driven approach to life is learning to value our own opinions and feelings about what is best for us more than those of other people.

In childhood, we adopt our parents' opinions and beliefs as our own. We may do the same with teachers and other authority figures. As friends and peers become more important to us, we try on their values and beliefs as well. In adolescence, as we rebel against parents' values and strive to forge our own sense of self, the shift begins. As we enter our twenties, our identity and our ways of thinking are challenged in college, and our sense of self continues to develop as we begin our first career. But when we enter adulthood, we must move our source of values and life philosophy from the external authority figures and peers of our youth to a more internal source. "To reach full maturity we must first rediscover our parents so that, now internalized and immortal, they become a source of fresh strength. In other words, to internalize and identify is to grow," writes George Vaillant in *Adaptation to Life*.

It is truly liberating to learn to trust our own judgment, whether it means choosing which car to buy or deciding whom to marry. We become less concerned about what others think and more concerned with whether or not we are true to our authentic sense of self. We begin to realize that the answers we seek are within ourselves. Thrivers embody this confidence in their intuitive, internal senses. This enables them to make change when it is appropriate, not just when crisis demands it.

RECEPTIVITY TO NEW IDEAS

"How does that work?" "Oh, really?" "Tell me more." These are examples of how a Thriver responds when confronted with a new experience, opinion, or belief. Inherently open and inquisitive, they want to understand how life works, and aren't afraid to ask, if the answer is not readily apparent. New experiences challenge them beyond their comfort zone, and they recognize fresh ideas as food for their souls.

Psychologists have found that people who are open and receptive in this way deal better with change than those who are close-minded:

> Those [subjects] described as open to experience tend to seek out and resolve challenging experiences, express a broader range of interests, and seem to be active participants in and creators of their world. Adults who are more open to experience exhibit more advanced levels of ego development, and are characterized as internal on measures of locus of control.[6]

Openness is critical if we are to enhance our self-awareness and hone our "impending change sensors" to detect the first signs of discontentment. Individuals with closed belief systems, heavily steeped in stereotypes, must consciously designate any experiences or beliefs unlike their own as "different"—often "wrong"—in order for their belief system to stay intact. Each time they do so, their belief system becomes more rigid and impenetrable. They are virtually guaranteeing that they will increase their intolerance of others and become more difficult to live with, and will age less easily than people who continually challenge themselves with new experiences. To the extent that we adhere to fixed ways of thinking and hold moralistic rules and requirements concerning ourselves and others, we close ourselves off from the deeper parts of life. We won't know how much more is possible for us until we relax those boundaries and let new experiences in, as Thrivers do.

In physics, systems which are closed (like people with rigid belief systems) inevitably become more and more disordered, deteriorating to the point of total chaos. Open systems, on the other hand, evolve into higher and higher levels of order as new elements enter the structure.

Thrivers' lives are marked by an ever-upward spiral of growth and evolution.

That is not to say they never have setbacks, or that they never question the choices they have made. But if their growth were charted over the course of their lives, it would rise in a generally upward direction, with a quantum leap here and a setback there. Copers' life courses, by contrast, take on a linear or even downward direction, as they become more and more the victim of their circumstances, and less and less open to allowing life's experiences to act as a catalyst for their personal development.

Receptivity to the new, in combination with an acute sense of self-awareness, becomes even more important because of the nature of change in the New Zero. Since new paradigms are emerging all the time, both at a macro- and a micro-level, it is in our interest to be on the lookout for the first signs that a Quantum Transformation is emerging. As soon as we notice that the existing rules are not solving some key problems in the system (whether the system is society, our career, or our life), the system is ripe for a new paradigm to appear.

You may have noticed an apparent paradox between the trait of internal motivation—trust in one's own judgment and viewpoints—and openness to new ideas. Such paradoxes will occur throughout our discussion of the Thriver personality.

Thrivers have the ability to engage others' ideas and experiences while maintaining the ability to generate their own. There is a simultaneous in-flow and out-flow. Retaining an open mind, the Thriver continues to trust his or her own intuitive hunches without always needing to be "right" or have things a certain way.

In his extended research of the "survivor personality," Dr. Al Siebert found that these paradoxical sets of traits, which he calls "biphasic," are characteristic of people who become stronger through adversity. Dr. Siebert began investigating survivors when he joined the paratroopers after his sophomore year of college. The training cadre at his basic training in Fort Campbell, Kentucky was from a unit that had been trapped by Communist armies at Inchon, Korea. Only one man in ten came out alive. Dr. Siebert sensed that it was not just luck or fate that caused these few men to return; something about them tipped the odds in their favor.

Both his military experience and over forty years of subsequent research has proven that survivors are both serious and playful, trusting and cautious, independent and dependent. How can they be both? Says Siebert, "Biphasic personality traits increase survivability by allowing a person to respond in one way or its opposite in any situation. To have biphasic traits is to be 'and' rather than 'this way but not that.' You are proud and humble, selfish and unselfish, cooperative and rebellious." In short, the survivor response varies, depending on what is appropriate to the situation. They have developed a flexibility in choice of strategy which enables them to face even the most challenging situations successfully:

The secret ingredient, if it can be called that, is that surviving difficulty comes more from an orientation, an attitude, an expectation, than from any specific element. It is the intention to survive and to do so in good shape that brings it all together. This is an emotional commitment of the total self. Once made, the how of survival is to be discovered.[7]

If we want to awaken to truly seeing life in all of its splendor—and its ugliness as well—we must work diligently to pierce the fixed boundaries of our beliefs about life and how it "should be." By consciously choosing to respond to new stimuli with questions such as "How does that work?" or "Tell me more," we begin to open ourselves to allow new information into our minds and selves. We deliberately adopt an orientation to *thrive* in the midst of our transitions. Gradually, we begin to experience the wonder that comes when we are constantly reinventing our lives, over and over, and allowing the image of our highest self to emerge.

TEN WAYS TO DEVELOP ATTENTIVENESS

Thrivers pay attention to their internal state as much as to the external events in their world. As they do so, they become keenly attuned to the first signs of discontentment, or the need to correct their course. To develop your own capacity for attentiveness, follow these ten simple principles:

1. Learn to recognize your own signals of discontentment (whether physical, mental, emotional, or other).
2. Loosen your labels and preconceptions of the world. Ask yourself, "How can I see this differently?"
3. Avoid self-deception, denial, and perfectionism.
4. Cultivate "bare attention" through meditation, journaling, and weekly planning and renewal.
5. Practice Continuous Self-Improvement. Learn something new each day.
6. Make your choices from the "inside out." Remember

Terry McBride's message: "You can choose your own reality."

7. Trust your own judgment about what is best for you, what course of action you should take. All of your answers are inside of you.

8. Be willing to pursue new experiences and ideas.

9. Ask probing questions to open yourself still more: "How does that work?" "What could that mean to me?" "Tell me more."

10. Learn the value of "both . . . and" rather than "either/or." Life need not be black and white; shades of gray, and other colors, give life its variety.

As your attentiveness increases, you will find yourself less and less frequently in acute crisis, for you will anticipate the need for transition before it reaches a crisis state. But for those times when you must deal with a crisis, the next chapter guides you through the three key elements needed to face its challenges squarely.

NOTES

1. Levine, Stephen, *A Gradual Awakening,* Doubleday 1989, p. 1.
2. *Ibid.,* p. 10.
3. Dhiravamsa, *The Way of Nonattachment,* Crucible 1989, pp. 16 and 33.
4. "When I Stopped Being Perfect, I Got Better," *Parade* February 6, 1994.
5. Goldstein, Joseph, *The Experience of Insight,* Shambhala 1976, p. 21.
6. Lonky, Edward, et al., "Life Experience and Mode of Coping: Relation to Moral Judgment in Adulthood," *Developmental Psychology* Vol. 20, No. 6, 1159–1167 (1984).
7. Siebert, Al, "The Survivor Personality," *Northwest Magazine,* January 27, 1980. For further elaboration, see Siebert, Al, *The Survivor Personality,* Practical Psychology Press 1994.

6

GROUNDING OURSELVES IN TIMES OF CRISIS

❧

At that crisis point, when there's no other option but futile resistance, if we choose the [peaceful] warrior's path, we go through the pain, like a dark bank of clouds, and emerge in a place of clarity; we come out from our hiding place and find the will to heal our lives. Most of all, we never give up.

—Dan Millman
No Ordinary Moments

As thirty-two-year-old singer-superstar Gloria Estefan awakened from her nap, it was snowing on the road outside her customized tour bus. Heading for a concert in Syracuse, New York, the Miami Sound Machine expected a sellout crowd. The bus had stopped to avoid a jackknifed truck. "Then it was like an explosion when another truck suddenly slammed into us from behind," Gloria relates. "There were no seat belts on the bus, and I must have been thrown off the couch, because the next thing I remember is lying on my back on the floor in excruciating pain. I had the strangest taste in my mouth, almost electrical, and I knew instantly I had broken my back." All she could do was call out, weakly, "What happened?" as the bus was hurled into still another truck, carving out a gaping hole in the bus so that now it was snowing *inside.*

Gloria was afraid to move. She couldn't see her husband, Emilio, who had been forced out of his laced tennis shoes by the force of the crash. She then realized she was lying on the floor in a pile of debris as Emilio looked down and asked, "Baby, are you all right?" "I think I broke my back," Gloria answered.

Her next thought was "What's happened to Nayib?" Nayib, their nine-year-old son, was covered by shoes, purses, bags, and other things that had fallen from the bunks. He clutched at his shoulder and murmured, "I think it's broken." Though she felt relieved that both Nayib and Emilio had survived the crash, Gloria couldn't shake her first thought after the crash: "My God, it's happened. The thing that I had always feared most." Certain that her back was broken, she wondered if she would become wheelchair-bound like her invalid father had been. Fear gripped her as she waited for the ambulance to arrive.[1]

No one escapes the sudden impact of crisis at some point in life. Suddenly, unexpectedly, our life is in utter upheaval. The crisis event is so far outside our expected range of experience that there is a "gap" between what was and what is now, after the incident. And while not every transition begins with a crisis, certainly each life crisis initiates a transition.

Quantum physicist Dr. Fred Alan Wolf suggests that such crisis events may represent the temporary escape of the essential spirit "trapped" inside all matter—including our physical bodies. When a quantum leap occurs, whether it be an electron suddenly leaping into another orbit or an individual faced with crisis, the innate essence of the particle or individual momentarily transcends its physical form, resulting in a permanent shift in perception. We catch a glimpse of the true essence of things, and from then on, we are not the same. Our crisis is a "parting of the ways," in the meaning of the Greek root of the word. But the passageway through this process is far from easy.

Crisis is designed to build our inner strength through a trial by fire.

The story is told of a man who saw a butterfly exerting great effort to extricate itself from its cocoon. The man had compassion for the creature and tried to help it by taking a sharp knife and lightly cutting the cocoon. To his dismay, the butterfly died. His subsequent research disclosed that during the struggle to get out of the cocoon, the butterfly pumps fluid into its wings, which gives it the strength to fly. By trying to "help" the butterfly out of its crisis, the man had inadvertently deprived it of the strength it needed to survive outside its protective shell. People, too, sometimes need the ordeal of crisis to allow their greater self to emerge.

VARIETIES OF CRISIS

The forms of crisis are as numerous as the individuals who experience them. But they fall into two basic types, each with its own strategy for facing it. First, there are the *unavoidable crises,* such as freak accidents, the sudden death of a loved one, or a diagnosis of serious illness. These can be the most difficult to deal with, since they make no logical sense. There are no simple explanations for why a child is born with a disability or why a murder occurs. All we can say is that "Sometimes life isn't fair." Like the sudden leap of the electron to a new orbit, these involuntary crises are random and unpredictable.

When confronting unavoidable, seemingly unfair crises, it is often best to simply accept the reality of what has happened and shift our attention to the Sorting-out Phase of feeling our feelings, exploring our options, and moving on. This is not denial; rather, it is a mature response to confronting the kinds of crisis which cannot be prevented or anticipated.

Avoidable crises, the second type, involve health problems, divorces, job losses, or financial difficulties which result from refusing to make lifestyle changes we suspect are necessary. They only occur when we have ignored the messages of our inner voice which has been beckoning us to make an adjustment, or even a radical transition, over a period of time. These "wake-up calls" present fertile opportunities for our growth. In fact, they often result in wholesale quantum leaps from one paradigm to another.

Thrivers are not content merely to deal with such crisis events as they arise—they strive to prevent the crisis from happening at all. They learn to notice when their discontentment is reaching the saturation point, and begin considering their next step at that juncture. Avoidable crisis is thus an endangered species of experience in the Thriver's life. Their attentiveness sharpens their perception, both internally and externally, so that they can take action before it reaches crisis proportion. Instead, they calmly make a decision to consider alternative behaviors or new approaches to situations they wish to change. Psychologists have found that much inner work is required simply to reach the point of readiness from which effective change can occur. Thrivers make sure they have progressed to this point before moving to the next task of their transition. And when a crisis does occur, they learn from it so that it can be avoided next time.

HOW A CRISIS DEVELOPS

The transformative growth crisis engenders is not unlike the emergence of revolutionary scientific discoveries. The emergence of quantum physics from the old Newtonian paradigm, the discoveries of the X ray and the lightbulb, each represented a marked departure from existing thought and only came forth after a sequence of preparatory events. Thomas Kuhn, who coined the term "paradigm" and examined the phenomenon of scientific revolutions in depth in his work, *The Structure of Scientific Revolutions,* found that crisis (whether in science or in life) begins with an anomaly: something which is irregular, which deviates from the common rule or predominant paradigm. The discovery of the X ray, for example, occurred when a substance being used in an unrelated experiment exhibited unusual properties, which were later applied in X ray photography.

Similarly, we recognize an anomaly when our spouse has an unusual reaction to a familiar remark: usually, he smiles and complies when we ask him to take out the garbage, but today he explodes into a tirade at this simple request. Or perhaps we notice an unusual sensation in our body, a nagging pain or a sore that isn't healing.

Taken alone, these events may mean nothing. Such anomalies of experience can occur many times, both in the scientist's experiment and in our own lives, without generating any apparent need for change. They either disappear, or are resolved in a routine fashion.

So what is it that makes an anomaly lead to a crisis, or to a resolve to change longstanding behaviors? At least three possible situations will do so.

First, the anomaly may call into question fundamental generalizations of the existing paradigm. This is the case when, after fifteen or twenty years on the job, rumors of downsizing and eliminating divisions begin. We can no longer assume we have job security with this company, and we seriously question our job security paradigm. A crisis has begun as our familiar paradigm becomes blurred.

Second, the anomaly by itself may not appear to be fundamentally significant, but the limitations it causes are significant. If minor pain or other physical ailments began to impair our ability to perform our job, this kind of crisis would result.

And third, the simple progression of time and the evolution of our lives may transform anomalies that were initially merely "vexing" into crisis. If our spouse's incident with the garbage combined with other seemingly unrelated occurrences to culminate in a full-fledged midlife crisis, this third type of crisis would exist.

Once the shift from anomaly to crisis has occurred, the anomaly begins to draw more attention. We may talk about it with others, but that does not make us any more willing to shed our old beliefs before the new paradigm is clear. We hold to our familiar patterns of thinking long after they have served their purpose, simply because they are familiar and we do not yet have anything with which to replace them.

Resolving a Crisis

Crises resolve themselves in one of three ways. In some cases, our old paradigm proves able to handle the crisis-provoking problem, even though it did not appear at first that it could. No further action is necessary. Other times, the problem resists new approaches, even radical ones, and it is shelved to be dealt with in the future. We simply don't have the tools to resolve this issue right now. In these situations, we can be assured that another crisis will occur in the future to bring the issue to the forefront once again, hopefully for final resolution.

The third type of crisis resolution is when a new paradigm emerges that appears to solve the problem. Then a battle follows for the acceptance of the new paradigm.[2] The crises that produce our quantum leaps in growth are of this third variety. Merely applying or extending the principles or techniques that have worked for us in the past will not suffice; if they were still effective, we would not be in crisis. Crisis involves "a reconstruction of the field from new fundamentals," according to Kuhn. And during that process, we need three kinds of support to ground ourselves:

- a spiritual belief system
- a strong support network
- inner resilience

SPIRITUALITY: THE BASIC FOUNDATION

Virtually all of the Thrivers I have examined incorporate spirituality into their lives in some meaningful way. This helps them manage crisis more effectively. Spirituality, for Thrivers, does not require that they believe in any particular type of god; rather, it contemplates a perspective on life which has a supernatural dimension.

To say that Thrivers are spiritual people does not mean they are necessarily religious in the sense of regular church attendance or adherence to a particular denominational creed. An estimated two-thirds of the baby boom generation have dropped out of the mainstream religious organizations in which they were raised, but more than one-fourth of those who left have recently returned.[3] Three out of five individuals in this postwar generation shun organized religion, but nevertheless consider themselves to be on a spiritual quest.[4] The form of that quest varies widely. Some Thrivers belong to traditional Christian or Catholic churches; others meditate or subscribe to Buddhist practices. Some find spiritual nourishment attending twelve-step groups; others find their deepest centering being in nature.

Spirituality serves five important roles in times of crisis:

- reduction of internal conflict
- comfort
- context
- centering
- courage

Reduction of internal conflict. A particular gift of spirituality, during crisis as well as non-crisis, is that it diminishes the disorder, or what physicists call "entropy," that we feel. It helps us to see the order, the connectedness, and the harmony among the seemingly disparate segments of our experiences. Thrivers are able to see through the "haze" of crisis by turning to their spiritual source for insight. But even as spirituality diminishes our sense of inner conflict, it can make our situation seem worse as life's various aspects become clearer. And that is a natural part of the crisis experience, as described by Marianne Williamson in *Return to Love:*

> It often seems, in fact, that our lives get worse rather than better when we begin to work deeply on ourselves. *Life doesn't actually get worse; it's just that we feel our own transgressions more because we're no longer anesthetized by unconsciousness.* We're no longer distanced, through denial or dissociation, from our experience. We're starting to see the truth about the games we play. This process can be so painful that we are tempted to go back-

wards. It takes courage—this is often called the path of the spiritual warrior—to endure the sharp pains of self-discovery rather than choose to take the dull pain of unconsciousness that would last the rest of our lives.[5] (emphasis added)

When Joanne was selected to attend a two-week-long professional workshop, she didn't know that she was actually being chosen for a spiritual awakening. Successful in her career, but pondering divorce and feeling generally unclear about her future, she describes the experience as going "through my deep hole." Though Joanne was usually a very gregarious, talkative woman, she found herself saying nothing during the entire first week of this intensive seminar. "I felt absolutely removed from everybody," she remembers. She had stayed in the hotel room alone, which was also uncharacteristic. She felt an emptiness, a hollowness, for no apparent reason.

During the second week, each participant was asked to present to the group a symbol of him- or herself, something sacred or special to that individual. Joanne went into the session in which these items were to be presented, still unsure what she would offer. Then, suddenly, she blurted out, "I knew McNair, who was killed in the space shuttle. He was a speaker at a graduation at one of the colleges where I was going to school." She explained that the theme of his message at the graduation had to do with being "better than good enough," and she then began crying uncontrollably. In that moment, Joanne experienced what she calls her "breakthrough":

> That is the moment that everything changed. I became really open to observing other people, who they were, and what their issues were. It was like this floodgate that came through. That was where spirituality opened up to me.
>
> That was where . . . [I saw] that there is a guiding force other than what I believed "God" was . . . that things happen in your life for a reason and that the Universe is guiding and that there is a path for you [even] if you don't know what it is.

From that point on, Joanne has never been the same. Through this pivotal experience, Joanne confronted her shadow self—those parts of herself that she had hesitated to face—and realized that she had to be true to her purpose, even if it meant creating temporary upheaval in her life. She recalls the new depth and sense of direction she contacted at that workshop as "absolutely distinctive" and credits it with transforming her life for the better, as it empowered her to divorce her husband and, later, to launch her own consulting business.

Comfort. The belief that life continues after physical death provides an invaluable sense of comfort to those dealing with the death of a loved one, a serious medical condition, or other disorienting transitions. Bereavement counselor Kelly Osmont notes that people with spiritual beliefs have a decided advantage when it comes to facing the crisis of a loved one's death. And not just any kind of spirituality works in this situation:

> [It is important that people] have some sort of spiritual base that [also] honors them as a human being on this planet, too. In other words, Christians that believe they shouldn't cry because after all, their husband is better off with God or Jesus deny their humanness. So those that are willing to honor their humanness as well as find some peace and comfort from their spiritual beliefs do much better.

The faith of singer Mary Wilson, formerly with the Supremes, was tested recently when her fourteen-year-old son Raphael died in a car accident in which she, too, was injured. In an appearance on "Sally Jessy Raphael" just a month after the tragedy, she recounted the experience. Her son was alive at the accident site for forty-five minutes or so, as people came over to assist the injured. Mary managed to pull herself out of the car, climbing over her son, who was on the passenger side. As she lay on the ground, she "saw him becoming an angel. I mean, I just actually saw him now, going alongside God."[6]

Wilson's radiance during this television appearance was striking. She exhibited a calm sense of acceptance, saying that "I know that he is wherever good people are supposed to be. I'm not in shock. I feel blessed to have had a very special young person in my life, and because of that blessing, I cannot grieve." Many claimed that Wilson was in denial, that she was not reacting as one might expect following such a loss. But her close friend, Rita Coolidge, who was at the hospital for the entire week following the accident, responded, "She's not in denial, because she talks about it all the time, and she talks about the loss of him and all the beautiful things that they shared and that he brought into her life."

Wilson credits her faith with providing her with this sense of comfort and peace in the face of what would otherwise be considered a tragedy. Her parents taught her and her siblings how to love, and that God would take care of them. And Wilson has always thought of herself as spiritual. "I'm not the religious person [in the sense] of being born again, but I never do anything without my prayers." Wilson's experience is just one example of the comfort spiritual beliefs can bring in crisis.

Context. Spirituality can also help put the events of life into a context which was lacking before. Jay, the man who had multiple bypass open-heart surgery whom we met in Chapter 5, had a spiritual awakening at age fifty-two, following his surgery. While he had attended various churches since childhood, he had never sought to nurture his spirituality on a deeper level. But the newness, the fresh sense of wholeness he felt after his surgery prepared Jay for the concepts he heard when he visited a Religious Science church some time later. "It's like I didn't know that I was missing that spiritual development until I found it," he says.

Since this discovery, Jay has found "a forum to express lifelong concerns, lifelong desires, lifelong things that I felt inside about life and this planet and how we live here and how we relate to each other. And I met people that were expressing like feelings to what I had, and some were expressing feelings that weren't exactly like mine, but didn't judge me." The experience changed his life. He now has a sense of strength and purpose that he lacked previously. "And even more importantly, I have an impact. I have some say-so about what happens to me here, and what I do here does impact my world. . . . That's a real sense of power, and that's a real sense of accomplishment for me," he says.

Thrivers find that by adding the spiritual element to their life perspective, the achievement of their goals and desires takes on a new meaning.

Spirituality gives significance to what would otherwise seem trivial, adding a dimension to life that is ongoing both now and after our life on earth is complete.

Centering. Another important role of spirituality for the Thriver is to provide an inner place to which they can go to find peace, even when the world around them is in utter chaos. Rev. Mary Manin Morrissey, director of the 2,500-member Living Enrichment Center, has had to call on her spirituality for centering on more than one trying occasion. In 1987, she discovered that her son, John, was addicted to marijuana. He went through outpatient treatment, but because he was primarily motivated to do it for his parents rather than himself, he returned to drug use after a short time. This time, he "graduated" from marijuana to cocaine use. Thirty days of in-patient treatment followed, but sixty days later he was again using. His sponsor then asked Manin Morrissey and her then husband to do the hardest thing they have ever done: He said, "You've got to tell him he can't come to your house, he can't stay at your house, you won't talk to him unless he gets solid in recovery. And that's the basis on which you'll have a relationship with him."

They did so, and Manin Morrissey didn't hear from John for a month, during which time he lived in his car. It was agonizing for her, since she worried and fantasized about every horrible scene imaginable. So she turned to her inner center:

> Finally I built an altar for him in the house, and I put out baby pictures and pictures up to the time of his age, and wrote the Prayer of Protection all around it, so that I had a focus for my mind. I would say, "John, the light of God surrounds you, the love of God enfolds you . . ." and that's where I would put my attention.

It worked, both to keep her mind focused and to get John to make the decision he needed to make for himself. Three days later he called his mother and said, "I'm ready." He checked into a detox center, then to a halfway house, eventually making a solid recovery, which continues as of this writing.

More recently, Manin Morrissey faced the end of her twenty-six-year marriage simultaneously with the move of the Center she directs from a rented facility to a forty-two-acre permanent site. She was surrounded by change and chaos on a daily basis. She realized she couldn't get rid of the chaos, at least not for a while.

> So I had to be different in the midst of it. I had to have it around me but not in me. And it's okay to be in confusion if you don't get the confusion in you, or to be in chaos if you don't become chaotic. And that was very difficult at first and then became almost a challenge and then a learning and then a joy, because it could all be going on around me and I was unmoved [by it].

What she learned through that process of centering and relying on her inner sense of Spirit was this:

> **"Everything is bounced off your own state of inner peace. So I know I'm okay with me when I'm in my inner state of peace."**

Courage. For some Thrivers, spirituality provides the way out of an intolerable situation. Singer Tina Turner endured years of physical and emotional abuse at the hands of her husband, Ike, until she was introduced to Nichiren Shoshu Buddhism. Turner describes her discovery this way: "I listened to this and something inside me went *bling!* I guess it was intuition—I knew that this was something that was being given to me."[7] She began to test the chant she had learned when Ike wasn't around, and it began to impact her life. As she continued to develop her spiritual awareness through the Buddhist practices, "I could feel myself becoming stronger—becoming less and less afraid." Ultimately, she developed enough inner strength to leave Ike for good.

What was it like when I walked out and left Ike? Yeah—I was afraid. But sometimes you've got to let *everything* go—purge yourself. I did that. I had nothing, but I had my freedom.[8]

The success she enjoys today, following her rise from virtual poverty to become a powerful woman in her own right, Turner credits to "something I found within myself—something that's in all of us, I think, a little piece of God just waiting to be discovered."[9]

Regardless of what role spirituality currently plays in our lives, becoming a Thriver demands a deeper experience of it than we have had thus far. And it is important to understand the uniqueness of our spirituality. We learn to walk our own spiritual path and to live a life that reflects the values, priorities, and beliefs we find helpful to guide us on our journey. It may mean challenging our old ways of thinking, taking risks, or simply paying attention to our deepest yearnings, which have gone unheeded. And when crisis strikes, we can lean on those beliefs to steady us when the world around us seems shaky.

For those who are skeptical about spirituality, the following key questions we often asked as children, and the kinds of answers we give, can be revealing:

- Where did I come from?
- Is there life after death? What is it like?
- Why am I here?
- What is God like?

We may look for the answers in churches of various types, or by "sitting quietly, doing nothing," as the Eastern mystics express it. We can explore nature, attend support groups, or embrace unconventional religious organizations if mainstream religious denominations do not suit our spiritual needs. But by opening ourselves to the *possibility* that there is more to life than what we see, we will find the path that is right for us.

SUPPORT SYSTEMS AND CRISIS

The symbol used to represent the Oregon Attorney Assistance Program, which assists lawyers with career transitions, stress, burnout, and substance abuse, is the red crane, a painting of which hangs on the director's wall. According to the Micmac Indian artist who painted it, the red crane was a bird that would ferry people from one side of the river to the other. In the process of the journey, the people would change, so the red crane has come to be known as the bird of transformation. This story is a perfect illustration of how our support system is there to ferry us from one side of our river to the other through acknowledgment, listening, questioning, providing a reality check, or offering assistance when needed. By relying on it, and giving those things back to the people supporting us, we find ourselves transformed in the process.

At no time does it prove to be more critical to have a network of close family and/or friends than in a time of crisis. Following her harrowing bus accident, Gloria Estefan found the balm of public support she received to be as important to her recovery as her medical treatment. She received more than 4,000 floral arrangements, 3,000 telegrams, and over 48,000 postcards and letters. "It definitely helped: so many people concentrating positively, praying for me," she said in an interview shortly after the accident. "It was like an energy I could feel in the hospital. It helped me bear all that pain."[10]

But crisis can also test the relationships which matter most. Emilio and Gloria Estefan emerged from the bus crash and its aftermath feeling even closer than before. "When there's no real love in a relationship," Gloria says, "hardship tends to separate you rather than bring you closer together. The healthy one loses patience. When this happened, Emilio showed me how much he really loves me. He was there every second for me."[11]

The Benefits of a Strong Social Network

A strong social support network offers many benefits when dealing with transition. Psychological studies demonstrate that if family support is strong, individuals are less likely to experience depression and other "negative life events" than if family support is weak.[12] In addition, Thrivers draw at least five other strengths from their support system:

- acknowledgment
- listening
- challenge
- grounding/reality testing
- assistance

Acknowledgment. Not just during crisis, but each day, we crave acknowledgment. It feels good when someone recognizes us for who we are: "I acknowledge you for being such a loving and important person in my life."

We also receive acknowledgment when someone recognizes that we have done something beyond the ordinary: "I acknowledge you for being willing to stretch yourself beyond your comfort level to try something new."

Freely offering such expressions of appreciation for who someone is, or for what they have done, is particularly self-affirming during crisis.

If we are in crisis and are not receiving the acknowledgment we desire, we can feel free to ask for the acknowledgment we want.

It may take some coaching at first, but people who are committed to being supportive will be glad to know how they can best provide support in difficult times. And incidentally, one of the best ways to break out of a depressing or negative frame of mind is to acknowledge the people we meet each day. That simple act will not only warm their hearts, but holds a hidden benefit: Our own problems will seem to shrink in size as we focus on the positive aspects of others.

Listening. Our support system also provides the invaluable gift of listening. When we are in the midst of a difficult transition, we often simply need a safe environment in which to express our confounding feelings. Talking about them helps us understand our own feelings better, and just knowing that someone cares enough to hear us is an invaluable gift. Studies of the use of support networks when one is approaching career burnout,[13] as well as my own research, demonstrate that those who use support systems experience transition more easily than those who do not.

It takes a special skill to truly listen, and not try to give unsolicited advice. Too often, when spouses (particularly women) want to talk to their partner about a challenge they are facing, or feelings they are having about their relationship, their partner will try to "fix it" by offering advice. The person sharing their feelings ends up feeling invalidated, as though his or her feelings don't really matter.

To avoid giving advice, Thrivers have learned to engage in *reflective communication.* Using this method, the response to our sharing our feelings may be, "What I hear you saying is . . . ," or "I hear that you are feeling . . . ," thus reflecting back to us what they heard us say. That's all. No easy answers. No pat advice. Just communicating that our feelings have been listened to and heard (even if they were not entirely understood).

Through verbalizing how we feel in a non-threatening environment, we can more easily understand ourselves and find the answers we need.

Challenge. Providing challenge may not, at first blush, sound like a proper function of a support system. But when we are in the midst of crisis or an extended transition, we sometimes need a push from someone who knows us well to get us off our excuses. They may ask, "Is this *really* the way you want to spend your time?" or "Isn't there another way to do this?" When the foundation of the friendship is solid, friends can question each other on these levels without risk of rejection, knowing that the emotional challenge is based on love and caring.

Our support system also helps when, during a crisis, a logical decision must be made and we are too emotionally distraught to make a sound decision. The supporting person may then serve as an interface between us and the necessary authorities (e.g., the funeral director when dealing with a death, or the attending physician when facing a serious medical condition), lobby for postponement of major decisions when possible, or ask us probing questions to help stimulate our rational thinking process.

Grounding/reality testing. When our world has just been blown apart by a crisis, we may at times fear that we are going crazy, or that we are the only one who feels this way. At such times, our support network can provide "grounding" by serving as a forum in which we can share our perceptions and elicit opinions as to whether we appear unstable and should seek outside help, or whether others feel or have felt the same way.

Assistance. Crisis demands quick action. And yet when it happens to us, the added stress of the disturbing event may make us feel unequal to daily tasks such as preparing our meals or performing our job. This is where our support system can come to the rescue by reaching out during this difficult time. When we have just received the news that a crisis has occurred, the first thing we should do is telephone those in our support system, and let them know that we need their help. Bereavement counselor Kelly Osmont suggests that you tell them "that after a while you may get tired of asking them, so you'd like them to tell you specifically things that they'd like to do. Because sometimes we don't even know what we want." Or, if we know we need someone to mow the lawn every Saturday, we could make that specific request. Perhaps a good housecleaning every other week is what seems most necessary. By making specific requests, we give the people in our support system the opportunity to respond to a particular need, and enable them to feel comfortable volunteering the services that we most need.

Building a Support Network

The time to build the key components of a support network is before, not during, a crisis. When she lost her only son in a freak accident some years ago, Kelly Osmont found that she lacked the kind of close friends she really needed to help her through the painful grieving process. She ended up calling on acquaintances for some assistance, and trying to do the rest herself, which only compounded her grief.

Thrivers find support in people they encounter every day—at work, at the gym, at church, or while doing activities they enjoy. They understand the importance of a support network in maintaining their physical and mental equilibrium, and have taken the necessary steps toward cultivating meaningful relationships that allow them both to receive and to give support. In light of her experience, Osmont advises married people to cultivate friendships with single people as well. "They're the ones who are going to know what loneliness is about, because they're living it." Besides friendships, we can also reach out to our family—immediate and more distant—by planning regular activities together and becoming more involved in each other's lives.

BOUNCING BACK THROUGH AN INNER CENTER

Wally Amos had a setback that would have stopped most of us. But after losing not only his ownership of the $80 million cookie company he had founded and the fortune it generated, but even the right to use his own name in future business ventures, he is happier than ever. "It did not change me to lose all of those things," he said in a recent interview. "It didn't diminish who I am. It's still me—the best Wally Amos I can be."[14]

What is it that causes some people to be devastated by setbacks, whereas others can seemingly bounce back from anything, no matter how catastrophic?

"There are two reasons why people fail," says Amos. "One is irresponsibility. The second is fear."

Retailer Tom Peterson agrees. When his multimillion-dollar furniture and appliance business was at its peak, Peterson developed what he calls the "walk on water syndrome." "I thought I could walk on water because I had just gone through five or six years of fabulously successful times. And I assumed that even a bankrupt company I could turn around and pull out." So he purchased Stereo Super Stores, a small chain of electronics stores, out of bankruptcy and attempted to turn it around. Within a year, the venture had dragged his entire operation into Chapter 11 and ultimately liquidation, putting him through the trials of financial devastation and public scrutiny. "It was a difficult time to go through, but I'm a relatively strong person. I just pulled myself up by my bootstraps and went on."

Like most Thrivers, Peterson has learned from the experience. Now working in a similar store owned by his daughter and son-in-law, he recalls thinking his financial problems were just temporary and would go away, but they didn't. So now his motto is: "If you have a problem, solve it today, not tomorrow. Don't sweep it under the rug, because it just festers, gets infectious, the whole body gets sick. I knew that all the time, but I thought I was above problems." Another key to Peterson's resilience and positive outlook is, "Don't worry about tomorrow. Tomorrow will take care of itself. Just worry about today and do the best you can. I think all you can do is get up in the morning, do the very best you can, and when you're tired say, 'That's it.'" He points out that people who worry are usually worrying about the same things now that they were a year ago. These things don't go away. We just have to put them away, and go on with our activities.

Resilience

We become resilient by changing our focus, thereby putting ourselves in the position to recover easily and quickly from adversity. Copers see themselves as victims of their circumstances, which keeps them anchored in them. Thrivers, on the other hand, focus on the positive aspects of their situation. "You have to focus on what you *can* do," advises Amos. "There are people who convince themselves that they can't do anything with their lives because of what's happened to them—and they're right. They can't. But the reason is that they've told themselves they can't. They've said, 'I am a victim. Somebody did something to me that paralyzed me for life.' If you believe that, you'll never move forward."

Resilience is often developed through a refusal to give up despite apparently overwhelming odds. Thrivers may recall their past successes, or the difficulties they have overcome, to remind themselves that they can do it again. And once cultivated, resilience results in seemingly endless energy and drive to activate our purpose. Thrivers refuse to let the changing circumstances of their lives get them down, even when bouncing back is hard to do.

To be resilient is to continually adjust our priorities, our commitments, and our activities to adapt to changes that life brings.

It takes inner strength and a determined will to survive and overcome a setback such as Gloria Estefan's bus accident. Upon arriving at the hospital, Estefan was examined and given two choices: wearing a body cast for six months with little hope of full recovery, or surgery with the possibility of infection and even paralysis. Estefan chose surgery. Estefan was in extraordinary physical shape before the accident; to be suddenly unable to walk or take care of herself would have been devastating. Her recovery and return to performing her demanding stage routines are nothing short of remarkable.

Every step along the way she focused on the "firsts": the first walk, the first time she climbed a few steps, the first time she wore high heels since the accident. "Some days it seemed I was just trudging along and I would never be able to do anything again," she recalls. Her comeback is due largely to a rigorous daily workout schedule with a personal trainer, the unconditional support and assistance of her husband, Emilio, and the clear goal she set to be back in concert by January of the year following the accident—which she was. Her trainer, Carmen Klepper, noted that "Gloria is recuperating faster than anyone. She has drive like I have never seen." Of her road to recovery, Estefan says, "I'm enjoying every second; every little thing is just that much more fun. When I think of what could have happened, I feel better—and luckier—every day."[15]

Grounding ourselves through our spiritual beliefs, our support system, and our inner ability to bounce back are key resources for facing the "acute," or initial phase of crisis. But what about later on, after the life-altering event but before we feel life is back to normal? This is the confusing Sorting-out Phase that is part of every transition (crisis-based or not). Our next task is to weather it without becoming "stuck," and learn to touch the deeper parts of ourselves that are ready to emerge during this transition.

The Do's and Don'ts of Facing Crisis Effectively

DON'T:

- take instant action that will have a broad impact
- try to solve it all at once
- be a victim or blame others
- deny your feelings
- try to be a superwoman/superman
- turn to drugs or alcohol for relief
- isolate yourself unduly

DO:

- narrow your life focus—defer important decisions until after the crisis has passed
- take care of yourself—pursue activities that give you pleasure
- know the feelings and experiences to expect, and allow yourself to have them
- ask yourself what you can learn from this: Was it an avoidable crisis?
- develop a positive outlook; refuse to be a victim
- see yourself as more than the sum of your problems
- start small and build your success experiences as you become stronger
- ask for help—use your support network
- when you feel ready, take action
- make a list of the good things coming out of your crisis
- be sure you are ready to initiate a change before moving on

NOTES

1. Estefan, Gloria, "My Miracle," *Ladies Home Journal* August 1990, p. 99.
2. Kuhn, *The Structure of Scientific Revolutions*, University of Chicago Press 1970, pp. 83–4.
3. Ostling, Richard, "The Church Search," *Time* April 5, 1993.
4. Gerzon, Mark, *Coming Into Our Own*, Delacorte 1992, p. 261.
5. Williamson, Marianne, *Return to Love*, HarperPerennial 1992, p. 135.
6. All quotes in this section are from transcript #1443, "Sally Jessy Raphael," air date March 18, 1994.
7. Turner, Tina, *I, Tina*, William Morrow 1986, p. 156.
8. *Ibid.*, p. 223.
9. *Ibid.*, p. 223.
10. Dougherty, Steve, "One Step at a Time," *People Weekly*, June 25, 1990, p. 78.
11. Dougherty, Steve, *Op. cit.*
12. Roehl, Janet and Okun, Morris, "Depression Symptoms Among Women Reentering College: The Role of Negative Life Events and Family Social Support," *Journal of College Student Personnel* Vol. 25(3), pp. 251–254 (May 1984).
13. Pines, Ayala, and Aronson, Elliot, *Career Burnout: Causes and Cures*, Macmillan 1988.
14. Ryan, Michael, "Why People Fail—and Why They Don't Have To," *Parade* May 22, 1994.
15. Estefan, Gloria, *Op. cit.;* Dougherty, Steve, *Op. cit.*

7

TRUSTING THE SORTING-OUT PHASE

&

The world is not in chaos, but is instead changing in a quite orderly fashion.

—John Naisbitt

Going through the Sorting-out Phase of transition is like being lost in a forest without a compass. Lacking our usual surroundings to ground us, even the smallest decisions become arduous. We don't know whether to go forward or back. In this territory, our old map is of little use: The entire landscape has changed. The Sorting-out Phase is a time of reorientation, of completing our past, and of exploring new directions.

The Newtonian model, which governed the Old Zero, viewed transition mechanically. We thought that if we could reach the end result—just get from "here" to "there" as quickly as possible—we would feel better. In that model, there was no place for a Sorting-out Phase, with its call to self-examination. And if we *do* find ourselves in that tenuous place of "in betweenness," where our goals are unclear and we feel lost and confused, our Newtonian friends would only try to "fix" what is "wrong." What they failed to realize is that nothing is "wrong" when the Sorting-out Phase appears; it is the winter of our transition. Rather than succumb to the temptation of quick action to fill the void, however, Thrivers surrender to it, knowing spring will follow.

There are two kinds of Sorting-out Phase. In relatively minor transitions, such as a change of job within the same industry and geographic location, the Sorting-out Phase may amount to nothing more than appreciating the job we have left, analyzing what we need in a new job, creating a vision, and conducting our search. Transitions involving such a simple Sorting-out Phase do not cause the kind of upheaval of the "dark night of the soul" variety.

In these latter cases, discontentment may take us into an entirely new field, out of a long-term marriage, or into a new lifestyle. Death of a loved one can also lead to this kind of Quantum Transformation. Much of the discussion which follows addresses the dark night species of Sorting-out Phase, since it is so difficult to negotiate without guidelines.

In the Sorting-out Phase, we are often called upon to look deeply into ourselves. If we have not yet been overwhelmed by our pain or are not entirely ready to conquer the issue we face—in addiction treatment this is called "hitting bottom"—we may try simply to skip over the introspection demanded by the Sorting-out Phase in favor of impulsive action. In *Care of the Soul,* Thomas Moore cautions us against submerging our feelings in this way:

> Maybe we have to broaden our vision and see that feelings of emptiness, the loss of familiar understandings and structures in life, and the vanishing of enthusiasm, even though they seem negative, are elements that can be appropriated and used to give life fresh imagination.[1]

Like the transformation of the caterpillar in the cocoon into the butterfly, the Sorting-out Phase is a time for gestation—that invisible, but pivotal, growth period.

The danger in skipping the Sorting-out Phase is that our core issue will re-emerge in the next job or relationship, again demanding attention. For example, if our last several relationships have been frustrating, simply moving on to a new one immediately following a break-up will not heal the self-esteem issues, codependency, or other concerns that may underlie our apparent inability to relate intimately. Or if we have just lost our fourth job in two years for a reason such as "poor fit within the company" or "discipline problems," rushing out to polish our résumé for the next new job will not resolve any inherent mismatch between ourselves and the position or field we have chosen, or any long-standing authority issues.

Dr. Frank Colistro, a psychologist who works with individuals in transition, has seen some clients who have made needed change with his coaching, and others who have not.

> Some people don't move through it. They go through a kind of revolving door, or it's maybe more like a pendulum, where they'll get real dissatisfied; and that will motivate them to do something, but then as they start working on it, they get so fearful of the change that they back away from it.

Colistro has found that the key to transcending this fear "starts with a willingness to allow themselves to go through a pretty shaky period." That willingness is what Colistro calls the "make-it-or-break-it point" in making a transition. This "shaky period" includes feelings of confusion, lostness, uncertainty, fatigue, and fear, interrupted periodically by bursts of excitement and new insight as we discover new aspects of ourselves or new possibilities to explore. Thrivers draw on the Trust Cluster of traits to carry them through the trying Sorting-out Phase, practicing six principal activities:

- feel their feelings, no matter how uncomfortable
- resolve issues from their past
- become comfortable with ambiguity
- explore new options (but don't try to settle on one just yet)
- trust the process
- nurture themselves

142 THRIVING IN TRANSITION

DARING TO FEEL

Many of us have been taught since childhood to deny our feelings. Our anger, hatred, frustration, and hurt were uncomfortable for our parents to deal with. To alleviate their own discomfort, they forbade us from expressing strong emotions. During the Sorting-out Phase, when emotions run deep through uncharted territory, restricting their natural flow can stunt our growth as adults.

Sally spent ten years in a marriage governed by those rules:

> I was living with behaviors from my partner that were repugnant to me. He would charge purchases to my credit cards without my permission, and then try to make it my problem that I was upset about it! Showing and expressing anger or upset was not okay—it was a sign of weakness. I couldn't be sad or cry. If I did, he would leave the house, or leave the room. That was typical. I felt I had to compromise myself to keep the family intact.

During the Clarence Thomas confirmation hearings, Sally, a sexual harassment consultant, commented on the Anita Hill sexual harassment allegations while she and her husband were socializing. Says Sally: "When I expressed an opinion about it, I was told that I didn't have any experience in government agencies and didn't know what I was talking about." Such public put-downs characterized their relationship.

After trying to "fix" the problem, fix herself, and fix her partner, Sally realized she was caught in an endless spiral of codependency. She began group therapy and discovered how other couples related in healthy ways. And since therapy provided a safe environment to express her true feelings, Sally became more aware of her emotions. This awareness led to her decision that she could not stay in the relationship.

> I had talked about divorce for at least eight years. And finally . . . I was ready to hear my own true needs. I had denied my emotions for so long because it wasn't "safe" to express emotions in my relationship. It was an abusive relationship. And I couldn't understand or fathom that I was being abused, because I didn't understand what that was. I knew I was very unhappy

and that I was not acknowledged or valued as a person or respected. So once I began to work with people who knew how to communicate in respectful ways and to value everyone . . . then I could contrast. But as long as I was in the bubble of the relationship, I was second-guessing myself constantly.

Was leaving the marriage worth it? Sally definitely feels it was.

> Now I really feel at peace. I don't have all the answers, but day to day, moment to moment I just feel so much more at peace. It's like I don't care whatever else ever happens—I don't feel like I'll ever not be at peace anymore.

The primary gift Sally received from this painful situation was an enhanced attentiveness to how she *really* felt. From that awareness, she could then take appropriate action.

The Sorting-out Phase is troublesome because our feelings often appear before any logical cause is apparent. Our best approach is to let ourselves experience them, and *allow the feelings themselves to teach us what we need to know.* We need not feel pressured to explain our feelings to our spouse or friends. We may share our emotions in some cases, and defer explanation in others. By using the mindfulness we are cultivating in our Attentiveness Cluster of traits, we can train ourselves to simply "be" with our feelings: "I know that I feel a certain way, but I don't know where the feeling is coming from. I'm open to the feeling and am willing to allow it to guide me into the experience it has for me." As we adopt an open, nonclinging attitude toward our feelings, we free ourselves from the pressure of having to *know* and thus enable ourselves to access other related emotions and memories.

The Pain of Grieving

When a loved one dies, the pain of the void we feel is devastating. Grief has been called "a sacred time, where we can rearrange our fragments into a new definition of wholeness."[2] After facing and moving through the devastation of losing her only son, Kelly Osmont went on to become a bereavement counselor to help others confront the pain of grief. In *Parting Is Not Goodbye,* her autobiographical account of the freak horse accident and subsequent hospitalization and death of her nine-teen-year-old son, Osmont notes that most people experience two to eight months of what she calls "hard grief" immediately following a loved one's death. During this period, daily crying periods are common, as are a host of physical, emotional, and mental symptoms ranging from sleeping and eating distur-bances to hallucinations, overactivity, and preoccupation with the deceased.

Following this initial period, the balance of the mourning process (in death-related grief or other kinds of loss) is de-signed to integrate the death into one's life—a process which can take years. Kubler-Ross's often-cited stages of grief actually apply to anticipatory grief when approaching death, and are in-appropriately applied in the context of grieving the death of an-other. Osmont and her mentor, William Worden, Ph. D, recommend a different approach:

By thinking in terms of accomplishing key "tasks" of mourning, rather than going through an artificially con-structed set of stages, we can discover the key benchmarks in our individual grief process.

"Stages to me are feelings," says Osmont. "Sadness is a feel-ing, it's not a stage. I could in one hour feel several feelings." Clearly, that does not mean she also moved through several stages in the course of that hour.

There are four tasks in dealing with grief feelings:

Accept the reality of the loss. Worden explains that "When someone dies, even if the death is expected, there is always a sense that it hasn't happened. The first task of grieving is to come full face with the reality that the person is dead, that the person is gone and will not return."[3] Of course, this means that our denial must be overcome.

Experience the pain of grief. It may be a literal physical pain, or it may take on emotional, mental, and psychological dimensions. "Sometimes people hinder the process by avoiding painful thoughts," Worden notes. "They use thought-stopping procedures to keep themselves from feeling the dysphoria [unhappiness] associated with the loss." Others entertain only pleasant thoughts of the deceased, idealize the dead, or avoid situations or places that remind them of the departed. These tactics must give way to feeling the pain of our loss.

Adjust to an environment in which the deceased is missing. This may include becoming aware of the many roles played by the deceased, and learning to take on some of those roles ourselves.

Emotionally relocate the deceased and move on with life. To "relocate" the person is to gain a sense that the person is not in the grave, or under the ground, but is "in my heart," or "in heaven."

Osmont illustrates how these tasks often "loop," or repeat, many times before the Sorting-out Phase of grief is complete:

> A widow is driving along and she hears a joke on the radio, and her husband had always been a jokester, so she'd always memorized them. She started memorizing the joke, and all of a sudden it hit her: he wasn't around to hear it. So she faced the reality; once she realized it, and faced the reality again, then the feelings came up. And then she had to adjust [and ask herself], "Do I finish listening to it? Do I memorize it? And if so, who do I tell it to?" She has to readjust what she's going to do about it.

Repeating these tasks until we feel "complete" is as important in divorce or job loss transition as it is with the death of a loved one. In one psychological study, in which seventy adults in transition were interviewed, the researchers found "no difference in coping score" between subjects dealing with death and those dealing with dissolution of a relationship.[4] The reason? "The subjective interpretation of loss is the important factor rather than the specific kind of loss."

In a job layoff, the tasks might work like this: the evening after the layoff, the laid off employee starts to set the alarm clock as he normally would and then realizes, "Wait a minute, I don't need to set the alarm." Then he has the feelings about it, and finally readjusts: "Do I set the alarm anyway? Do I want to get up early or not?" Following a divorce, we must learn to care for the children and develop a new routine *without* the spouse in the household.

These tools can be helpful in accepting painful feelings during the Sorting-out Phase.

RESOLVING ISSUES FROM OUR PAST

When Susan's boyfriend of three months ended their relationship, Susan was heartbroken. And while any kind of relationship separation is difficult, Susan's reaction seemed out of proportion for such a short-term relationship. She wept constantly, couldn't concentrate at work, felt irritable, and experienced a tremendous longing to have her deceased father to talk to. What was happening?

Resonance

Susan's experience reflects the phenomenon of *resonance,* in which the energy of any unfinished similar transitions "joins forces" with the emotions from the immediate event, compounding the transition process. The term was coined in physics, to describe the process in which the air in a cavity would respond only weakly to a sound wave coming from outside the cavity, but would begin to "resonate," or vibrate very strongly, when the sound wave reached the "resonance frequency."[5] The Sorting-out Phase sounds the "resonance frequency" in which past experiences are processed.

Susan's resonance arose from a number of relatively brief encounters she has had with men over the past ten years, each of which was terminated by the man. Her father died when she was a child, and her older brother retreated into his own interests after their father's death. Susan developed a belief that men she loved would always leave her, and this has been the case thus far. Only now, as she experienced the resonance effect and realized the pattern in her life, did she become open to the possibility that she can assume a more active role in ending her relationships.

What we must do, in any transition, is to ask ourselves whether any of our past similar transitions may be influencing or compounding our reaction to the current event. If we have not allowed ourselves a Sorting-out Phase in those transitions, have not forgiven those who have wronged us, or have failed to make peace with past events, they are likely to impact our current experience. In this way, what began as a simple Sorting-out Phase can quickly escalate to a dark night of the soul.

Making an Inventory. In twelve-step work, the fourth of the twelve steps is to "make a searching and fearless moral inventory of ourselves." This inventory includes persons we have wronged, persons who have wronged us, our character defects, and similar issues which have, in many cases, unknowingly driven us into our addiction. Sharing this inventory with a trusted professional or sponsor, and making amends when possible to those on our list, releases a tremendous healing energy in our lives, causing us to feel lighter, more "right" with the world, and at peace within ourselves.

A similar process can be helpful in any transition in which the Sorting-out Phase is particularly dark, and in which we are facing a pattern of behavior which has caused us ongoing pain and heartache. Where have we been wronged? Where have we wronged others? What are the roots in our personality of the troublesome behavior? Counseling can be invaluable at this juncture, as we face key life issues.

The Use of Rituals. Another powerful tool to help us complete past issues and live fully in our present is the use of rituals. Our culture has largely abandoned ritual to the forces of commercialization and an increasingly rapid life pace. The recent resurgence of Native American practices such as sweat lodges and drumming, as well as more traditional customs such as weekly churchgoing, birthday parties, weddings, and funerals, stem from our inner drive to mark the cycles of our lives.

Ritual can lend meaning to many key life junctures:

- On my thirtieth birthday, I had my first wedding ring reset with a pearl as a gift to myself at this turning point in my life.
- When a roommate moved out after a long friendship, I lit a candle and walked from room to room, blessing what had been and invoking joy for what was to come.
- On New Year's Eve, it is becoming a common ritual in many churches to do a "burning bowl" ceremony, in which one's past wrongs and situations needing forgiveness are written on small pieces of paper and burned in a large bowl as a symbolic cleansing and releasing process.

Individuals in my workshops have related many imaginative rituals and ceremonies which have assisted them in making life transitions:

- writing a letter to a former spouse, parent, or other individual with whom one still has unresolved issues—but not mailing the letter
- inviting one's friends to join on the eve of moving into a new home to do a "house blessing"
- doing a mental visualization of release and forgiveness, such as those described in *You Can Heal Your Life,* by Louise Hay
- conducting a separation ceremony in conjunction with a divorce
- celebrating an adolescent girl's onset of menses, or an elder's menopause, in a women's circle
- planting a tree in a deceased loved one's favorite park
- preparing pieces of artwork to express one's feelings toward a deceased parent
- conducting an "energy-renewal process" following divorce or death of spouse by returning to places they had frequented with their spouse and changing their view of those places

The list is as long as the number of individuals who design the ceremonies. Books such as *Ceremonies for Change,* by Lynda S. Paladin, are helpful to suggest ideas for ceremonies to ritualize particular occasions. The ritual has been successful if, by going through it (even if you do it several times), you feel complete in your experience of the past and have no emotional residue to carry forward into future situations.

In her work with grieving individuals, Kelly Osmont stresses that ritual plays a critical role at two stages in the grief process. First, immediately after the death, she advises people to view the body of their deceased loved one. This helps the mourner accomplish the first task of mourning: accepting reality. If they have not viewed the body, they can stay in denial and tell themselves that the death has really not occurred. Osmont has seen individuals go through an encapsulated grieving process upon viewing photos of their deceased loved ones (when they had not viewed the body initially), even months after the death:

> One woman for the first time two days later had memories— good memories of her husband who died of a drug overdose. Another was a bereaved parent whose son had been found after he killed himself, many, many days later, and she finally was looking sad—part of her had been denying it, she always looked sort of "right" out there, everything's fine. But she couldn't get away from the sadness. And the third person for the first time accepted the possibility that her husband wasn't murdered, out of what we saw in the pictures and the questions she finally asked.

The second function of ritual in grief work is when facing anniversaries—one year after the loved one's death, the loved one's birthday, and similar events. Osmont's guideline when one is facing a significant date is "to do one thing to honor the deceased, and one thing to take care of themselves, and have it all on the same day." Honoring the deceased may mean going to the gravesite with their children, laying down some flowers, holding hands and singing a birthday song together, followed by an outing to a special place for them. Or perhaps one of them wants to treat themselves to a professional massage, or another wants to go for a run following the ritual at the grave site. That allows them to do something for themselves, which is a shift, focusing back on them.

However we use ritual in our transitions, they serve a key role in helping us come to terms with our past and setting the tone for a positive present and future. And they can be particularly helpful in the throes of an extended transition (such as a company reorganization or rebuilding our lives following a personal tragedy), when many of the usual stable elements in our lives are absent.

DEALING WITH AMBIGUITY

One of the most vexing aspects of the Sorting-out Phase is its ambiguity. From the root word meaning "to wander," ambiguity denotes the frustrating experience of being without bearings: not being able to use the old rules, not yet knowing the new rules, and realizing that the rules we have been told to use will probably be obsolete tomorrow. In a divorce, for instance, when one spouse initially decides to move out, there is a temporary readjustment to the house without Mom or Dad, and some kind of informal, temporary arrangements for the departed spouse to visit with the children. Just as the family gets accustomed to that way of doing things, a court order may upset the temporary stability by dictating when and how visitation must occur. Complicating things further are the usual negotiations (or disputes) conducted between the spouses—as to whether or not to try to reconcile, property settlement issues, child custody, and the like. Following final disposition of the case, visitation may change again. It is not easy for either parent, or for the children, to process this rapid succession of logistical adjustments, as well as emotions ranging from denial, pain, and anger to fear, defensiveness, and guilt.

Charles Garfield's study, spanning over twenty years, of peak performers reveals that they "enhance their skill in managing change by cultivating an unusual degree of tolerance for ambiguity,"[6] somewhat akin to "expecting the unexpected."

Tolerance for ambiguity allows Thrivers to discover new information along the way, adjusting their goals and balancing between change and stability.

The Newtonian paradigm compelled us to see times of ambiguity as puzzles to be solved. If we can just find "the answer," we will once again feel at peace, we thought. Sometimes that approach works. But while we are looking for our "answer," we miss the important experiences of our lives. We are too focused on the future result to fully appreciate the present.

In order to thrive, we must remain open to the gifts the situation has to offer, even in the face of raw emotions and being pushed to the edge of our ability to adapt. There is a positive side to the pain and frustration of ambiguity: Now that the old rules no longer apply, anything new is "fair game." Creativity and innovation are welcomed. The next chapter will explore ways to capture this fertile energy and channel it into a new vision.

EXPLORING THE POSSIBILITIES THROUGH VIRTUAL TRANSITIONS

The creative energy of the Sorting-out Phase culminates in the exciting process of exploring options for our next step. Many possibilities exist for how the next stage of our lives will look and feel. In fact, the opportunities may seem endless at one point and absolutely barren at another as we face our own shortcomings and disillusionment. The new options often have no apparent order or sequence. They may be direct opposites of each other. Our only task now is to remain receptive to choices which may seem crazy or irrational (from the viewpoint of our former, limited self). We need not necessarily act on those choices, but can mentally "try them on." If the precise form in which the idea comes to us is not a practical one (e.g., moving to India to find our purpose), perhaps there is a seed within the idea that we *can* internalize (e.g., a need for solitude and introspection).

Quantum physicist Danah Zohar explains how this phenomenon occurs on the level of quantum particles. When an electron is about to make a quantum leap to a new orbit, "it puts out temporary 'feelers' towards its own future stability by trying out—all at once—all the possible new orbits into which it might eventually settle, in much the same way as we might try out a new idea by throwing out imaginary scenarios depicting its many possible consequences."[7] These temporary feelers are

152 THRIVING IN TRANSITION

called "virtual transitions," and the actual transition of the electron into its new, permanent home a "real transition." These virtual transitions are not a trivial matter. Quantum physicist David Bohm goes so far as to say that "Virtual transitions 'are often of the greatest importance, for a great many physical processes are the result of these so-called *virtual* transitions.'"[8]

Any major life change should be preceded by some "mental rehearsal," a kind of virtual transition. Thrivers are well skilled at virtual transitioning, because they have learned that doing a "practice run" of the potential new choice in their mind it saves them time, energy, and disappointment. They imagine the possibility all the way to the end, to determine its probable consequences. For example, the individual considering leaving an unsatisfying marriage may mentally rehearse how life would be if they did not live with their spouse, or if they could not be with their children as much as they are now. The worker considering leaving a dead-end job may do the same kind of mental exercise, practicing his or her termination speech, contemplating how life would be in a different kind of job, and strategizing how they might manage their finances if they were unemployed. Neither of these individuals has to actually leave their spouse or their job before they are mentally ready for it (unless, like Mike Long in Chapter 4, they have denied their dissatisfaction too long and other circumstances remove from the source of their unhappiness).

Yet making these virtual transitions can also compound the ambiguity of our situation. With so many options, how can we choose? Because of the importance of the Sorting-out Phase of transition, however, the best decision we can make (for now) is not to make any choice. We can allow ourselves a period of exploration, as did Ellen from Chapter 2, who spent six months doing "anything I wanted to do, within reason, and with a method through which I can support myself," and so looked at all kinds of what she called "wild ideas," from another job in computer sales to selling art, working at Saks selling clothing, and other possibilities. Narrowing our focus and actualizing our vision will come later.

But for now, reining in our tendency to bring our issue to

resolution, "staying in the question," as I like to think of it, can result in an internal deepening which pays great dividends. It pushes us beyond our normal range of choices—and perhaps beyond our comfort zone—to remain open longer to new possibilities.

Staying "in the question" can result in an internal deepening which pays great dividends.

With the advent of twenty-four-hour televised entertainment, cellular phones and pagers that stay with us everywhere we go, and a constant barrage of stimulation from all directions, we have become fearful of our own internal quietness. The Sorting-out Phase beckons us to reawaken to the tranquil beauty of our own inner Self. Thomas Moore describes this as a sense of "soulful emptiness," which becomes a precursor of authentic power if we "withstand temptations to fill it prematurely."[9] We might ask ourselves, "When was the last time I spent even an hour alone, doing nothing: just pondering my thoughts, my breath, or the meaning of my existence?" During a dark-night Sorting-out Phase, a practice of even thirty minutes a day spent in quietness can yield incredible insight, calm, and new direction.

I remember, in the early weeks of my recovery from alcohol abuse and chronic fatigue, being concerned because I felt absolutely unmotivated to work or do anything productive (very atypical for me). I felt confused, and unfamiliar emotions (fear, anger, confusion, sadness) would arise at unexpected times. It was suggested that, as a way of centering, I spend fifteen to thirty minutes each morning doing nothing but staring out the window—noticing the trees, the scenery, the sky, the wind. Initially, no thoughts about health, money, relationships, or other daily issues were to be entertained, just a quiet concentration on the beauty of nature. Though difficult at first, that practice provided a grounding for me during a time of tremendous turmoil. Slowly, I began to feel more comfortable within myself. And gradually, as the weeks and months wore on, the external issues in my life began to resolve themselves. My motivation eventually did return. But first I needed to focus on my inner healing—physical, emotional, and spiritual. Such simple practices can be very helpful during challenging transitions.

THE IMPORTANCE OF TRUST

In our mechanized world, everything is timed, dated, and synchronized—to the minute, if not the nanosecond. We want to know how long each event or experience will last so that we can plan the one to follow. But when we face pivotal transition times, this mechanical view is unhelpful. The dark night of the soul calls us to a more organic view of our life process, one which accommodates unanticipated sequences of events, periods of pain and confusion, and sudden leaps forward into unexpected directions. The terrain of the inner self is unpredictable and uneven. Its movement cannot be timed on a calendar or on a stopwatch; it has its own sense of right timing.

It has been a challenge in our Western culture to balance the individual need to experience the pain of grief with cultural expectations concerning how long grieving should take. During the past century, the acceptable grief period has shrunk from three years for a widow in 1927 (according to Emily Post) to six months in 1950, to the unrealistic advice of Amy Vanderbilt in 1972 that the bereaved should "pursue, or try to pursue, a usual social course within a week or so after a funeral."[10] Most corporate bereavement policies limit bereavement leave to immediate family, thus facilitating what author Jeremy Rifkin calls "a trend toward less community participation in mourning duties and rituals."

The shortening of expected time duration is not limited to grieving. Our culture allocates only a certain amount of time to finding a new job, to starting to date again after a divorce or separation, to healing from a heart attack, and to returning to work after childbirth. This mechanistic view of dynamic life events constitutes the apogee of Newtonian reasoning. And it is as outmoded as Newtonian physics has become. Each individual's experience of grief and other transitions is unique. Its timing cannot be preordained. Rather than attempt to legislate an "acceptable" time for transitions to occur, we must learn to trust our own process of growth. Some job transitions will be easy, others will be difficult. And the process will vary depending on whether one is facing a quantum leap or a rather ordinary change.

> During the Sorting-out Phase, when numerous options present themselves, feelings run wild, and our usual sense of time is skewed, the phrase "I trust the process" can serve as our mantra.

This powerful affirmation tells us that we accept what is happening—even though we don't understand it and don't know where it will ultimately lead us. It allows us to feel cradled by a Higher Power, guided by what is best for us. This kind of trust is built by relying on it in small transitions and seeing the hand of Providence rush in to support us and provide the resources and information we need. We build on a track record of success, each step opening new possibilities for our growth. And eventually, we can make even major changes—a cross-country move, a radical career change, or a divorce after years of marriage—with confidence. Even if it doesn't turn out the way we think it will, we are growing each step of the way.

TAKING CARE OF NUMBER ONE

Self-nurturing is the final aspect of the Trust Cluster of traits which is so critical during the Sorting-out Phase. And this is precisely the time when we may feel *least* like taking care of ourselves, especially if we are feeling pressure to get to the Action phase. One of the gifts of the Sorting-out Phase, particularly of the dark-night-of-the-soul variety, is that we are invited to slow our lives down. While these lifestyle adjustments may increase our stress temporarily, they are counterbalanced by the relief we feel as the deadlines and pressure of our fast-track life evaporate. And since doctors tell us that 75 percent of all medical complaints are stress-related, we may see an increase in our physical health in the process.[11]

It is common to feel a desire to spend more time than usual alone when going through the dark night. We may wish to journal, to meditate, or to resolve issues from our past through rituals or other means. But above all, it is a time for the soul to be alone, and until that time has passed, no one else can truly share the experience with us. Mystical experiences are also commonplace during the Sorting-out Phase, as we touch the deeper spiritual aspects of ourselves and our destiny. These desires and experiences are not to be feared, but honored, and as we do so, the natural process of transformation will continue its course.

Thrivers nurture themselves in four key ways during times of transition:

- preserve their stability zones
- pamper themselves
- keep up physical activity
- give voice to their experiences

Preserving stability zones. No matter how much change we are experiencing, we can find at least one thing in our lives that remains stable. It can be anything: our family structure, our morning routine, the neighbors, or our pets. As we undergo the upheaval of a major transition, we must also recognize what is *not* changing. These stable elements of our lives are forms of "stability zones," a term coined by Alvin Toffler to denote habits and relationships which are carefully maintained despite ongoing changes.[12] We can consciously establish additional stability zones to support us during our transitions by developing daily habits we sustain regardless of external shifts: maintaining long-term friendships and family ties, and postponing any unnecessary changes until the major transition is completed.

It is tempting, when one area of our life is shifting, to rally together a number of changes we wish to make and orchestrate a wholesale lifestyle change, while we're at it. But this strategy is ill-advised except for the highly skilled Thriver who can manage such a radical transition.

Pampering. During times of stress (from a rough day at work to a divorce or major surgery), we need to find ways to treat ourselves well. This may mean a walk by the water or in a nearby park, buying a bouquet of flowers, buying a symbolic item to mark our progress toward an important goal, or a bubble bath at the end of a long day. What too many of us do in budgeting our time is to give ourselves what's left over after we have fulfilled our boss's and our family's demands. The result is that there is no time left for us.

I was struck to learn that authors Ken and Marjorie Blanchard (*The One Minute Manager*) plan their personal time and time together *first,* before meeting the demands of their busy lives. Their other activities are planned around those personal times so that they are guaranteed the time they need to recharge themselves and nurture their relationship.

One way to begin self-nurturing is to make a list of our "special treats" and schedule at least one of those things daily.

Nurturing ourselves also entails heeding creative urges and honoring them.

Perhaps we feel the desire to return to painting, to play the guitar, or to write poetry as the Sorting-out Phase begins. Though these activities may seem unlikely to lead us to a new job or heal a cancer, they are important to pursue. Surprisingly, by accessing our creativity in one form, we may tap innovative solutions to our transition dilemmas which were not apparent before.

Physical activity. Regular physical exercise, proper diet, and adequate sleep are prerequisites of physical health. But in times of transition, as with any other kind of stressful experience, these practices tend to be ignored just when they are most important. Keeping ourselves in top physical condition during transitions not only increases physical health; it does more to alleviate depression than any other practice. Nearly all of the Thrivers I interviewed and included in the focus groups relied on physical exercise as a key component of their transition management skills. Some, when faced with a particularly diffi-cult transition, overindulged in exercise and reached extraordi-nary levels of fitness as a kind of escape from the pain of their loss. There are certainly more damaging vices!

Giving voice to experiences. As we gain the insights of the Sorting-out Phase's inner reflection, we need an outlet through which to express them. The people who comprise that "sound-ing board" will vary. It is important not to share our thoughts too soon—particularly new ideas about what we *might* do next—because in their embryonic form, they will be trampled by the voices of practicality and fear. Some people rely almost exclusively on their own private journal for their self-expres-sion; others will turn to therapists, church groups, support groups, seminars, and friends for support. Sharing our feelings during this confusing time helps us feel that we are not alone. The benefits of a close support network discussed in the previ-ous chapter apply equally here.

The Sorting-out Phase, with its darkness and its inner-direct-edness, can have varying degrees of intensity. Sometimes it will only last for a day or two. But the dark-night experience, which often results in a quantum leap, can go on for weeks or months. Fortunately, after we have experienced one severe dark night of the soul, those that follow will not usually be as deep or as long lasting—provided we have internalized the message of our first experience. Thrivers learn as much as they can from the Sorting-out Phase and allow themselves to be transformed by the process. The next step is to use the insights drawn from this period of gestation to formulate a new vision and put it into action.

PRACTICAL IDEAS FOR FINDING NEW BEARINGS

- Don't deny your feelings—feel them, journal about them, talk about them.
- Take time off if possible; otherwise, find an hour every day for reflection.

- Pay attention to your creative urges and follow them through.
- Make a list of what's *not* changing—your "personal stability zones."
- Take time to mourn your past.
- Pay attention to your dreams.
- Design a ritual to mark what is passing from your life.
- Look for new options in your transition area; list them in a notebook for later review.
- Seek counseling or other support as needed.
- Stay in the question before you; don't settle on the first answer you encounter.
- Take care of yourself physically by getting enough sleep, exercising regularly, and maintaining a healthy diet.
- Feed yourself positive mental food.
- Lean on your support network.
- Don't be afraid to say you don't know yet, you don't have the answer, or you're exploring.
- Don't take action just to avoid your uncomfortable feelings.
- Postpone decisions and other transitions until your current transition is complete.

NOTES

1. Moore, Thomas, *Care of the Soul,* HarperCollins 1992, p. 141.
2. Stephanie Ericcson.
3. Worden, J. William, *Grief Counseling and Grief Therapy: A Handbook for the Mental Health Practitioner,* Springer 1982, p. 11.
4. Lonky, Edward, et al., "Life Experience and Mode of Coping: Relation to Moral Judgment in Adulthood," *Developmental Psychology* 1984, Vol. 20, No. 6, pp. 1159–1167.
5. Capra, Fritjof, *The Tao of Physics,* Shambhala 1991, p. 269.
6. Garfield, Charles, *Peak Performers,* Avon 1986, p. 243.
7. Zohar, Danah, *The Quantum Self,* Quill/William Morrow 1990, pp. 31–32.
8. Bohm, David, *Quantum Theory,* Constable 1951, p. 415.
9. Moore, Thomas, *Ibid.,* pp. 121–22.
10. Rifkin, Jeremy, *Time Wars,* Holt & Co. 1987, pp. 48–66.
11. Charlesworth, Edward and Nathan, Ronald, *Stress Management: A Comprehensive Guide to Wellness,* Ballantine 1984.
12. Toffler, Alvin, *Future Shock,* Random House 1970, p. 334.

8

A VISION
WITH PURPOSE

❧

*The soul is explosive and powerful. Through
its medium of imagination, which is always
a prerequisite for action and is the source of
meaning, it can accomplish all things.*

—Thomas Moore
Care of the Soul

In the Vision Phase, we generate the mental images that ultimately become our next experience—the new job we desire, an
enhanced level of health, or life without our former spouse.
Our world is the result of these mental pictures, coupled with
strong emotions, which bring each picture into being. Mental
images are used proactively by the Thriver during the visioning
period of transition.

People who are unskilled in transitioning may try to skip
over not only the Sorting-out Phase, but this phase as well, believing that they should move directly into action following a
crisis or minor discontentment. One of two outcomes can result from this approach.

If we take action without consciously choosing what we
want to create, we may overreact and find ourselves "throwing
the baby out with the bathwater." That is, we may pursue a

new mate or opportunity that is so different from the one we just left that we forget to include critical positive elements from our former situation. For example, suppose we separate from a spouse who is overly disciplined and rule-bound—albeit responsible and stable—and partner with someone who is artistic, intuitive, and "goes with the flow"—but can barely pay his or her rent and has no sense of commitment to work. We have escaped the tyranny of our former spouse's rigidity, but we have given up the security of his or her sense of responsibility and willingness to care for us. We haven't yet considered the possibility that we could have *both* the sense of responsibility of our former spouse *and* the spontaneity of our new partner—if we can dare to imagine a higher vision of a partner!

If we fail to consciously visualize what we want to create, our new situation will just perpetuate the mistakes of the past. We will remain in our "comfort zone" of experiences created by our standard of living, our peer group and their lifestyle, our willingness to risk and try new things, and our beliefs about ourselves and about life.

Unless we challenge ourselves through imagining how our lives could be better, we will tend to make choices that fall within the parameters to which we are accustomed.

In quantum physics, the probability that something will occur is determined in part by the amount of energy that is required to make something happen. Since it takes less energy to repeat what we have done before, it is the most probable choice—it is the easier one! As quantum physicist Danah Zohar states it, "Habit is a kind of free ride; it requires very little mental work."[1] So given a set of options concerning our future, we will tend to choose the options that allow us to make about the same amount of money, work in approximately the same kind of job, choose the same kinds of friends and intimate partners, and make similar selections in our hobbies and leisure activities.

Although the habitual option is our most probable choice, we are always free to choose an alternative that requires greater energy (and therefore greater perceived risk). Many factors combine to determine which of the infinite number of choices available to us we will select, including our genetic disposition, our experiences, and our relationships with others. This is not to say that we are governed by fate, or that some third force is determining our destiny. Rather, as co-creators of our lives, we choose certain experiences, which lead to other experiences being more likely. As Danah Zohar observes:

> Thus, while reasons themselves don't *determine* the choices we make, they do play a crucial role in making some choices more likely than others. . . . Each choice that I do make has an influence on the next choice that I will make, because it increases or decreases the probability of that choice. None of my choices, however small, is without some significance for the rest of my life.[2]

Viewed in this way, psychological claims that our environment influences our choices may be true—but not for the reasons usually given. Rather, our environment becomes familiar because it includes choices of lifestyle and values which we have made repeatedly, to the point that they have become instinctive. Making future choices in accord with past choices is more probable simply because of the relatively small amount of energy required to perpetuate the familiar. Until we are prodded to expand our boundaries and explore other levels of being, our comfort zone will dictate the outcome of our passages in life. But, as Zohar observes, "We are always free to choose against the weight of probability, to make more energy-demanding choices, and this freedom makes us responsible." When we encounter the dark night of the soul, the likelihood of such a shift occurring increases exponentially, because we have reached a point where the pain of the familiar choices forces us to consider new options.

It is not happenstance that the Vision Phase is the first of the three phases on the left, or upward-tending side of our diagram (see Diagram 4-1 in Chapter 4). The Discontentment, Crisis, and Sorting-out Phases generate a negative, downward (or inward) pressure, driving us to reexamine our life in critical ways to determine what we want more of, what we want less of, and what we want to change. As our new vision begins to emerge, a positive, upward impulse begins. In fact, the vision provides the fuel to fire us into action, moving us into the next level of the upward spiral of our growth. The change in momentum is noticeable at this phase: We begin to smile more, we feel excited about our new possibilities, and a mental widening occurs as we contemplate the potentiality of a new, higher experience.

The Right Time for Visioning

What marks the end of the Sorting-out Phase is when we notice that we keep returning to one or two of the options we have been exploring. We saw this in Chapter 3, when we revisited Ellen's transition from the Thriver perspective; the possibility of a career combining her medical and computer expertise hounded her—until it became a reality. Tina Turner finally left her abusive marriage after dozens of false attempts and innumerable mental rehearsals of how she could claim her freedom.

Congressman Mike Kopetski also made this critical shift from introspection to imagining. He found himself longing for more time to pursue his hobbies and be with his family, but his demanding career as a legislator required him to spend most of his time away from home. As his second marriage deteriorated and his son got closer to high school graduation, a fishing trip with a core group of long-time friends revealed the startling decision Kopetski had to make: He would quit Congress when his term expired (after twenty-five years in politics) to spend more time with his son and live a more balanced life.

Just before the vision emerges, a dormant period occurs, much like what happens in quantum physics during phase transitions, such as the transition from water to ice. In these changes, there is a point where both the ice and water are the same temperature, and where energy is extracted from the water to make it into ice, but there is no temperature change. Dr. Fred Alan Wolf explains: "There is a certain point where there's a sort of rearrangement or restructuring going on, which takes energy, [but] there doesn't seem to be any real change taking place."

When we feel this period of greatest frustration, when nothing tangible is happening and there is no obvious energy change, we can be assured that the energy needed for our new vision is being extracted for formulation into a specific image.

Though we may typically think of visioning as a task to be used in a voluntary transition, it is also applicable in the wake of a crisis. Eventually, there comes a time when we begin to envision a new life for ourselves, without the loved one following his or her death, without our work following a layoff, or without our former level of health following an accident. We may at first feel as though we don't know what our new life's possibilities are. But as we talk to our support group and begin to tap into our own dreams, our imagination opens new options we had not known were there. The acute pain of the crisis begins to subside as our vision gathers momentum and draws us toward it.

The power of imagination has been undervalued in our society, as our entertainment comes prepackaged in the form of movies, television, theater, concerts, and video games. Rarely do we engage in spontaneous, creative activities such as storytelling, playing games, gardening, writing, singing, and the like. Reading for pleasure is giving way to video-based entertainment. Our mental images govern our experiences, even if most of our input is from external, prepackaged sources, a fact Thrivers understand only too well. Hence, they carefully censor their mental input, restricting it to the kind of material that will lead to their desired results.

To proactively construct and materialize our vision as Thrivers do, we need three primary qualities, each of which can be learned or developed:

- a strong sense of purpose in life
- big dreams that go beyond what appears practical
- proficiency in using the eight principles of proactive creation

DEVELOPING A SENSE OF PURPOSE

Much of my work with individuals and groups during the past eight years has involved facilitating the discovery of one's life purpose. What I have found is that prior to considering what our life mission or purpose may be, any goals we set—as well as any results we achieve—lack cohesiveness. We wander aimlessly through our lives, perhaps accomplishing some results, but with no thread holding the various activities together. A kind of emptiness exists when we are purpose-less (at least at the conscious level) which drives us in whatever directions we believe will provide the answers we need. In fact, the need to satiate this hunger can lead to a profoundly deep Sorting-out Phase.

When Roxanne contacted me for counseling, she was alternating between discontentment and crisis on a regular basis. With her marriage of fifteen years in jeopardy, she could hardly bring herself to perform her duties as manager of the beachfront motel she and her spouse owned jointly with his parents. She knew her life had to have a purpose, but it had eluded her during ten years of searching for it. We worked through the "ten clues" (described below) together, allowing her raw emotions to emerge during the process, and her purpose became clear: to have fun expressing God's love through joyful means. For her, these "joyful means" meant realizing her dream of designing and selling T-shirts and other items that spread love and positive messages. She located a company in her state that did just that, and became their sales representative as a "rehearsal" for starting her own business. When we ended our work together, Roxanne was literally beaming as she integrated her life purpose into her newfound work and commenced an amicable divorce proceeding.

All Thrivers share a sense of purpose, both about their overall life mission and about each course of action they choose. Thrivers draw on their sense of purpose to fuel their vision, to inspire their actions, and to enable them to create consistently excellent results in their lives. Their life purpose statement thus becomes an organizing principle for the rest of their lives. (See Diagram 8-1.) Beginning by evaluating our purpose (in the center of the circle), we next sort our roles and decide how we want to spend our time, and to what ends (a set of exercises for this is provided in Appendix B). This leads to our setting goals and visions for each individual area of our lives, followed by objectives and action plans. The tools of time management and stress management then assist us in carrying out our action plans with ease.

Diagram 8-1
LIFE PURPOSE AS AN ORGANIZING PRINCIPLE

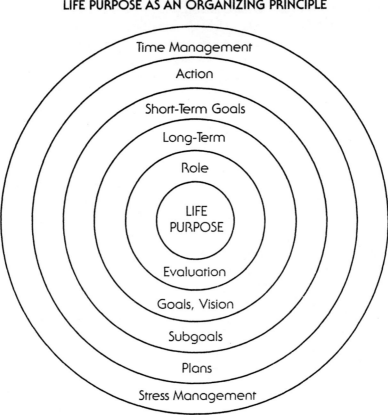

Time Management
Action
Short-Term Goals
Long-Term
Role
LIFE
PURPOSE
Evaluation
Goals, Vision
Subgoals
Plans
Stress Management

Reviewing our life purpose statement during times of major transition provides an anchor in the rough waters of change. When Rev. Mary Manin Morrissey announced to her congregation of 2,500 that she and her husband of twenty-six years (who was co-founder of the church) were divorcing, the church was simultaneously preparing to purchase a forty-two-acre facility, make a major transition from renting to owning (thus taking on added expenses), and move twenty miles south to its new location. Manin Morrissey admits that "there are times when you feel so scared and so alone and so desperate and frightened that what you want to do—what I wanted to do—is run." It felt like a firewalk to her, but her sense of mission sustained her through it. In firewalks, the participants must keep their mind focused on their goal. If they allow their attention to wander to the heat underneath their feet, they will get burned, but if they keep focused, they find they can actually walk on 2,000-degree coals. Manin Morrissey relied on this analogy during her time of challenge:

> So I kept my focus on my intention, and my focus on serving, and why I was doing what I was doing, and I said to myself, "I have a right to be happy" over and over and over and over again because of the criticism that came with a minister divorcing. And I just kept feeding myself that kind of nourishment. And I knew that no matter what, at least I'd have myself.

One day, months later, she was able to feel the benefits of walking through that time: she felt grateful for having the courage to "step into the life I want to live in."

Only by having something to focus on—a mission statement, an affirmation, or a strong vision—can Thrivers keep their heads above water when everything around them is pulling them down.

Most of us acknowledge the importance of understanding our life purpose. And as the New Zero shifts our balance toward an emphasis on internal authenticity and personal responsibility for finding fulfillment in our work, an increasing number of individuals find the issue of life purpose squarely before them. It is frequently during key life transitions that we find this inquiry once again presented for resolution.

Many methods are touted for accessing a solution to this elusive inquiry. In my last book, *When 9 to 5 Isn't Enough: A Guide to Finding Fulfillment at Work,* and the accompanying tape, "Discovering Your Life's Purpose," I articulated ten clues to our purpose which allow us to examine the mission of our life from many different angles.

I have shared these clues, as well as the Symbol Meditation found in the same book and tape, with dozens of clients and thousands of seminar participants. Some have had tremendous

Diagram 8-2

TEN CLUES TO YOUR LIFE PURPOSE	
1	What do you love to do when you have spare time?
2	What parts of your present job or life activities do you thoroughly enjoy?
3	What do you naturally do well?
4	What have been your 10 greatest successes to date (in your eyes)?
5	Is there a cause, value, or quality that you feel passionate about?
6	What are the 10 most important lessons you have learned in life?
7	Are there some issues or perceived problems that have occurred over and over again in your life?
8	What do you daydream about doing?
9	What would you like to be remembered for?
10	What would you do if you knew you could not fail?

breakthroughs working with these tools; others have made little apparent progress. Whether or not these tools (or any others) will reveal the sought-after life mission for a given individual depends on a number of factors, including the individual's level of commitment to its discovery, the time and effort already invested, how aware the individual is of his or her own feelings, and the extent to which that individual has already followed his or her inner guidance. Often, one's purpose is so obvious that it is overlooked or taken for granted until pointed out to us by a perceptive observer.

Following our sense of purpose sometimes demands that we relinquish some aspect of our life that we are reluctant to give up. One client with whom I worked had been frustrated for years in his work. He loved to work with wood, and had a fully equipped shop in his home to pursue this passion during his non-work hours. Since his personality was best suited to self-employment, his occupation as an engineer in a series of large corporations led him to butt heads with managers. He was fired several times, which increased his frustration. As we worked together over a period of months, the source of his seeming inability to pursue his passion became clear. He was married to a woman with whom he had an extremely codependent "contract." Whenever he took steps to turn his woodworking into his occupation, his wife sabotaged his every effort. Her complaints would set off arguments, which resulted in my client retreating to his more traditional (if less fulfilling) path of engineering work.

After months of counseling, filing for divorce and actually moving out of their house at one point, he thought he could—at last—reclaim his sense of self. But he became unwilling to maintain that arrangement. Eventually, he moved back in, withdrew the divorce proceeding, and kept trying to find work as an engineer (including temporary jobs when necessary to pay the bills). Because he was unwilling to follow his heart concerning his marriage, he was ensuring that he would remain stuck in his quest for occupational fulfillment.

This is not to say that everyone who has an unfulfilling marriage will fail to find satisfaction in their work. However, because it was so clear that my client needed to exit his relationship, and that he had explicitly refused to follow the guidance his inner Self was giving him, he closed himself off to making similar moves in other areas of his life. As we will see in the next chapter, we are often called upon to take just *one step* toward our vision. We may not know what will follow from that, or what the ultimate result will be. But we are summoned to build our trust, to fortify our faith, by taking just one step. After that, the "fog" on our path moves ahead a few more feet and we see the next step to take. Eventually, the result becomes clear, but only because we have dared to step out and follow our inner guidance in one small way.

THE EIGHT PRINCIPLES OF PROACTIVE CREATION

To thrive in times of transition, we need to do more than simply undergo another round of goal-setting or wait for fate to show its hand. Thrivers are *proactive* in initiating what happens in their lives, without insisting on a precise timetable or specific form for the result of their vision. By using visioning, rather than goal-setting, we can escape from the drudgery of pursuing "ends toward which great effort is directed," which is the literal meaning of goals. Instead, we envision "desired results"—our larger dreams of how our life can be. I have, in lectures and an article,[3] called this "intuitive goal setting," and here call it "proactive creation." It involves following our "hunches," staying open-minded, and daring to act on our passion. This approach contrasts sharply with traditional goal-setting, which emphasizes close-mindedness and an adherence to a particular focus, all of which can lead to an overly rational mindset and the achievement of shallow external results.

The following eight principles demonstrate how to use this approach effectively.

Principle 1.   Develop a clear vision statement

Our vision statement is the largest dream we can imagine for the area of our life that is in flux. Designing and utilizing a vision statement to set in mind the kind of relationship, work, health, or living situation we desire is at least half of the process of actually making it happen. This statement begins to bring one's overall life purpose into application in a particular area of one's life.

Thrivers' visions for themselves stretch their comfort zone beyond its existing boundaries. While their dreams may not seem practical, the Thriver embraces the dream with commitment and a belief that it can be realized. As we saw in Chapter 3, Ellen's desire to combine her nursing background and her computer/sales skills eventually evolved into a vision for her new career. She knew she was unlikely to find such a position in the "help wanted" ads. But she also knew that developments in the health care field and technology would create an opportunity for her to use her combined expertise as she desired.

Michael, too, had a dream that was beyond what would be considered practical. His crisis came when his marriage began falling apart. Michael and his wife worked together in a family advertising business, following his departure from the field of law, after burning out. In both his marriage and his work environment, Michael discovered that he felt compelled to take care of the people around him. The counselor he was seeing for these difficulties recommended that he leave the business— even though he enjoyed it—in order to cleanly end the marriage and allow Michael to continue with his own life path. Michael recalls:

> I never went from one place to the next without knowing where I was stepping career-wise. And it had all been so easy—I had always gotten what I chose for myself, or thought I was choosing for myself. And this last time, I left the business on December 31, and I had nowhere to go. And that was really scary. . . . I was receiving unemployment, and I knew that that had a six-month period, and then that was out and what was I going to do for money? At first I didn't think it was going to be difficult finding a job. Well, all of a sudden as I entered the job market, I was not even getting interviewed. And then I started to panic.

Michael sought out a career counselor, and together they discovered four career areas that would be appropriate for Michael. And when the counselor asked him, "What would you really like to do, if you had a magic wand?" Michael declared, "I want to write my own job description." The counselor suggested he hold on to that, recognizing that it was an important piece of what Michael needed. Also important to Michael was a large dose of independence—either working for himself or working with minimal supervision.

Michael began volunteering at the liability insurance company for attorneys in the state where he lived, just to have something to do to alleviate his feelings of panic as his unemployment wound down. He suggested that they expand their counseling services for attorneys into other areas. His 10 hours a week became 20, and then 30, and he was still not getting paid—but it did give him an organizing structure for his day. He turned down a job offer in his fifth month of unemployment, clinging to his dream of writing his own job description. A week later, the liability insurance company offered him a full-time position managing the programs he had begun. The director of loss prevention said to Michael, "What we'd like to do is propose this position to the board of directors, but we need one thing from you. Would you write up a job description?" Michael was quick to accept, and realized that he had asked for this, and that "you have to be careful what you ask for, because you just may get it." Michael was true to his vision—which appeared impossible at first—and he now runs the nation's model program for attorney assistance.

Designing your vision statement is an art form which requires practice to perfect. Effective vision statements share the following characteristics:

Present tense. Vision statements are written in the present tense, just like affirmations are. Sentences begin with "I am" or "I have" or "I feel," rather than "I will be," "I will have," or "I will feel." This helps the visioner begin to see the image of what he or she is creating as occurring *now,* not at some indefinite future time.

Open-ended. Our vision statements should leave room for something to happen that is even greater than what we have imagined. Open-ended vision statements use words such as "at least" or "this or something even better." This language prevents the self-limiting effect of using close-ended dollar amounts, time limits, or descriptions that allow only one interpretation. For example, it is better to formulate a vision as "spending at least eight hours of quality time with my children this week" than to state the goal as "four trips to the park with my children every week."

Sufficiently specific. A vision statement should be specific enough that it can be recognized when it appears. By simply reading the statement, the desired image should become tangible. Can we see that new position as we read it? Can we feel the kind of body we desire?

We must avoid becoming too specific, so as to close ourselves off from other possibilities which we have not considered. This happens when we believe only one form will fulfill the essence (or "ultimate intrinsic desire," as Peter Senge calls it in *The Fifth Discipline*), of our vision. To avoid becoming trapped in these narrow channels with our vision statement, we need to look for the "essence" of our desired experience. What do we *really* want that we believe a particular person or situation will give us? Love? Acceptance? Freedom? Do we in fact see our vision, as we have stated it, as a means to another end? If the vision statement is framed in terms of the ultimate end, rather than these secondary objectives, then the realization of our vision will be more fulfilling—even if it is different from what we thought we wanted.

I know of a woman who struggled each year to set aside enough money to pay her two sons' tuition to the private school they attended. As the time for payment neared once again, she began to visualize herself receiving $4,000—the amount needed for the tuition. However, after receiving coaching on writing vision statements, she restated her intention as "I pay my children's tuition easily and without struggle." The result? She was hired as an office assistant by the school her sons attended, and one of the fringe benefits was free tuition for all dependents. She no longer had to worry about coming up with that money each year!

Stretch our limits. The vision should stretch us beyond our comfort zone, but it shouldn't be unrealistic or overly ambitious. It should challenge us to reach further than we have before. If we do this at each of our transitional junctures, we will be constantly growing into greater possibilities. So if we think we can easily earn $25,000 in our next position, a minimum salary of $27,500 or $30,000 should appear in our vision statement. While we don't want to push ourselves relentlessly, ever striving toward elusive new goals that we believe will bring us success, we do want to expand our vision into the highest and best situation we can imagine—knowing that what we attract may be even better than that!

Focus on feelings. The final critical element of an effective vision statement is that it must describe how we will *feel* when we have achieved the vision. Merely chanting an affirmation or a vision of how we want our life to be will prove ineffective without an emotional commitment. And the clearer we can articulate the emotions we expect to feel as the vision unfolds, the more likely it will be realized. If we feel passionately about doing some type of work that we love—even if we have never done it before—we are more likely to bring it into being than we are a job about which we have little passion.

Following are two examples of actual vision statements integrating these five key elements—one in a work setting and one in the context of attracting a mate (have you ever considered doing a "wish list" for that?):

> *Vision Statement #1:* Upon graduating from the school of occupational therapy, I am employed in an autonomous position doing healing work 20 hours per week with children which honors the mind/body connection and includes art therapy. I have my own practice with adults as well, spending 10 hours per week doing bodywork, music, counseling, and art therapy. I speak to groups regularly about the psycho-social-spiritual process.
>
> I make $50,000 or more per year from these activities. I feel energetic and fulfilled. I have time to enjoy life with my daughters, going camping, singing, and sharing meals together. I am enjoying and supporting my daughters through high school. I own my home, have a garden, and earn enough that I can hire help to clean the house and maintain the yard so I can enjoy my creative projects.
>
> *Vision Statement #2:* I am open to the expansion of my concept of 'relationship' to that relationship most perfect for me. I now draw to myself a companion who is compatible with me and very comfortable to be with. He is a joyful, happy man, deep and thoughtful and also filled with fun. He has a sharp mind and a fit body. He is gentle, patient and compassionate, a lover of beauty and music. Our lives merge easily and naturally. We bring out the best in each other. We live in a beautiful, simply but elegantly furnished home in a secluded location, which includes woods and walking trails nearby. I feel honored, respected, and

cherished as an equal, not in a codependent way. This or something better comes to me, easily and gracefully, for the highest good of all.

Each of these statements is worded in the present tense, as though the individual is living her dream now. They are open-ended ("$50,000 or more," "This or something better") to allow room for an even greater manifestation to occur. They are sufficiently specific, so that the visioner can recognize the position, lifestyle, person, or home when she sees it. Each is stretching beyond the visioner's current experience in setting this vision in motion. And the visioner's feelings are described as well ("I feel energetic and fulfilled," "I feel honored, respected and cherished as an equal"). These individuals can be assured that their vision is well on its way to being realized.

How do you decide what to imagine in your vision statement? As Robert Fritz explains in *The Path of Least Resistance,* most creative individuals—including musicians, writers, painters, sculptors, and others—conceive of the result they desire by simply "making it up." There is no magical formula, no one telling them what they "should" make. They choose a project, out of an infinite number of creations in which they could invest their creative talent, simply because they want to bring it into being—and for no other reason. We can begin to bring artistry and creativity to our own lives by using this approach in choosing our next career, our next mate, our next home, or our level of health. To open our imaginations, we can ask ourselves questions such as these:

- How would my life be if I had no restrictions on what I could do or be?
- Where would I live?
- What kind of work would I choose?
- Who would I spend time with?
- What would my primary activities be?
- What would my priorities be?
- What are the characteristics of my ideal mate?
- What are 5 ways I could generate money without working a 9 to 5 job?

- What are 5 possible strategies for turning my number one passion into a moneymaking venture?
- If I could live anywhere in the world, where would it be?

Principle 2. Find a model of what we wish to create—and study it

Nearly all of the Thrivers I have encountered had one or more role models for some aspect of their lives. It may have been a career mentor, a parent or other relative who displayed ethical values they emulated, or someone who took a nontraditional step in following their heart.

To be successful in realizing a vision which is beyond our current level of experience requires what psychologist Dr. Frank Colistro calls "cognitive restructuring." This can best be accomplished if we find (or create) a clear model of a person who is doing what we want to do. Then, when presented with a decision, we can ask ourselves, "What would he or she do in this situation?" It thus helps us to shortcut our journey from where we are to where we desire to be. I did this as I entered the field of speaking and writing. I sought out others who were very successful as speakers and writers, and watched them. I read about them and invested time and money counseling with them to learn from them.

To choose a role model, we should find the most successful person we can identify, and find out how they achieved their vision. If we cannot get a personal interview with them (though that is usually the best resource), we should do research on them through the available literature, or by asking others who know them what they are like and how they got where they are. Even in selecting our role model, we can demonstrate to ourselves that we deserve the best, and that we are striving to be the best.

Principle 3. Add other sensory dimensions to the vision

We have discussed clearly *seeing* what we want to experience, and describing the *feelings* we want the vision to produce. To enhance the intensity of the vision even further, we can add other sensory dimensions. For example, are there things we *hear* each day that are important to us? When my husband and I began looking for a home to purchase, we longed for a home which was quieter than the busy neighborhood in which we lived. We knew that we could have *both* the convenience of the city and the quiet of a rural neighborhood. And that, as well as all of the other features on our vision statement, manifested itself perfectly in the house we bought.

The same can be done with *smells, tastes,* and the sense of *touch.* A vision statement for a new car can include the "new car smell" and the texture of the upholstery. If we associate certain smells with harmonious family times, or the sound of the ocean with tranquility, we can use those as a metaphor in our vision statement. This increases the chances of our vision coming into being—including the wonderful feelings with which we have infused it.

Principle 4. Refuse to let the vision be suppressed by what appears to be "practical"

So far, we have focused on the vision itself, and the elements which comprise it. As we imagine what is possible for us, a little voice in the back of our mind will interject at some point with a comment such as, "You can't do that!" or, "Don't you know you tried that before and failed?" or, "You can't support yourself doing that. Aren't you being a bit *impractical?*" These doubts and questions are the voices of our comfort zone dissolving. Each time we stretch, we find ourselves at the threshold of what simultaneously excites us most and scares us most.

It is natural to have doubts. But the Thriver will do no more than acknowledge those doubts and return to his vision. He gives the voice no further heed—except in the Evaluation Phase (which we explore in Chapter 10), where if a doubt is recurring and is blocking a dream from emerging, it will need to be examined and dealt with. If Thrivers allowed practical concerns to circumscribe their visions, they would never achieve the remarkable results they do. They are only able to do so because they keep their eye firmly on the vision (like Mary Manin Morrissey and her "firewalk") despite the logical, rational, practical concerns that say it can't be done.

Principle 5. Maintain "structural tension" between the vision and current reality

Robert Fritz, the author of two books on the creative process, has found that maintaining a sort of "structural tension"—like a giant rubber band—between our current level of experience and where we want to be is key to the manifestation process. Diagram 8-3 illustrates this phenomenon.

Diagram 8-3
STRUCTURAL TENSION

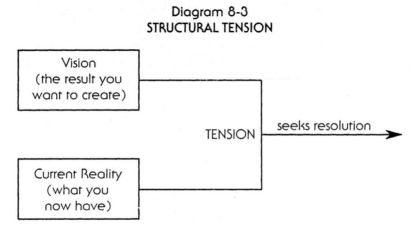

Reprinted by permission from *The Path of Least Resistance*, by Robert Fritz, copyright 1981.

Structural tension means simultaneously visualizing an objective image of where we are right now, and a clear vision of how we want our life to be. As we hold these two images in our mind together, the gap between them begins to narrow as the tension resolves in favor of the path which offers the least resistance. This structural tension can mean the difference between a Pollyanna approach and one which moves us to a higher level. Without it, we might envision ourselves as becoming a millionaire within the next year when our current reality is that our business just failed, we filed bankruptcy, and we have a long road of rebuilding ahead.

Principle 6. *Refuse to be daunted by the voice of discouragement*

Visioning a better life for ourselves can be threatening to those around us. Thrivers have learned not to seek the counsel of the gainsayers, but to surround themselves with individuals who will support them in their growth, challenge them when appropriate, and encourage them when their vision becomes clouded. As I discussed in *When 9 to 5 Isn't Enough,* our best defense against such discouragement, resistance, and sabotage is twofold: a strong support system, and a clear commitment to our vision, which is reinforced daily. Encouraging ourselves with four simple words—YOU CAN DO IT!—can keep us going when the lions are at the door.

Principle 7. *Don't insist on knowing the entire plan in advance*

Competent managers in the business world would be reluctant to proceed with a merger, a downsizing, or the launching of a new product without formulating a plan for the entire sequence of events, complete with the ramifications for each department, each market, and each customer. While this may be good business practice, it is not always the best advice for individuals in transition. There are times when we feel a calling from deep within ourselves to take a drastic step, whether it be a career change, ending a marriage or other long-term relationship, or going on a diet. Mike Long, whom we met in Chapter 4, is an example. His soul was crying out for him to quit the law long before the partners in his firm asked him to leave. Perhaps part of the reason he stayed was the security of a steady job, or an unwillingness to abandon a career in which he had invested so much time, energy, and money. But it may be that if he had obeyed his soul's call for redirecting his vocation, he could have avoided much of the pain he suffered by forcing circumstances to make his decision for him.

When we feel strongly that a change is needed, we may only know the first step to take. And we won't know the next one until we take that first known step into our future. Although it is true that things may not turn out the way we planned, "a lot of times the process of going through the change is just as valuable as the outcome," says psychologist Frank Colistro. "And even if nothing comes of it—in other words, even if they take a few years off and go back to school and then decide they want to go back to what they were doing, they'll still be the better for it because they'll know that they've tried something different, and just that process will have enhanced their self-confidence and self-esteem."

It is not unusual to envision one result and find that once the process is completed, we find ourselves in another. For example, when I became unhappy working for the law firm which employed me following law school, I began proactively creating a new "work situation" that would fulfill me. To my surprise, the result of that vision was an opportunity to start my own firm from a strong base provided by a client who wished to retain me part-time. While I could never have imagined that such an opportunity existed, my vision was open enough that I could welcome this situation when it presented itself.

I frequently advise my career counseling clients to develop a "transition plan" by which they can move more gradually from their current occupation to their ideal one, but not to be so tied to their plan that they close themselves off from other, even more desirable alternatives. Perhaps they can begin a business or take a job moonlighting in their chosen field. Or they can reduce their current working hours to part-time (assuming they can support themselves financially on a part-time salary) and pursue their passion part-time until it begins to sustain itself. Thrivers think through possible scenarios such as "What if I start my business and it doesn't grow as fast as I expect," or "What if I leave my spouse and end up in a bitter custody battle—could I deal with that?" Then, they consult their inner self to decide whether they are ready to take that critical first step, trusting the rest of the process to work itself out for the highest good of all concerned. I believe there is no greater tragedy than to find ourselves near the end of our lives and regret that we never dared to explore our true passions.

Principle 8. Be open to synchronicity

The final Principle of Proactive Creation is to be open to synchronicity. We now know that the Newtonian notion of cause leading mechanically to a specific effect is outmoded. In the New Zero, the phenomenon of "nonlocality" makes it possible that events in Australia can influence activities in New York, and that our choices today can affect individuals in another country tomorrow (or even yesterday, according to some quantum physicists!). Cause and effect are now connected in surprising new relationships, often circular or cyclical in nature.

Synchronicity is a term coined by psychologist Carl Jung to denote the order which exists in the human psyche in a noncausal manner.[4] If we make a decision to explore a career in radio, for example, and we find ourselves next to a local disc jockey in line at the movies, synchronicity is at work. There is no logical (i.e., linear and causal) reason for that person to have come into our orbit—and indeed if they had done so prior to our decision, such a chance encounter would have much less significance. But in some seemingly mysterious way, we have drawn that person to us because of the focus we have placed on the radio industry.

When we set a vision in mind, synchronicity often follows. Suddenly we find ourselves encountering books, resources, financial support, mentors, partners, and other pieces needed to complete the "puzzle" comprising our vision. Michael's opportunity to write his own job description reveals the working of synchronicity, since at the time he verbalized that desire he had no idea how—or whether—it would become manifest. The power of his vision, coupled with the action he took in taking the steps he knew (working as a volunteer at the liability insurance company), fueled the unfolding of the work situation he desired. We can view synchronistic events such as these as validation from the Universe that we are on the right path.

As I watched the 1994 Wimbledon women's tennis finals, I

saw twenty-two-year-old Conchita Martinez triumph over long-time tennis veteran Martina Navratilova. That in itself was remarkable, but even more noteworthy is the fact that Martinez spent years in her childhood hitting the tennis ball and imagining Navratilova was on the other side of the net. Little did Martinez imagine that Navratilova would still be playing by the time she reached the professional level, so that her childhood vision could manifest itself before millions of spectators.

By holding our vision firmly in our minds, we will experience synchronicity at every turn. Though it will continue to amaze us, we will soon begin to anticipate it. And this only increases our trust in the ability of our Higher Power to support us in pursuing our highest good.

THE EIGHT PRINCIPLES OF PROACTIVE CREATION	
Principle 1	Develop a clear vision statement
Principle 2	Find a role model and study it
Principle 3	Add other sensory dimensions to the vision
Principle 4	Refuse to let "practicality" suppress the vision
Principle 5	Maintain "structural tension"
Principle 6	Refuse to be daunted by discouragement
Principle 7	Don't insist on knowing the entire plan in advance
Principle 8	Be open to synchronicity

How to Use the Vision Statement

We have explored how Thrivers craft a vision statement that will be most effective in capturing the positive momentum which begins with this phase of transition. But a vision statement, like the business plan for a business, is not something to write and put in a drawer. Rather, it must be a living, breathing, dynamic document we keep with us throughout our transition.

I have found that it is very effective to write the statement out each night before going to bed. Minor changes may be incorporated into the statement as we learn more about what is involved in creating it. Even if we don't have time to write it out freshly each night, it is also effective to read it to ourselves out loud at least once a day, bringing all of our senses to it: feel it, taste it, smell it, hear it, see it. This transforms mere words into the kind of vividly imagined scene that will rally our subconscious into action. And now that we have a vision of what we want to experience clearly in mind, it is time to begin taking action.

NOTES

1. Zohar, Danah, *The Quantum Self*, Quill/William Morrow 1990, p. 185.
2. Zohar, *Ibid.*, p. 184.
3. Perkins-Reed, Marcia, "Intuitive Goal Setting," *Science of Mind* February 1991, p. 13.
4. Wolf, Fred Alan, *The Dreaming Universe*, Simon & Schuster 1994, p. 54.

9

MOVING CONFIDENTLY INTO ACTION

❧

When you work with Wu Wei, *you have no real accidents. Things may get a little Odd at times, but they work out. You don't have to try very hard to* make *them work out; you just* let *them.*

—Benjamin Hoff
The Tao of Pooh

There comes a time in the unfolding of a transition when action is inevitable. The springtime of our transition has arrived. We have dealt with the crisis and examined our discontentment. We have undergone the introspection and transformation of the Sorting-out Phase. And we have formulated a vision that embodies the highest possibility we can imagine for our new experience. Now it is time to take a step to realize that vision. But mere action for its own sake will not suffice.

Thrivers think in terms of processes and wholes, not results and segments. The outcome of the transition is not as important as how they have approached each step along the way.

Copers tend to move directly to action—any action at all—to avoid the Sorting-out Phase and the visioning process. Thrivers, on the other hand, embrace the Action Phase with excitement, enthusiasm, and a unique kind of reserve that tempers what might otherwise become feverish activity. They understand the need to approach action as a process, not a simple means to an end. In the Buddhist tradition, this kind of action is paradoxically called "non-action." Stephen Levine defines non-action as "acting without a sense of 'self': appropriate but not attached action. Non-action is doing what's right in the moment."[1]

When it is time to act on our vision, we are again called to spend time centering and consulting with our inner guide: What action is best to take now? What is our motivation for acting? Is it for selfish purposes? Are we considering a career move solely to obtain more money? Or are we acting because we feel guided by our Higher Power to do so? Is it because the choice we are making is the best for all concerned? Or because we *must* make this important change to preserve our sense of self, our integrity, or another important aspect which has been threatened by our prior circumstances?

When Mary Manin Morrissey was in her "firewalk" period, she admits she felt like running at times. Yet she was determined that she would not leave her work in anger, frustration, weariness, or resentment. If she did leave, it would be because she felt guided to do so, and because it was a peaceful move. In other words, she chose the emotional energies that would be her driving forces. This prevented her from making a rash decision in the midst of her pain that she may later regret.

We can each decide what emotions we will allow to drive us into action.

It can be the wisdom of our inner guidance and the impetus of our vision, or it can be fear, doubt, insecurity, and guilt. The emotional motivators behind our action will color the outcome, and will determine whether we have another dark night of the soul ahead in which to again face the possibility of a higher level of being. By choosing their driving forces in life, Thrivers can triumph over seemingly insurmountable challenges because they have taken control of their experience of the events which confront them.

To take effective action in the New Zero requires that we continue to draw on our skills of attentiveness (see Chapter 5). As we remain vigilant to *all* of the shifting circumstances around us—as well as our own internal changes in emotional state, vision formulation, and commitment—we can make decisions that are better-informed and more likely to lead to the result we prefer.

It is the optimistic confidence cluster of traits that propels Thrivers into purposeful action to fulfill their vision. They draw on the following four well-cultivated skills to do so:

- self-confidence
- playful risk-taking
- optimism
- flexibility

SELF-CONFIDENCE

After living in southern California for nearly twenty years, Sally began to have nagging feelings of being suffocated. She no longer felt nurtured in the hustle and bustle of the nation's second largest metropolitan area. And her soul began to call her to return to nature. She walked more, went on weekend trips to the desert, and spent as much time as possible near the ocean, connecting with the forces of the waves and the origins of being. She felt torn when she considered leaving the area, since both she and her fifteen-year-old daughter had long-time friends there, and her consulting clients were largely in Los Angeles as well. But when she attended a professional conference in Denver, she fell in love with the region. She spent one afternoon driving to a small town outside Denver where a fellow consultant from the conference lived. And almost on impulse, she decided she wanted to live there.

As her vision became clearer, she decided she would maintain an office in Los Angeles to service her clients there, but her primary base would be a home office in a suburb of Denver, where she could write, meditate, and return to nature, and where her daughter could enroll in the community's school system. Sally kept busy with the preparations of moving: finding a place to live, packing, notifying her clients of her impending change. And it was the prospect of living in a relatively remote location, seeing the elk grazing near her new home, and being surrounded by trees that kept her going.

> I think it was so busy that I could mask some of the fears that I had . . . was I doing the right thing. But when I finally crawled into bed the first night, I looked up at the six-foot skylight over the bed and I could see stars for miles. And I looked up at the stars and the dark sky, and I looked out the side windows at the mountains and the trees and I thought, "I guess this is it. This is where I am supposed to be." And then I felt okay.

It certainly took courage for Sally to make the move she did, particularly when she was also emerging from a divorce. But she had the confidence in herself that she could do it. This assurance was built through her previous experiences in counseling, other geographic moves she had made, and an earlier career transition from employee to self-employed consultant. Sally's strong self-confidence enabled her to transcend her fears and make a lifestyle change which validated her soul's leading to a more nurturing environment and a slower pace of life.

Thrivers possess remarkable confidence in themselves and their abilities. Without becoming egotistical, they have developed, over time, an internal belief that they can handle what their life hands them, often "making lemons into lemonade." Yet even Thrivers feel uncertain at times. Whether during a dark night type of Sorting-out Phase, or following an action step that didn't generate the preferred result, Thrivers turn again to their self-confidence, knowing they have a degree of composure which enables them to try again.

When motivational speaker Terry McBride graduated from college with a degree in marketing and finance, he went to work at an accounting firm. Later, he decided to become a CPA, not having studied accounting or having knowledge of the contents of the four-part CPA exam. The first time he took the CPA test, there were a number of questions he didn't understand. But because he knew he could eventually accomplish his goal—despite the remarks of people who told him he couldn't pass it unless he was an accounting major—he studied on his own and took the exam again every six months for two and a half years. Finally, after taking it five times, he passed all four parts.

Terry describes this as understanding that "I could create a reality that I wanted, and I didn't have to fit into anybody else's box." His self-confidence was greatly enhanced by the lessons in creating his own reality that he learned from his thirty spinal and abdominal surgeries. He was then able to apply what he had learned in dealing with his health to the accounting exam, to dealing with divorce, to becoming a professional speaker, and to other areas of his life, knowing that he could always choose his attitude, emotions, and to some extent, his outcome.

Cultivating such self-confidence generates an additional benefit when dealing with simultaneous change or crisis situations:

Thrivers can remain calm and clear-thinking in the midst of external chaos because they know they are capable of handling the situation.

Thrivers have internalized the often cited maxim that "Life never gives us anything greater than we can handle." New situations may call for new approaches, for tapping our creativity, and for improvising. But whatever is demanded, Thrivers know they can respond.

Thrivers' self-confidence also allows them to defer temporary gratification for the sake of longer-term rewards. Brian Tracy's studies of wealthy individuals discloses that one of the traits shared by people who become wealthy is that they have a "long time perspective." Parents in Europe, he says, enroll their children in Oxford or a similar university when the child is born, even though the child won't attend college until eighteen years hence. Unlike many American parents, who tend to postpone college enrollment and financial arrangements until their child is in high school, European parents begin thinking twenty years into the future upon the birth of their son or daughter. They understand the importance of making decisions now that will assure a secure future with the outcome they desire.

Thrivers also trust their instincts and their intuition—even if what these inner senses are saying does not make logical sense (as is often the case). Many Thrivers (myself included) have learned that it is usually less costly and more in our best interest to heed the wisdom of our intuition than to follow the musings of our rational minds. I had a mystical experience one New Year's Eve in which I knew, beyond a doubt, that I would be the next board president of the church in which I was then involved. At the time I had the experience, the existing board was still in place, but the minister had just resigned. My experience, my intuitive knowing, made no rational sense. But due to its intensity, I trusted it, and through a series of circumstances (without any intervention from me), I did in fact become the next board president. As I experienced the wonderful dynamics of working with a new board, and even more importantly, trusted my instincts, the church rallied together and a remarkable new minister was hired who remains at the church to this day. I had to stretch myself, and my concept of what I could do, to follow this inner guiding. But it gave me a foundation from which to launch my own business a year later with a newfound confidence that I could do it.

PLAYFUL RISK-TAKING

Thrivers are willing to take risks others would not take. Where do Thrivers get the courage which empowers them to take action? In most cases, its source lies in how they view life. Unlike Copers, who see life as a series of problems to be solved, Thrivers perceive life as a game to be played, a glorious adventure to be experienced. As a result, they view the actions they take with a certain detachment, much like the Buddhist notion of non-action described above. They have an uncanny ability to participate fully without being overly attached to their results. "If this doesn't work out, then that will," they tell themselves. They don't feel the need to have Plans A, B, C, and D in order, although they often have considered a number of alternatives before acting. Rather, they trust their own ability to adapt their approach if their first trial is unsuccessful, and they take their next step as if making the next move in a chess game.

The way in which Thrivers participate in creating their lives resembles the "creative play" which Hindu myth says occurred in the creation of the worlds. According to Hindu lore, the world was created by the self-sacrifice of God. But sacrifice here does not mean "giving over," as it does in Western culture. "Sacrifice" in its original sense means "to make sacred": the Divine becoming the physical world, and then becoming the Divine once again. This creative "play," called *lila* in Hindu, manifests itself in many physical forms which possess a common underlying Divine essence.[2] Thrivers continually remind themselves that the world they see is not the "real" world, but simply many manifestations at play, reflecting a Divine reality which underlies all.

Does this mean Thrivers do not grieve at the loss of a relationship or the death of a loved one? No. Here again we see the biphasic aspect of the Thriver. He or she can fully experience his or her feelings and live a life which is approached thoughtfully, but simultaneously realize that it is all a game, that what really matters is living life fully in each moment.

Seeing life as a game has the happy consequence of enabling Thrivers to find a sense of joie de vivre, or joy of living, which pervades every aspect of their life.

The "life is a game" approach can, of course, be taken too far. I am not advocating that we abdicate responsibility for our lives. But I have observed among my clients, seminar participants, and other individuals I encounter every day that most of us take life too seriously. We are so focused on making more money, getting a house in the "right" neighborhood, having the latest clothes and the newest model car, that we forget to enjoy what we have. We have lost the ability to cherish our loved ones, and have lost sight of the value of time spent just "hanging out," laughing, telling stories, joking, and reminiscing.

I am suggesting that we, like the Thrivers I have studied, find a middle ground in which we accept personal responsibility for our own self-fulfillment—in all areas of our lives, such as paying our bills on time, preparing for the future by formulating a vision, saving part of our earnings, and preserving our environment—but that we also make time to play, to rest, to relax, to spend time with our families and friends, and to laugh.

This approach often requires that we re-characterize our experiences. Thomas Edison commented, after hundreds of unsuccessful attempts to make a lightbulb, "I have just discovered 950 ways *not* to make a lightbulb." Similarly, rather than describing our previous trials as failures, we can train ourselves to see our experiences differently. Rather than a bankruptcy representing a "disaster," we can see it as a financial clean slate. Or instead of perceiving a bitter divorce as a heartbreaking experience, we can begin to see it as a wonderful opportunity for letting go of what is no longer in our best interest. By reframing each experience in terms of our own growth opportunity, we create a playground on which to play the game of life.

Although Thrivers may seem to take substantial risks in the action through which they realize their vision, they view it otherwise. Time after time, as I asked Thrivers how it felt to make a major change in their lives, they would say, "It didn't feel like a risk; it was something I had to do." This feeling that we "have to" take the needed action is the momentum of the vision progressing forward into action. This phenomenon of being gently prodded forward by the Universe was recognized by W. H. Murray when he said:

> The moment one commits oneself,
> then Providence moves, too.
> All sorts of things occur to help one
> that would never have otherwise occurred.
> A whole stream of events;
> all manner of unforeseen incidents
> and chance meetings and material assistance come forth
> which no one could have dreamt would appear.

This support from Providence reveals itself through the synchronicity which follows Thrivers' clear articulation of their vision, and becomes even more evident once they take a step to act upon it. The game becomes even more fun to play as others join with them in their venture, as financial support appears, as support groups assist them in rediscovering themselves, and as "all manner of unforeseen incidents" surprises them at every turn, confirming that they are on the right path.

OPTIMISM

We know that people who maintain a positive attitude—we call them optimists—are more enjoyable to be around than those who don't. But we are just now discovering that optimism is more than a luxury for a few exceptionally happy individuals: it actually holds potential medical benefits. A positive outlook, for example, has been shown to help heal the heart following a diagnosis of heart disease, according to a recent study of over 1,700 men and women by Dr. Daniel Mark of Duke University.[3] Fourteen percent of the patients said they doubted they would recover enough to resume their daily routines. After one year, 12 percent of these pessimists had died, compared with 5 percent of the optimistic remainder. And another study validates these findings. Dr. Nancy Frasure-Smith studied the effect of negative emotions on 222 patients, most in their sixties, who were recovering from heart attacks. Those who scored high on the psychological instrument she administered, which measured feelings of sadness and depression, were eight times more likely to die during the following eighteen months than the rest.[4]

Medical doctors are becoming increasingly aware of the power of negative thoughts, attitudes, and words on the healing process. According to Dr. Deepak Chopra, "it is now standard practice not to make negative remarks during surgery. The more positive the surgeon's expressed opinions, in fact, the more positive the outcome for the patient."[5] Negative feelings are known to lower our immune response and diminish our ability to heal, perhaps even weakening our DNA's ability to repair itself, says Chopra.

Terry McBride began to sense this principle intuitively as he became more and more frustrated with his doctors' apparent inability to remedy his back problems and related conditions after over two dozen surgeries. He soon made it a practice to keep a sign above his hospital bed which said "Be positive or be gone." He insisted that those who visited him and interacted with him maintain an optimistic attitude, supporting him in his healing, or he was not interested in continuing to talk with them. McBride credits this attitude with empowering him to recognize his power of choice—regardless of how circumstances appeared or what the doctors' opinions may be—so that, ultimately, he brought himself to perfect health, turning his doctors' medical predictions on their heads.

Optimism is invaluable not only in the context of physical healing, but in any situation involving positive personal action (such as the resolution of a transition). If two people are seeking a new job, and one believes the right job is available for him to find, and the other believes the market is tight and he'll be lucky to find a single opening, the first person has set himself up for quicker results—and a better position. Quantum physics tells us, through the Uncertainty Principle, that when we are looking at one aspect of an object, we cannot simultaneously see the other—and yet both aspects are necessary for a whole view of the object, like the right and left hemispheres of the brain. For example, we cannot see the wave aspect of matter when it appears as a particle, and we cannot see the green aspect of an object when we are perceiving its redness. And so with our job seekers: If they are looking for jobs, they will find them, but if they are looking for a tight market, they will find that as well. While both the openings and the restrictions may be present, and together create an image of the entire marketplace, each job seeker's experience will be directly determined by his attitude toward the prospects and not by the prospects themselves.

If we feel ourselves becoming mired in the negativity around us, we can take comfort from the story of the prince who once asked a jeweler to inscribe his ring with something that would encourage him in good times and bad. The chosen inscription was "This, too, shall pass." Nothing is forever! If we are feeling depressed today, we will most likely feel better tomorrow. If our prospects seem slim today, they will increase tomorrow. We need only wait it out, know that our timing may not be the same as the timing that will actually play out, and trust that the best result is coming to us.

FLEXIBILITY

Thrivers have a unique ability to follow through on their vision that sets them apart from others who achieve fewer of their aspirations. It is paradoxical, in that it pairs commitment to a desired result with the ability to adapt to changes along the way.

Simultaneous Dedication and Nonattachment to Their Dream. On the one hand, Thrivers are dedicated to their dreams. Once they have explored the available options and "reduced the wave packet" to their chosen path, they pursue it with all their being. But at the same time, as they learn to let go of an insistence on winning or achieving, they may experience more outstanding results than any amount of effort could create.

Olympic skater Dan Jansen had a dream of obtaining a gold medal in the Olympics. In the first seven Olympic races in which he competed, he skated to please other people: his sister, Jane, who died of leukemia during the Calgary Games; his parents, who started him in skating at age four; his wife, Robin; and their infant daughter, Jane, as well as his coach. His desire to please others produced only mediocre results; the medals eluded him. As a recent article describes it, "Perhaps Jansen couldn't become a medal winner because he was thinking like a breadwinner, like someone who had to 'bring it home.'"[6] In the 1994 Olympics, he again lost in the 500-meter race. He came from behind to win the gold in the 1,000-meter by a surprising strategy: he simply stopped caring about winning. Says Jansen, "The way I got relaxed was not to care. No matter what happened in the 1,000, my family wasn't going to be gone. And losing the 1,000 wouldn't be as big a shock as not winning the 500. I went in with such low expectations because I didn't want to set myself up for disappointment." By focusing on his love for the 1,000 race, which he articulated by writing "I love the 1,000" at the top of daily worksheets for the past two years, he simply skated, removing his ego, his need to please others, and the pressure of the Olympics. And it worked. The dream hadn't subsided, but it came true almost in spite of the dreamer—once he released his grip on the coveted gold medal.

"Both And." Thrivers keep their eye on the prize, and yet are vigilantly aware of their results so that they can modify their

approach when necessary. Like the plants that change their structure to adapt to a new environment, Thrivers have an extensive repertoire of approaches from which to draw. And they look for ways to have "both and" rather than "either or." Often we believe we must make choices between two seemingly competing alternatives, when in fact we can have it both ways. Sally, for instance, found she could return to nature and still maintain her Los Angeles consulting base by maintaining two offices. Ellen found that she did not have to choose between her computer sales skills and her nursing background—she could incorporate both into one job. No one can predict exactly how the "both and" approach will work in all given situations.

It is the openness of the decision maker to the possibility of having both of the things they want that allows new possibilities to become clear.

Critical Path. On the Apollo flights from Earth to the Moon, the rockets were off their charted course more than 90 percent of the time. Many of us feel that way in our lives. Despite our best efforts to follow our dreams and fulfill our goals, we get distracted and pulled off course. The amazing result of the Apollo flights, however, is that they reached their destination. By constantly correcting their course, they stayed close enough to the path to reach the target as planned. Rather than being on a perfect course, they were on what is called a "critical path," which Charles Garfield, who worked on the missions, defines as "the most efficient or appropriate trajectory to take toward a target. Within it there is room for mistakes and corrections."[7]

Thrivers, too, find the critical path toward their vision and expect to make course corrections along the way. Perhaps the job they thought they wanted turns out not to be as fulfilling as anticipated. They may then explore ways to move laterally within their new company, to build other responsibilities into the job so that it does meet their needs, or to propose structural changes to their management which will allow the entire department to experience greater satisfaction. Or they may decide to look for other employment after a few months' trial reveals an improper fit. There is nothing "wrong" with such an approach. As we will discuss in the next chapter, it is one kind of "interactive experimentation" which is critical if we are to avoid feeling "stuck" in an unsatisfying situation. Garfield further explains the meaning of such course corrections: "*On course* does not mean perfect. On course means that even when things don't go perfectly, you are headed in the right direction."[8]

GETTING STUCK—AND GETTING OUT

In a perfect world, we could envision a result and immediately experience it in our lives. But in our world, most transitions are not so straightforward. It is not uncommon to confront setbacks, to have things not turn out as planned, to find ourselves sabotaging our own efforts, or to feel paralyzed with fear at the very prospect of letting go of our familiar lifestyle—Sorting-out Phase and new vision or not!

Setbacks and Disappointments. Kelly Osmont finds that among her grieving clients, many are disappointed when they get through the first year—with its holidays and anniversaries reminding them of the deceased—and find that as the second year begins, they still feel sadness. Haven't they dealt adequately with their grief? The answer, says Osmont, is that they probably have. But in the second year, they have an opportunity to enter another phase of the grieving process in which they decide how they want the holidays to be from now on— without the deceased.

Many would-be Thrivers find themselves caught in a seemingly hopeless cycle which I call the *Cycle of Frustration* (see Diagram 9-1). Their visions tend to be unrealistic idealizations of an idyllic existence. Because they are never realized, the visioner becomes frustrated, leading to an overall sense of depression and demoralization. He turns to idealizing to bring himself out of the depression, initiating the cycle again.

The law of averages dictates that some (or even most) of our attempts at change will not reach their desired end. This is especially true when we are new to the process. However, as we become more skilled at visioning—designing our statement

Diagram 9-1
CYCLE OF FRUSTRATION

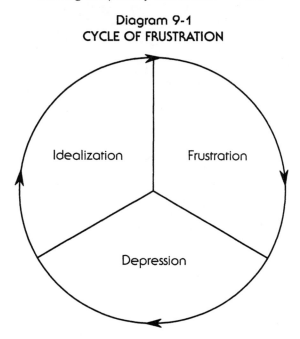

with just the right amount of specificity, open-ended in just the right places—we find that more often than not, we can manifest the result we seek. And it occurs more quickly than it did initially. Often the breakthrough comes by using suggestions such as those given in Chapter 8 for designing an effective vision statement. We then move into the *Cycle of Proactive Creation* illustrated in Diagram 9-2. By choosing a vision which stretches us—but not too much—we notice that it has a result, which we then evaluate (more about that in the next chapter). This leads us to the next choice, made with a detachment that frees us from constant emotional ups and downs and allows us to improve our ability to realize our dreams, choice by choice.

When they find themselves disappointed or in the midst of an apparent setback, Thrivers have several resources on which to rely. First, they turn to their inner resilience, their support system, and their spiritual beliefs (discussed in Chapter 6 relating to crisis). Second, they ask themselves, "What can I learn from this turn of events?" Even if no lesson is apparent, they reserve judgment on whether the shift is "good" or "bad," for the passage of time may show it to be either. Napoleon Hill once said that "Every adversity has within it the seed of an

Diagram 9-2
CYCLE OF PROACTIVE CREATION

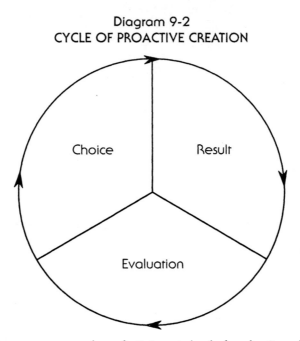

equivalent or greater benefit." As we look for the "seed of the greater benefit," our eyes become focused on the positive aspect of the situation and not the setback that was perhaps our first reaction.

It is important to avoid taking a setback personally. Psychologist Martin Seligman explains in his book, *Learned Optimism,* that optimism can enhance the persistence that is needed to get through particularly difficult times:

> Some people, the ones who give up easily, habitually say of their tragedies, "It's me, it's going to last forever, it's going to undermine everything I do." Others, those who resist giving in to tragedy, say, "It was just circumstances, it's going away quickly anyway and besides there's much more in life."

The key difference between Thrivers' reactions to setbacks and those of Copers is that Thrivers recognize the event as something that is temporary, whereas Copers immediately conclude that *they* are at fault, that *they* have done something wrong and it will be long lasting. It's the difference between "I'm a failure" and "This is just something that happened."

Fear and Self-Sabotage. It is not uncommon to unwittingly stop ourselves from making needed changes in our lives by focusing on our fear, or by sabotaging our progress through accidents, busywork, or procrastination. These blocking strategies must be examined closely. Sometimes, if we dare to ask the fear or sabotage to speak to us, we will discover that it has an important message.

There may be an unresolved past transition which, through resonance, is now emerging for resolution before we take further action. Perhaps the last time we followed our dream to pursue an entrepreneurial venture, we did not attain financial profitability, and had to return to a job that was less satisfying. When we again consider starting a business, the fear of re-creating our past "failure" is likely to arise. Learning from that past experience, our inner wisdom will guide us to the best strategy for working through these issues so that we can move forward with ease.

If it is not a matter of resonance of a past similar situation, these reactions may be due to fear of the unknown. By embracing our vision with love and caring, and by mentally rehearsing the action we desire to take, we can make peace with these feelings so that our entire being joins in the action step.

Our next area of growth is the thing that scares yet also excites us more than anything else.

Our fear can thus help us locate the issues we need to address. Therefore, fear is not to be stomped out or avoided, but honored by allowing it to speak to us. Once we listen to its message and understand it, we can continue with our action plan.

Another possible explanation for self-sabotage is the gradual obsolescence of the vision we formulated. At first, it was what we wanted, but now our passion has changed or other factors have withdrawn the "heart" from the vision. To determine if this is so, we can query, "Is this still what I want?" Thrivers do not hesitate to adjust their vision when appropriate, whether due to new information, a change in motivation, or a change in circumstances. We need not feel guilty for failing to follow through on a vision which may now be outmoded. Things move quickly in the New Zero, and we must adapt quickly to keep pace.

The Problem of Feeling Worthy. A final obstacle that can lie behind setbacks, fear, and self-sabotage is the problem of not feeling worthy of having what we desire. If we don't believe, deep down, that we deserve to have what we are envisioning, we will experience conflict between our conscious and subconscious, which will inevitably lead to mixed or confusing results.

In their work with couples as relationship therapists, Gay and Kathlyn Hendricks, authors of *Conscious Loving* and *At the Speed of Life,* have defined this issue as the "upper limits problem." "We are programmed [so] that we cannot feel good for very long without invoking some negative experience to bring us down," they explain. The challenge for the Thriver, as for the co-committed couple, is to learn "how to let yourself expand continuously into more positive energy."[9] Some of the behaviors in which we engage as we approach the "upper limits" of our ability to accept good are to deflect positive energy (e.g., deny a compliment someone makes to us), to worry about what might happen, to start an argument with a mate or friend, or to simply go on "automatic pilot" and revert to old behaviors. We may lie, conceal our feelings, or break our commitments to other people or organizations. We may temporarily "forget" our vision or our goals.

As Thrivers, we pay attention to these behaviors and become aware that our subconscious is telling us something. Before proceeding further in such situations, we should stop, reflect on our vision, and build our feeling of worthiness with an affirmation such as "I deserve to be happy," "I deserve to be financially secure," or "I deserve to be fulfilled." Then, we can revisit our vision, and "check in" with our subconscious to ensure that we are still committed to achieving it—as well as the unexpected positive consequences it is generating—and consciously open up to more of the good in our experience.

It is important to know when to act on our vision, and when to defer action, and when we do act, we want to choose the best course. Following are some guidelines for this key transition phase:

THIRTEEN KEYS TO TAKING EFFECTIVE ACTION
TOWARD YOUR VISION

1. Adopt the practice of non-action, i.e., do what seems deeply right in this moment. Ask, "What action is best to take now?"

2. Discern your motives for wanting to act: Are you just uncomfortable with the uncertainty of being in the question, acting out of fear, or do you genuinely sense your vision calling you to take a step toward its manifestation?

3. Choose the emotional energy that will be your driving force.

4. When you doubt your own confidence or ability to move ahead, recall past risks or challenges and how you overcame them.

5. View your transition from a longer time perspective: what will the impact of this action be in twenty years? Is that the outcome you want?

6. Trust your own intuition—particularly if one idea, vision, or action step keeps recurring in your mind as the step you should take next.

7. See life as a game to be played, not a test to be taken. Take reasonable risks that will move you toward your vision. Remember the saying that angels can fly because they take themselves lightly!

8. Avoid being dragged down by the past by recharacterizing past experiences as learning experiences or opportunities for growth, not disasters, problems, or failures.

9. Limit your thoughts and other input to those that are positive and which contribute to your desired result. See grand possibilities for your vision!

10. Cultivate a passionate dedication to your vision, while simultaneously remaining nonattached to the specific result you believe will occur.

11. View your action as simply a choice with a consequence, rather than a once-in-a-lifetime, success-or-failure event.

12. When you have a setback or unexpected disappointment, ask yourself, "What can I learn from this turn of events?" Don't take the setback personally.
13. Continue to build your sense of worthiness by affirming, "I deserve to be/have [your desire]."

As we take the action that is called for by our vision, we will find ourselves moving ever closer to our dreams. We will feel a positive change occurring, much like that described by Tarthang Tulku in *Skillful Means*:

> Life can be approached as if it were just another chore, but when we decide to make use of the many opportunities to change in positive ways, we can make our lives vital and healthy. We develop a genuine appreciation for ourselves, a sense of well-being which radiates through all our actions. When we accomplish change, we can see it, and take pride in it. Seeing the change in us, others too, will be encouraged. When we support one another's growth in this way, work is smooth and our hearts are joyful.

But taking action is not the end of our transition. We must continue through one more critical phase if we are to truly thrive and allow our transitions to facilitate our highest growth.

NOTES

1. Levine, Stephen, *A Gradual Awakening*, Doubleday 1989, p. 113.
2. Capra, Fritjof, *The Tao of Physics*, Shambhala 1991, pp. 87–8.
3. Haney, Daniel, "Positive Thinking Has Power to Heal Heart, Study Shows," *Oregonian* April 16, 1994.
4. *Ibid.*
5. Chopra, Deepak, *Quantum Healing*, Bantam 1990, p. 163.
6. Wolff, Alexander, "Whooosh!", *Sports Illustrated* February 28, 1994, p. 19.
7. Garfield, Charles, *Peak Performers*, Avon 1986, p. 199.
8. *Ibid.*, p. 200.
9. Hendricks, Gay and Kathlyn, *Conscious Loving*, Bantam 1990, pp. 124–5.

10

SELF-EVALUATION FROM A SYSTEMS PERSPECTIVE

✿

The good life is a process, not a state of being. It is a direction, not a destination.

—Carl Rogers

A commitment to constant self-evaluation is what separates Thrivers from Copers. Whereas Copers act aimlessly, unsure of their ultimate goal or direction, Thrivers use the Evaluation Phase of their transitions as a time to determine the value of the action they have taken. Is it bringing their vision into being, or not? This crucial inquiry gives them essential feedback so that they can either correct their course, or continue in the direction they are heading. In short, evaluation gives the action step its meaning.

The Evaluation Phase has not been addressed by most current transition theories. According to such theories—which bear the imprint of Newtonian physics—a transition stretches only from crisis to action step. And when evaluation is considered, it is done in a mechanical fashion by labeling the event: was this a "good" or a "bad" step for me? Was my action plan a "success" or a "failure"?

Such shortsighted thinking is no longer appropriate. We have seen that transition is a circular process, by which the end of one transition often leads directly to another. Evaluation gives us a chance to "catch our breath," to step back from our vision and our actions and analyze them with the eyes of a scientist. That is, evaluation calls for us to take a "laboratory perspective" on our lives. It is as though we are performing a scientific experiment by trying out the new job or working through the uncharted territory of grieving.

The only standard against which we weigh the consequences of our actions is this: "Did this action take me closer to my vision, or further away from it?"

If we find that it took us further away from it, that does not necessarily mean it was a failure. Indeed, as we will see in a moment, our greatest growth, and a majority of our true successes, occur when we discover what does *not* work to take us toward our goal. And if it doesn't, we have a simple choice to make: a change of course, another trial, or a new approach to reaching our desired end. Life becomes a series of choices, each of which has a consequence. We no longer think in terms of success or failure, but of consequences. The events of our lives become neutral; it is up to us to determine their meaning. And as we free ourselves from judgment, we develop a certain detachment from those consequences that enables us to better understand our own unique creative cycle. And it puts us in control, not of all the things that happen to us, but of our experience of them.

To evaluate effectively the actions they take, Thrivers draw upon the Systems Thinking Cluster of traits, which includes:

- systems perspective
- interactive experimentation
- sense of humor
- balance

SYSTEMS PERSPECTIVE

The Old Zero has programmed us to reduce problems to their least common denominator, to break every system or project into its component parts. In the industrial workplace, for example, each process of production is divided into "minute parts, so that the final product can be produced at great speed without anyone having to contribute more than a totally insignificant and, in most cases, unskilled movement of his limbs," as one economist describes it.[1] This "division of labor" results in work that is boring at best, and torturous at worst:

> From the point of view of the workman, it is a 'disutility'; to work is to make a sacrifice of one's leisure and comfort, and wages are a kind of compensation for the sacrifice.[2]

Or as I have often stated it in workshops, we feel like we are serving a "life sentence" of working, with retirement denoting the beginning of our "time off for good behavior."

To thrive in the New Zero requires that we begin to think in wholes, looking at each of the elements of the system as intimately interrelated.

From the systems perspective, each element is vital if the system is to remain healthy. Our finances are connected to our relationships and emotions, which are in turn related to our work and creativity. The marketing department must coordinate with the production department to ensure adequate supply to meet coming demand. Without this outlook, we are destined to live a life in which each of our roles is more and more separate from the other, and in which we feel ourselves being torn in a myriad of different directions, ever seeking to consolidate our separate selves.

Whether they are appraising the workplace, health care, or the environment, Thrivers have learned to take a flexible, balanced approach to life. They can appreciate the value of Western medicine in some instances, and can also avail themselves of Eastern alternatives in others. In Europe, alternative health care is referred to as "complementary health care," and is covered by all major insurance companies. Thus it is made clear that acupuncture, homeopathy, massage, chiropractic, and other alternative processes do not supplant more traditional methods, but complement them. They can coexist, each being utilized in the situations for which they are appropriate.

Regarding work, Thrivers understand that making an income at the individual level, and a profit at the company level, is part of the system. But they also know that the primary role of work is as creative self-expression and collaboration with others in a meaningful way. They have learned to balance these often seemingly conflicting objectives by identifying and pursuing work that is meaningful for them, but that also generates an adequate income.

A change in the overall structure of a system can entirely obliterate certain troublesome behaviors. For example, removing a child from an abusive family environment at an early age may markedly decrease the likelihood of that child's developing addictions, acting out, or perpetuating the cycle of abuse. Stanton Peele, an addictions expert, cites studies demonstrating that 95 percent of the soldiers who were heroin addicts in Vietnam ended drug use upon returning to the U.S. This result implies that the addiction was developed as part of a situation (a system, if you will), and when the system changed and the soldier returned to his home system, the addiction—and the need for it—disappeared.

As we recognize our individual lives as a living microsystem, and our employer, our community, our nation, and our planet as living macrosystems, we can begin to channel our creativity to envisioning new models for systems that thrive in the New Zero. These new systems, which arise out of the high level of complexity that increases daily, are called "self-organizing systems" by Nobel Prize winner Ilya Prigogine. Danah Zohar describes them as follows:

> The kind of order created by living systems is not the order of tidying-up operations. . . . The creativity of living systems . . . arises from their ability to create the kind of order that gives rise to relational wholes, systems that are greater than the sum of their parts,

and to do this spontaneously whenever a critical level of complexity is reached.[3]

When evaluating a transition after it has resolved itself, Thrivers examine not only the short-term results (i.e., did buying that new house result in less commuting time, less housing expense, or more room for the children to play?), but also the "big picture" outcomes, such as how the new home fits into their long-term investment plans, their life purpose, and the other aspects of their lifestyle, such as their health, relationships with their family, and their overall satisfaction with their living environment. Thrivers are cognizant of the entire system of their lives, and consider the impact on that system of each transition, each action, and each thought. They have a high commitment to maintaining a workable balance between their career and their key relationships, between being with others and being alone, between responsibility and play, so that their life system is optimally healthy.

INTERACTIVE EXPERIMENTATION

The Newtonian paradigm has isolated us from our environment. Rooted in the philosophy of René Descartes, it has conditioned us to see nature as divided into two separate, independent realms: mind and matter. This "Cartesian dualism" has allowed scientists (as well as human beings in their daily living) to "treat matter as dead and completely separate from themselves. . . . As a consequence of this division, it was believed that the world could be described objectively, i.e., without ever mentioning the human observer . . . ,"[4] according to physicist Fritjof Capra. In this view, the world is as it is, and no allowance is made for differing perceptions or for any intimate interaction between us and the things and people we encounter.

Quantum physics has upset this notion. By labeling the consequences of our actions as "observables," which can only be observed once we act, quantum physics unites us with our environment in an integral way. Like the creator who envisions and executes a project just for the sake of creating, "We 'do' to observe," explains Dr. Fred Alan Wolf in *Star Wave.* "We must bring out or cause something to occur in order that we observe anything at all." This paradoxical interaction of ourselves with our circumstances, by which reality is revealed to us through our participation in it, is called "contextualism" by physicist Danah Zohar,[5] and "interactive experimentation" here. It acknowledges us as the co-creators we are.

After we have noticed it, the observable fulfills a second role: "it 'sets up' the physical conditions that will enable [the observer] to continue observing the same value for the desired observable."[6] That is, as we make one choice and heed its results, that option will tend to sustain itself over time as we pay attention to it, and to replicate itself in future situations. However, not all observables are capable of being repeated. Due to the element of chance in every choice and every observation, we cannot predict with certainty what the outcome will be. This element of fate or chance helps make life a game for the Thriver.

We have talked previously about the observer effect, whereby the presence of the experimenter/observer in the laboratory influences the way in which the data or objects in the experiment behave. As we add the concept of observables to this observer effect, we find that a "self-referential loop" (to use Dr. Wolf's term) is set up through our observation. Diagram 10-1 illustrates this process of acting, observing, modifying our action if necessary, and acting again.

A similar process of trial and error occurs throughout the transition process. It is present when we decide to enter a particular occupation, find a position in a company in that field,

Diagram 10-1
THE SELF-REFERENTIAL LOOP

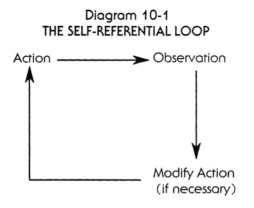

and discover, after several months, that we are making less money and experiencing less enjoyment through that work than we were in our former career. We are inventing the route to our vision's manifestation as we go along. And as we enter the experimental aspect of this process, it is a substantial departure from the conventional approach of "finding the one right answer" we learned in school. Robert Fritz, in *The Path of Least Resistance,* explains:

> Creating is a matter of *invention* rather than *convention.* Education emphasizes convention . . . Inventing is another skill that can be developed. When you take an action that is designed to bring your creation into being, the action may either work or not work. If the action works, you can continue taking it or discontinue taking it. Sometimes it will be useful to continue, sometimes it will not be useful to continue. **You will know what to do by watching the changes in the current state of the result.**[7]

In other words, we observe our results to determine our next step. As time goes on, we begin to develop a "sixth sense" about what works best. Indeed, Dr. Wolf tells us that "Creativity demands error. Through error, choice exists. Although all of us desire perfection in our lives, such perfection, if reached, would overwhelm us. Life, to say the least, would be horribly boring. Worse than trying something and making errors is not doing anything for fear of failure."[8]

In fact, as Wolf explains, the state of mechanical order and perfection which many seek in the Newtonian model would lead us to a kind of death, in the sense that it would entail the extinguishing of free will and choice.

Many people try to orchestrate their lives until they are "just so," in order to fulfill an unrealistic, static mental picture which, even if obtained, would only diminish their aliveness.

We all know people who are caught in a seemingly endless cycle of perfectionism, compulsively cleaning, making lists, and keeping up appearances to hide the deadness which exists beneath the facade. Extending ourselves through conscious action, and challenging ourselves with a higher vision, removes us from that deadening cycle. Of course, our lives may look a bit chaotic at first. We may relate to a sign I once saw in someone's office which says "I'm not coming apart; I'm just under construction." But how much more energizing it is to choose life—even if it looks funny and feels awkward as we first begin to experience new choices—than to remain locked into a routine which closes us off from the parts of ourselves that have been unexposed.

To avoid becoming discouraged, we must realize that a majority of our attempts may *not* directly further our vision. But through noticing which choices do not "get us there," and adjusting our approach accordingly, we develop our creative skills. Once we go through our third or fourth job transition, we know the steps to take and can usually traverse the emotional and logistic aspects of the search more easily than the first time. Dr. John Boyman, of the international outplacement firm Drake Beam Morin, has observed this phenomenon in the firm's outplacement enrollees: "With people who come through a second time, who have had the experience, particularly if they had outplacement help, they don't tend to have the shock that lingers on; they deal with their anger faster; they tend not to get as depressed, because they've been there."

Notice that I am not suggesting that if something doesn't work, to keep at it, hoping beyond hope that it will eventually succeed. There is a saying in recovery circles that "insanity is doing the same thing over and over again, expecting different results." And this is *not* what I am advocating here. It is the *ability to adjust our approach* as we notice we are getting further from our goal, rather than closer to it, that differentiates the Thriver from the Coper. As Robert Fritz so aptly states it, "It is not fortitude, willpower, or determination that enables you to continue the creative process, but learning as you go."[9] This is the critical difference between a life lived for others, satisfying their endless expectations without questioning, and the life of the Thriver, in which the individual makes choices based on which option will bring the greatest self-expression, the highest level of fulfillment, and the most genuine unfolding of their authentic Self.

"Learning as you go" also differentiates a machine which makes clay pots, generating hundreds of identical pots each day, from the child making a pot, using his own spontaneously generated design. A whole chain of free decisions—the idea to make a pot, the idea to make a particular style of pot, and the decisions involved in where to push or mold the clay to realize the design—leads the child through a process Danah Zohar calls "creative discovery," through which "the child makes both the pot and himself (his sense of beauty). . . . His creation has acted as midwife to the birth of a small bit of new reality."[10]

SENSE OF HUMOR

Thrivers rely on their sense of humor to overcome discouragement and keep their perspective. No matter how unpleasant the circumstances, or how strongly felt the interpersonal conflict, they find a way to laugh at themselves or the situation. Of course, such an approach can be taken too far, as in the case of people for whom making a joke out of a situation becomes an unbreakable habit, precluding them from dealing seriously with any issue in their lives. But as Freud has suggested, "Humor is a means of obtaining pleasure in spite of the distressing affects that interfere with it."[11]

When comedian Richard Pryor was critically burned in an accident in his home some years ago, it was his sense of humor, along with the support of his fans, that speeded his recovery. Two weeks after the incident, Pryor's friend, actor and former football star Jim Brown reported that "He's been joking and kidding. He's sharp as a tack—telling ten jokes a minute. He says, 'I can always open a flower shop if the doctors don't let me go back to work right away.'"[12]

Dr. Norman Cousins has reported cases in which cancer patients have literally laughed themselves back to health by watching old comedies from Laurel and Hardy and the Three Stooges. The laughter which they generate literally stimulates healing substances within the body. These in turn stimulate the immune system and result in quicker healing than would occur without the humorous input.

There are times in a transition, particularly a complex transition in which several major changes are occurring at once, when all we can do is laugh, both at ourselves and at our situation. Through doing so, we open ourselves to new ways of viewing our experiences. As astronaut John Glenn has said, a problem cannot be solved using the same energy with which it was created. Laughter can create the "different energy" that is needed to help us evaluate the results of our action in a more effective way and to find the solution that previously eluded us.

Laughing at ourselves can leave us with the "last laugh" too. When Ellen was going through her divorce, she dated a younger man, partly to inflate her ego and restore her sense of feeling attractive to men. When he broke up with her, he told her, "When you're fifty, I'll be forty-five, and you'll be all wrinkly and I won't." That only compounded other stress Ellen felt from an exploitive boss who had just fired her. She reports thinking to herself, "There must be a 'kick me' sign on my back. Why is this happening?" But Ellen had her revenge. A few years later, it turned out that the younger man she'd dated was losing his hair, and she was able to laughingly say, "I may be wrinkly when I get older, but you're not going to have any hair!"

Using humor can lighten up what would otherwise be a heavy load of adversity. As we look for the silver lining, using the optimistic approach that also characterizes Thrivers, we can train ourselves to see a funny side to our predicament.

BALANCE

The pace at which the New Zero challenges us to live our lives threatens to overwhelm us. Work responsibilities can easily overshadow our personal lives, forcing us to make difficult choices when conflicting demands occur. As our lives accelerate and the information age saturates us with endless input, stress inevitably becomes a part of life. The threat of corporate downsizing pressures us into working longer hours and taking fewer vacations in an attempt to guarantee, through outstanding job performance, that we can retain our jobs in a fluctuating marketplace. Only recently have we begun to demand a reprieve, to insist that our employers, our society, and the dizzying pace of our lives loosen their grip on us and allow us to craft a more balanced lifestyle.

Our perception of overwork is far from imaginary. As discussed in Chapter 1, we now work a full month longer than twenty years ago, and take shorter vacations and other time away from work. As this data comes to the public's awareness, polls of Americans show that fewer and fewer people are willing to let the trend continue. A 1990 University of Michigan survey showed that 70 percent of those earning $30,000 a year or more would give up one day's pay each week for a day of free time; 48 percent of those earning $20,000 a year concurred.[13] Another poll done by *Time* magazine and CNN in 1992 of 500 adults revealed that 69 percent of participants would like to "slow down and live a more relaxed life," whereas only 19 percent indicated they would like to "live a more exciting, faster-paced life."[14] And a 1990 *New Woman*/Yankelovich survey showed that 78 percent of men and 90 percent of women would sacrifice promotions at work, and 72 percent of men and 86 percent of women would sacrifice a pay raise, in order to spend more time with their families.[15]

Shifting Priorities. These statistics reveal a profound shift, which is mirrored in the Thriver Profile. By definition, Thrivers seek out novel ways to introduce balance into their lives. They are no longer willing to sacrifice themselves for their work, if it means a diminished family life or little or no time for themselves. Following a significant life transition such as a health crisis, the death of a loved one, an automobile accident, or a bitter divorce, one's priorities often undergo substantial reorganization. Over 60 percent of the Thrivers I interviewed said that following their transition, work was less of a priority than before. One-third indicated that their personal relationships became more important following a key transition, and nearly 20 percent said that improving their health and maintaining a positive environment became more of a priority. Time also became more precious to them after transition.

What seems to occur during key life transitions is that we confront our own mortality, and the fleeting nature of our lives. We realize that we will not live forever, and that we must use the time we have to its fullest. We become less willing to spend that time in a job that has no lasting value for us, or in a relationship which is inherently unhealthy. And we become more selective about the kind of people we allow into our lives. We give less time to petty matters, such as being upset with someone who cut us off on the freeway.

I discuss balance in the context of evaluation because it is often through a reassessment of our lives, or at least of one aspect of our lives, that we realize our time investment is out of sync with our true priorities. This can be the seed of the discontentment that leads us directly into a series of voluntary transitions that realign ourselves with our life purpose, our authentic priorities, and ultimately, our bliss.

When Sally took the courageous step of leaving her southern California home after twenty years, simultaneous with divorcing her husband of ten years, to live in a relatively remote area near Denver and take up writing and meditation, many of her friends were baffled. They frequently asked her, "Do you really think you're going to make it?" But that question had become a moot point for Sally. "It's like I don't think 'making it' is the goal anymore. And the deepest awareness I've had is that I don't feel like I have to push anymore. I don't feel like I'm competing. I'm not on a treadmill trying to get ahead. And that feels really great." Sally's priorities have changed. As she listened to the call of her soul to slow down her life and listen to her inner Self, it became clear that some external changes would also be required. Her spiritual growth became more important than the success of her consulting career, and living in the remote reaches of Colorado was the most nourishing and (to her soul anyway) reasonable thing for her to do *at this time in her life*. That is not to say that she won't return to the "fast track" with her newfound perspective in the future. But achieving balance is about heeding the inner calling in this moment, trusting that the cycle will lead us into the next phase as surely as it brought us here. Only then can we truly live from our center and fulfill our destiny in each moment of living.

Aligning Priorities with Actual Time/Energy Investment. Living a balanced life is defined uniquely for each individual. To determine what balance means for us, we must first be able to identify our individual purpose, priorities, and vision.

In the balanced life, our investment of time and energy is aligned with our priorities, so that we are spending the majority of our time doing what is most important to us.

Not surprisingly, authors Linda and Richard Eyre, the authors of *Lifebalance,* have found that, when asked about their priorities among work, development of personal character, family, and "other interests," most people ranked family or personal character first, with work coming in third or fourth. However, when asked about how they actually spend their time, they ranked work or other interests first, with family and personal character further down the list. My classroom use of a similar exercise has validated their results. In other words, most of us do *not* have the desired alignment between where our effort is invested and what is most important to us. Appendix B provides a series of exercises to help develop this important Thriver trait.

It is commonly acknowledged that the excess stress of our busy lives takes a physical toll on our bodies. There are far more heart attacks on Monday mornings at 9:00 A.M. than at any other time of the week, according to Dr. Deepak Chopra and others. Heart disease, cancer, and other stress-related diseases are rampant in Western society, but virtually absent in others who are less industrialized. Is this the price we must pay for modernization?

One thing is certain: we cannot wait for the system to change before we change our behavior. As Thrivers, we must learn to be proactive in standing up for our right to create a satisfying life, without the demands of excessive stress. If our company operates in a codependent or abusive way, the first step in its healing is to penetrate the layers of denial that often accompany such situations. Using a resource such as Anne Wilson Schaef's *The Addictive Organization,* we can identify the form the addiction is taking in our company and arrange an "intervention" of sorts. Or if that is too threatening for us, we can at least refuse to continue to participate in the addictive behavior, such as regular workdays in excess of eight hours, covering for management errors, and ignoring changes in the marketplace for the sake of preserving the status quo. We can confront our own tendencies toward workaholism or burnout, and as we begin our own recovery, others may choose to join us.

We can also set clear priorities on our personal growth and on our relationships with our family and close friends, and honor those commitments with *at least* the same degree of intensity that we give to our work. And if, on the other hand, we have been lax in our work ethic and spent excessive energy on unproductive ventures, perhaps we need to reverse our priorities. We can do this by arriving at work on time, giving our work our best effort, and acknowledging the interesting and varied people we interact with each day.

The Value of Breaks. Another key to balancing our lives is learning to take breaks. We are not designed to work mechanically, hour after hour, day after day, without breaks in our schedule. Approximately every two hours during our working day, we need to get away from our work environment and turn our mental attention elsewhere, even if for only ten or fifteen minutes. At lunch, it is best to leave the work structure and receive some nurturing from fresh outdoor air if possible (assuming we work in an office building or retail complex). We should not let our allocated vacation go unused, no matter how heavy the workload seems to be. We deserve these breaks—and we need them.

Over half of the Thrivers in my study have taken a sabbatical—a leave of absence from their usual work schedule—at some time during their working lives. And sabbaticals are increasingly becoming a fringe benefit of choice, in large as well as small- and medium-sized firms. Computer chip giant Intel Corporation discovered several years into its company's history that it was losing its best employees after an average of seven years of dedicated service. Some went to work for competitors, some took time out to travel, and others made drastic career changes. As the company investigated this alarming trend, which was costing them thousands of dollars in recruiting, training, and replacing employees who were literally irreplaceable, they discovered that the stresses of nonstop work were burning these employees out. Intel responded quickly by developing a sabbatical policy, allowing each employee several weeks of sabbatical leave every seven years, in addition to their regular vacation, with full pay. Immediately, the attrition rate decreased. The company was giving its employees the break they needed.

Other companies have made similar strides. IBM offers some employees full salary and benefits while taking a twelve-month-long Community Service Leave at the nonprofit agency of their choosing. And in 1991, AT&T began offering managers with five years' tenure to take a Special Enhanced Leave of Absence (unpaid but with regular benefits) of up to 24 months, during which they can pursue a serious personal interest.[16] Although most companies that offer sabbaticals are high tech companies, law firms, and consulting businesses, according to The Conference Board's *Redefining Corporate Sabbaticals for the 1990s,* other types of businesses are joining the trend. Less formal "sabbaticals," whether done with company consent or during a time of unemployment between jobs, are also becoming more common. However, there is still some risk of requesting such leave in professions in which the hard-driving, climb-the-corporate-ladder kind of mentality prevails.

Bringing balance to our life requires, above all, a commitment to set the personal boundaries necessary to create it. Learning relaxation techniques, taking breaks, and measuring time and energy commitments against our priorities at regular intervals will all contribute to a slower, more satisfying lifestyle. As we reach our own optimal balance between work, self, and relationships, we begin to learn what it truly means to thrive in the midst of even simultaneous transitions.

EIGHT GUIDELINES FOR EVALUATING A TRANSITION

1. Ask, "Did this action take me closer to my vision, or further away from it?"
2. Pay attention to the results that follow from your choice. If they did not further your vision, modify your action and make a new choice.
3. Be willing to engage in "trial and error" as part of your interactive experimentation process.
4. Learn to laugh at yourself.
5. Mentally step back and analyze the potential impacts of your decision on all areas of your life system—including the lives of your family, friends, and others.

6. If your desired change is not occurring, ask yourself if changing your environment or other aspects of your life would assist you in achieving what you want.
7. Examine your priorities and the way you spend your time and energy. Is your life balanced between self, family, work, and other interests?
8. Honor your essence as an organic, rather than mechanical, being; nurture your body, mind, and spirit. Are you taking breaks from the routine of working on a daily, weekly, and annual basis?

ATTRIBUTES OF A SUCCESSFUL TRANSITION

We have now come full circle in the cycle of transition. Beginning with a crisis or sense of discontentment, we have surmounted the initial acute crisis/decision phase, experienced the abyss of the Sorting-out Phase, begun to formulate a new vision, taken action on it, and evaluated our progress. Now that we are aware of the transition cycle, we will notice ourselves going through it multiple times in our lives, at various levels ranging from trivial issues to quantum leaps of transformation. Do we dare try to label our transitions as "successful" or "unsuccessful," "healthy" or "unhealthy," "good" or "bad"?

In the Old Zero, perhaps we would. And evaluation in this sense can have value if we use it as a tool for learning. Rather than asking, "Was that a good or a bad experience?" we might instead ask, "How could I modify my choices, my attitudes, or my way of being so that next time this transition will go more smoothly?" or, "How could I be more true to myself and my feelings as I go through another relationship transition?"

Psychologist Nancy Schlossberg, in her book *Overwhelmed: Coping with Life's Ups and Downs,* finds that three factors characterize those who negotiate transitions successfully and profit from change: a sense of increased options, an informed understanding of what has happened to them, and a feeling of control. It is like the feeling expressed by a man following a difficult job transition when he said, "If I can weather that, I can weather anything. I will never be that upset again. In addition,

I have more understanding of what one goes through after one loses a job and before one gets another one."

Evaluating Our Transitions

I asked each of the Thrivers I interviewed, as well as the participants in the focus groups how they knew that a transition came out well. Some of them had specific responses, such as these:

> [I know by] "how I feel."
> "Things kind of calm down and stabilize a bit. The elements have less intensity, but they aren't gone. [Later, I feel] a sense of inner peace."
> "I feel good. After a transition or challenge, I know that it's successful when I'm happy. I feel good, I feel comfortable, I no longer worry about it."
> "When I can look on it with fondness and enjoy telling people about it; I can share it in a way that helps other people."
> "When I can see it for what it is and I don't have quite so much emotion about it. When I can say 'This happened, I feel that, I made this decision, and these are the results.'"
> "I can sleep. And I'm thinking in positive terms."

But others felt that they *all* came out well, because each contributed to their individual growth:

> "Ultimately they all end well, because they become building blocks. When the transition is over, you start to feel comfortable with where you're at and what you're doing."
> "They have always come out well. So I trust that."
> "They never end."
> "I feel an internal happiness that has nothing to do with accouterments or things, but just a peace, a calm. And if that isn't there, I change course."

The truest indicators of whether a transition has had a positive result in our lives are our own internal senses. We can notice the "tendencies" in our experiences: Are we happier? more authentic? more fulfilled? more balanced? Do we exhibit more of the Thriver traits and less of the Coper characteristics? Did we surmount this relationship transition more gracefully than the last one? Or at least without getting into the same behavioral traps?

We compete with no one but ourselves in facing our transitions. We can model behaviors of others who appear to be more skillful than we are at dealing with a particular variety of change. But ultimately, we are each on our own path, developing in our own evolutionary spiral, in interaction with our interpersonal and social environment. All that remains in our journey together is to begin to practice the process. In the next chapter, we will apply the Thriver approach to specific transitions.

NOTES

1. Schumacher, E. F., *Small Is Beautiful,* Harper & Row 1973, p. 51.
2. *Ibid.*
3. Zohar, Danah, *The Quantum Self,* Quill/William Morrow 1990, p.190.
4. Capra, Fritjof, *The Tao of Physics,* Shambhala 1991, pp. 22, 57.
5. Zohar, *Ibid.,* p. 47.
6. Wolf, Fred Alan, *Star Wave,* Macmillan 1984, pp. 66–7.
7. Fritz, Robert, *The Path of Least Resistance,* Fawcett Columbine 1989, p. 53.
8. Wolf, *Ibid.,* p. 100.
9. Fritz, *Ibid.,* p. 54.
10. Zohar, *Ibid.,* pp. 192–3.
11. Vaillant, George, *Adaptation to Life,* Little, Brown 1977, p. 117.
12. Robbins, Fred and Ragan, David, *Richard Pryor: This Cat's Got 9 Lives!* Dellah 1982, p. 14.
13. Dobbin, Muriel, "Feeling Overworked? A New Study Says You Are," *Oregonian* March 1, 1992.
14. Jackson, Donna, "Making a Choice," *New Woman* April 1992, p. 67.
15. *Ibid.*
16. "Leaving Work Behind," *New Woman* April 1994, p. 75.

PART FOUR

LEARNING TO THRIVE

11

APPLYING THE
THRIVER APPROACH

❧

*If we listen to our hearts and watch our ac-
tions, we learn from ourselves. We learn
where we have work to do. We don't have to
superimpose any "do's" and "don'ts." We
discover for ourselves that the truth has no
single form, that truth is only in the moment
and can always be discovered right there.*

—Stephen Levine
A Gradual Awakening

It is one thing to understand intellectually the principles of
thriving in transition; it is something else to live them. But thriving is not a luxury in the New Zero—it is a *survival skill* as the
pace and amount of change continues to accelerate. All transitions include the six phases we have discussed, and require use
of the Thriver traits. However, situation-specific descriptions of
what to anticipate during various types of transition can provide a useful guide for us—particularly if we have not experienced those situations before.

This chapter, then, is a sort of "laundry list" of transitions,
by general type, with an explanation of how (or whether) they
differ from the typical model, representative emotions during

such transitions, and strategies for getting through them. While each individual's experience will be unique, I hope these somewhat generic pointers will be helpful both in seeing how the Thriver model works in specific situations, and in supporting you, the reader, in your own transition process. Included at the end of the chapter is a discussion of complex transition, or multiple simultaneous changes, and some suggestions for how to thrive even in the face of that challenge. (The reader is also referred to the Resource List in Appendix A, which enumerates books and other resources according to subject and type of transition, including some not discussed in detail here.)

THE CAREER CASSEROLE AND OTHER OPTIONS

The average employee today will have from three to six (or more) different careers during his or her working lifetime. Therefore, each of us will have multiple opportunities to perfect our career transition skills. Some work changes will be voluntary, while others will follow from a downsizing, burnout, or another "involuntary" event. Because of the differences between the voluntary career/job change and the involuntary one, we will address them separately. (Retirement, though a traumatic adjustment for some, is not discussed here, although substantially the same process can be undertaken in planning retirement as in planning a voluntary job change. The primary difference, of course, is that in retirement, the options to explore will not be full-time jobs [in most cases], but a collection of other activities which provide a fulfilling composite lifestyle during our post-working years.)

Voluntary Job/Career Change

The voluntary job or career transition usually lasts longer than the involuntary one because it sneaks up on us. Through a series of incidents of subtle dissatisfaction, it eventually reaches a point where our soul's cry for change becomes deafening. We feel the pain of a "mismatch" between our passion and our paycheck. But we may be hindered by what psychologists call "conditions of worth," if we have chosen a career because our parents or others told us that was what we "should" do. And as psychologist Frank Colistro points out, "There is a lot of identity wrapped up in the work even though they hate it. So for a lot of [these people] it takes a lot of courage to cut that all loose."

The Discontentment Phase in a voluntary work transition can continue for months or years. For the Coper, it is long lasting but ignored. Thriving when we feel work discontentment means to, as Dr. Colistro advises, "constantly be sensitive to your own satisfaction level, so that at the first sign that a job is starting to not meet your needs, you become aware of it and . . . intervene early to test whether it's fixable, because . . . it's a lot easier to make a change early on." Every time we feel those twinges of discomfort and ignore them, we tell ourselves we can't deal with it. And, he continues, "if you do that enough times, you're going to convince yourself and then you'll just be stuck." Colistro has seen clients—people we would call Copers—who ignore their dissatisfaction until they vomit when they pull into the parking lot at work. The message from their body is unmistakable. But when will they dare to listen to it?

If we heed our inner signals early, we can eliminate the need for crisis. In Mike Long's voluntary-turned-involuntary career change from attorney to social worker, his discontentment escalated to a crisis before he became willing to enter the Sorting-out Phase. However, chances are the next time he needs a work-related course correction, he will act sooner. Now he knows the job transition terrain, and he has developed some skills in transitioning that can be applied in future transitions.

In the Sorting-out Phase of a *career* transition, we must release our former work role and confront our tolerance for risk. A *job* change within our field, on the contrary, will entail relatively little role change, risk, or pain. In both cases, however, we may need to forgive bosses, co-workers, or others who we believe have wronged us, or who treated us unfairly.

After feeling the pain of loss and completing the past, we begin to explore new options. The successful job search in the New Zero marketplace relies on a complementary mix of

strategies to locate openings. If our next career is entirely uncertain, a reassessment of our life purpose will help to shed
some light on the best directions to consider. (See exercises in
Appendix B.) Doing informational interviewing with industry
leaders in the field(s) we are considering entering will give us
firsthand insights into the field. Further research in the local library and/or employment office will augment our in-person research.

**In addition to thinking in terms of one "right" career to
pursue, we can also examine innovative ideas such as a
career casserole, in which we work at two or more part-
time jobs to accommodate our various interests.**

We may also explore starting our own business or taking a
sabbatical (if time and money allow) to pursue a non-voca-
tional interest.

As we survey our career possibilities, we should *simultaneously* create a vision statement. Even if we do not yet know the
precise field toward which we will target our job search efforts,
we know more than we suspect about our ideal job. We may
know the kind of people we wish to work with, the tasks and
responsibilities we desire, our preferred income, important
fringe benefits, and the company philosophy and values that
complement our life purpose. If we phrase our vision in those
terms, we can add specifics such as field(s) and position(s) as
we progress with our research.

The Action Phase emerges naturally from this simultaneous
vision/exploration process. As we pursue the opportunities un-
covered by our networking and research, we will feel a resonance as we approach our ideal job. Acting on that opportunity
by arranging an interview is effortless once we recognize the
physical manifestation of our vision. Our primary responsibility
(think of it as "response-ability") is to notice our inner sensations as we proceed, seeking what futurist Barbara Marx Hub-
bard calls "vocational arousal." The passion we feel for our true
livelihood creates a unique excitement, as we realize we are
bringing our vision to life.

To validate our vocational arousal, it is helpful to build a template of objective criteria for our ideal job. Our vision statement can serve this purpose. It should incorporate the seven key aspects of an ideal job which I discuss in *When 9 to 5 Isn't Enough: A Guide to Finding Fulfillment at Work:* (1) our life purpose, (2) our work values, (3) the aspects of a work situation that motivate us, (4) the skills we enjoy using, (5) the facets of our past experience we want to perpetuate or recreate, (6) our ideal career area and job description, and (7) our preferred work environment. This template can provide checks and balances for the intuitive message that "This is the one!" It also avoids an affirmative response to a situation so different from our former position that we have omitted key elements. For example, John, a thirty-five-year-old salesman, felt so constrained by the rigid structure of his current job that his intuition rejoiced at an opening in a company with a laid-back, "go with the flow" mode of operating. But what his intuition overlooked was that the company had been operating at a loss for the past three years and could go bankrupt within six months due to its laissez-faire attitude. That is, in his hasty pursuit of a more relaxed environment, he forgot about the security that the more rigid company had provided. The ideal job template can help alleviate such rash decisions.

At intervals of a week, a month, three months, six months, and at least annually thereafter, we should undergo the Evaluation Phase, asking ourselves the questions we posed in Chapter 10 such as: Am I more fulfilled now than in my former job? Am I carrying out my life purpose, as I understand it?, Through interactive experimentation, proactive creation, and correcting our course of action when necessary, we will experience ongoing growth in our fulfillment at work. Ultimately, we will know that we are pursuing our right livelihood, and, through the self-referential loop process, will learn to refine that work to its highest level.

Involuntary Job/Career Change

Many involuntary job or career changes begin with no notice whatsoever. We had not become discontented with our work, and were in fact happy with the job we had. But when our transition stems from a corporate reorganization, layoff, or circumstances leading to our termination, we suddenly find ourselves in the unknown territory of unemployment—without a map. For us, transition begins with this kind of crisis event, and we proceed from there. (For others, a neglected Discontentment Phase culminates in a crisis—e.g., attorney Mike Long's partners asking him to leave the firm—when they have been unwilling to make needed change voluntarily.) The Thriver approach to such an event is to accept it, even if it is not what we would have consciously chosen.

Thrivers know that "when one door closes, another opens," and they then move masterfully into the next phase of their transition.

Dr. John Boyman, a managing director at Drake Beam Morin, has observed that the people who have the most difficulty with involuntary career change are those who have worked at one company for many years. Having become inured to the familiar setting of that company, they are often overpaid due to their tenure. They hold an Old Zero worldview, expecting job security despite the changing workplace. These individuals experience tremendous shock when their regular paycheck and retirement benefits are suddenly a thing of the past. Their shock can paralyze them, preventing them from taking any effective action for weeks or months without outside guidance.

If the individual is unskilled in transitioning, an involuntary job change in midlife can trigger a dark night of the soul type of Sorting-out Phase. In *Journey of the Heart*, psychologist John Welwood describes this as a time when "the weight of karmic accumulation starts to overpower our life force. Midlife crisis is the realization that time is running out and our karma is catching up with us."[1] So for the individual caught off guard by a job layoff, the Sorting-out Phase can be the longest part of the transition cycle. Dealing with the shock and self-esteem and identity issues (with counseling assistance if necessary) can lead to a rebirth of the self. Only then does exploration of new options make sense.

The balance of the involuntary transition is much like the

voluntary one: learning to network, updating our résumés, getting career counseling if needed, and doing informational interviews, all done simultaneously with crafting a vision of our ideal job. The Action Phase emerges naturally, and the Evaluation Phase is conducted periodically following the beginning of the new job to ensure that we are staying on our chosen path.

TWISTS AND TURNS OF THE HEART

Over the course of our lives, our hearts lead us through many relationships. From child/parent to husband/wife, mentor/mentee to friend/friend, each encounter we have with another person influences us in some lasting way. And changes in these relationships require adaptation. Break-up of a friendship, birth of a child, marriage, the "empty nest syndrome," and moving away from a mentor each demand mental and emotional adjustment. Our roles change. Our support system is transposed as we learn to act without the input of the person who left. And while each of these relationship transitions merits discussion, I will rely on other authors to address many of these transitions (see resource list); they are common but usually less disturbing than a divorce or marriage crisis discussed below.

More than half of all marriages in the United States end in divorce, and unmarried but committed couples who live together have roughly parallel breakup rates. Psychologists have found that the impact of the loss experienced in such breakups is as pronounced as that of the death of a loved one.[2] Serial monogamy (or consecutive marriages) is the norm in the New Zero.

Transitioning in and out of intimate relationships is commonplace. But the quality of the transition—and whether we grow through these relationship changes—depends on whether or not we apply the Thriver traits.

Arguably, there are voluntary and involuntary divorce experiences, just as there are in the career/job change arena. We are shocked if our spouse suddenly leaves us for someone else, or announces one day that he or she is no longer happy in the relationship and wants to end it. But in most cases, if we are honest with ourselves, such apparently unforeseen events are preceded by a period of weeks, months, or years of discontentment on the part of at least one of the partners. Perhaps we have deluded ourselves and refused to "see" what was occurring because we could not face the prospect of a marriage breakup.

Discontentment in relationships may arise from a critical individual transition for one partner, or the growth of one partner may detach them from interests and values previously shared with their partner. The "empty nest syndrome" which occurs when the children leave home, or the process of aging can also trigger discontentment. Relationships can also be severely challenged by one partner's completion of an extended course of education, a career change, insights gained through counseling, or return to health following a medical crisis. In this way, one key transition gives birth to another, as Mike Long's career change had the unexpected consequence of raising issues in his marriage.

During the Discontentment Phase, the partners engage in a back and forth kind of dance. One moment they believe the relationship is over, and the next they think to themselves, "Maybe we should try again." Much mental rehearsal goes into the final decision to separate. And oftentimes, the Crisis Phase can confuse the process: one partner moves out temporarily, or files for divorce and then withdraws the filing; or the couple has a "fight to end all fights" in which they dredge up all of their unresolved issues.

As this discontent/try again, fight/resolve cycle continues, at some point the couple must decide whether their relationship is ending, or whether they are just going through growth pains. In *Coming Into Our Own,* author Mark Gerzon points out, "What's important to remember is this: Encountering your shadow and feeling pain do not necessarily mean your marriage has failed. Indeed, it may mean that it is actually starting to work."[3]

Marriage and family therapist Daphne Rose Kingma, in her book *Coming Apart,* offers seven signs which indicate the difference between a terminal and a salvageable relationship: constant fights, irreconcilable differences concerning key issues in the relationship, pervasive boredom and restlessness all indicate the end of a relationship. Emotional distance, changes in location or circumstance, one or both parties having affairs, and even counseling can also portend the ending.

The first three phases of divorce transitions (Discontentment, Crisis, and Sorting-out Phase) are more intertwined than in many other transition situations. As the "push and pull" continues, and one partner eventually leaves, it is not unusual for each of the spouses to consider, from time to time, getting back together. And this constitutes the first phase of exploring options—along with counseling, talking with trusted friends about the situation, and imagining how our life would be without our partner. We also experience a whole plethora of feelings, from "I can't believe this is happening to me," to anger, shock, guilt, sadness, denial, resentment, a desire to withdraw—even relief, excitement, and anticipation of the new that can come.

Once the couple decides the relationship is really over, legal documents are filed, and it becomes more final, a new cycle of Crisis and Sorting-out Phase can occur, as the reality of the end of the relationship strikes. Rituals can be quite helpful here, whether they be a separation ceremony done with our partner (such as that described in Dan Millman's *No Ordinary Moments*[4]), practices such as those mentioned in Chapter 7 (e.g., revisiting places you and your spouse used to frequent, writing unmailed letters to vent your feelings), or others developed to fit an individual situation. These processes help to complete our feelings concerning the marriage and clear our mind and heart for future relationships. Relying on our spirituality, support system, and other stability zones in our lifestyle which remain can also help support us through this challenging time.

The Vision and Action Phases follow the confusing Sorting-out Phase. Now, we begin to envision life without our spouse, and perhaps without a full-time relationship with our children. Through visioning, we can imagine a positive lifestyle as a single person, and we slowly begin to recreate ourselves and our post-divorce life.

The Evaluation Phase following divorce does not necessarily analyze whether or not we made the "right" decision in divorcing (though that question may come to mind). Rather, we appraise our post-divorce lifestyle. Is it enhancing our fulfillment and betterment as an individual? Are we attracting more healthy relationships, building on what we learned in our marriage and divorce? If so, we have gained the benefits of thriving, even in the midst of the painful process of letting go of a key relationship in our lives.

ILLNESS, ACCIDENTS, AND OTHER PHYSICAL CHALLENGES

It is a truism that "If you don't have your health, you don't have anything." And that saying becomes only too true when we find ourselves in the hospital following a car crash; when we have just received a serious medical diagnosis; or during a bout with a chronic illness which defies conventional medical treatment. The process of healing is a difficult and often frustrating one, but it is possible to use the Thriver skills to find opportunities for growth, even at these times.

The Discontentment Phase is often underplayed in health transitions. Sometimes, we receive subtle physical messages telling us that a lifestyle adjustment is needed if we are to maintain optimum health. More typically, the medically-based transition begins with a crisis. We undergo a heart attack, an unexpected diagnosis, or an accident, and suddenly our life is turned upside down. We can no longer care for ourselves as usual, and we are faced squarely with our mortality and the often lengthy journey back to health. During this Crisis Phase, our primary focus is on logistics: how will I perform—or get help with—the cooking, housekeeping, dressing, getting in and out of bed, and managing my financial and other affairs while I am recovering? Following our doctor's instructions and complying with prescribed treatment occupies much of our time initially. And throughout the treatment phase, we must listen carefully to our doctor's explanation of our condition, and ask questions when they occur to us. By becoming more proactive, we develop the kind of control that fosters resilience.

Dr. Bernie Siegel, who has worked extensively with cancer patients, has found that patients' emotions and attributes, including their will to live, can literally make the difference between living and dying, coping and thriving. Coming to terms with this issue constitutes the beginning of our Sorting-out Phase. Siegel suggests asking the following four key questions, presented in his book *Love, Medicine & Miracles,* to determine these critical attitudinal components:

1. *Do you want to live to be a hundred?* This question leads to others, such as whether we love ourselves enough to take care of our body and mind, build a positive lifestyle, and pursue self-fulfillment.

2. *What happened to you in the year or two before your illness?* Answering this query can reveal psychological and situational factors which may have predisposed us to illness. In one study, doctors asked each of the heart attack patients in an intensive care ward the reason they had a heart attack. In each case, they could identify a situation in their lives that led to the physical event: a broken heart from a failed marriage, a child who had drug-related problems, or being passed over for a long-awaited promotion. Such inquiries force us to confront the connection between mind and body.

3. *What does the illness mean to you?* If the illness means death, then that fear or misconception must be resolved before any type of treatment will be effective.

4. *Why did you need the illness?* Again, this probes psychological needs that the disease may serve. Sickness can often be used to give us permission to relax, or to do things we would otherwise feel inhibited from doing. It can also be a useful tool for soliciting sympathy from others.

Once the will to live and heal is established, the Sorting-out Phase begins in earnest. If psychological factors underlie our condition, we do forgiveness work or self-esteem building exercises, or we seek counseling. Settling those concerns enhances our healing. We may join a support group of other patients with similar conditions to build our support network, provide an outlet for our feelings, and get our questions answered.

The options we investigate may vary widely. With a chronic illness which is "incurable" or unresponsive to conventional medicine, choices may include alternative health care techniques such as guided imagery, massage, acupuncture, Chinese herbs, nutrition therapy, yoga, kinesiology, homeopathy, or a host of other such practices. In the case of reduced physical mobility, such as Gloria Estefan experienced after her bus crash, we may explore physical therapy or lifestyle aids, such as wheelchairs, ramps, walkers, and crutches. Times of reduced independence are often periods of introspection, during which we ask questions ranging from "Why me?" to "How can I heal most quickly?" We vacillate between losing hope and regaining it at the prospect of one more treatment strategy that may cure us. And we begin to realize, as Terry McBride did in the midst of his thirty back surgeries, that we are at choice, and our answers lie within us. (See Resource List for books to assist with self-healing.)

As our alternatives become clearer, we formulate a vision of our desired life. It will incorporate our physical health, certainly, but it will also include our work, relationships, finances, and spirituality along with the new perspective which we have acquired through our illness. And even in the midst of our healing, we begin to take action to consummate our vision by adopting more healthy lifestyle practices, reducing our stress, vowing to approach our work in a more balanced way, and paying more heed to our family and other close relationships. Our perspective shifts, and one day we realize that we have created the vision we designed. As we evaluate our results, we find that each choice has helped us find the critical path toward health. And we realize that we have been transformed in the process.

ADDICTION RECOVERY

One of the results of our inability to cope with the nonstop, simultaneous change of the New Zero has been an increase in addictions, including "substance addictions" to alcohol, nicotine, street drugs, caffeine, and sugar, as well as "process addictions" to such things as shopping, sex, gambling, and work. Although we know that addiction is prevalent in society, the denial which accompanies addiction can keep us from acknowledging our own dependency for months or years before we enter rehabilitation treatment.

Discontentment occurs when the substance or process of choice no longer numbs our pain. At this relatively late stage of the addiction, the addict will display such classic symptoms as being under the influence at work, drinking or using their drug or process on a regular basis (though much of the use is typically done in secret, hidden from their family). Other signs include personality changes, depression, fatigue, blackouts (not remembering where they were or what they did for a period of time), frequent absences from work, poor nutrition, emotional deadness, and socializing only with other addicts.

For a successful recovery, the addict must truly be ready to change. And according to addiction researchers, fewer than 20 percent of people struggling with addiction are prepared for action at any given time.[5] Some addicts reach the point of readiness on their own, simply by realizing their lives "have become unmanageable," as the Twelve Steps states it. Through self-reflection, counseling, or the caring words of a friend, they come to understand the nature of their disease. The resulting sense of Discontentment leads to a turning point, at which time they enter a treatment program—in-patient or out-patient. This is the decision variety of the Crisis Phase of transition.

Other addicts remain buried in their denial, and an "intervention" becomes necessary, in which their close family and others affected by their addiction meet with the addict and tell him or her honestly what the addiction is doing to them, after which they are escorted to a treatment program. This scenario constitutes a true Crisis, since the addict has not voluntarily chosen recovery. Frequently, the crisis is preceded by a long period of unrevealed Discontentment in the addict's life.

The early period of recovery—up to the entire first year—is often a classic Sorting-out Phase. Since most addicts do not have a spiritual belief system on which to rely, developing such beliefs is encouraged in early recovery. Furthermore, addicts have no support system, since their former one had been comprised of other addicts. Thus they begin to substitute members of their recovery groups to build a new network. One of the most difficult aspects of this early period, once the addict has been detoxified, is the emotional roller coaster which follows. Feelings which have been suppressed by alcohol or drugs for years arise, and the addict feels as though he lacks the ability to deal with these emotions. Lack of motivation is common, as are marital problems. This period can continue for months, as the recovering addict faces his addiction and its consequences. Attending regular meetings with other recovering addicts, such as Alcoholics Anonymous, Narcotics Anonymous, Codependents Anonymous, Gamblers Anonymous, or Overeaters Anonymous, can help the newly recovering addict find ways to live effectively without addictive behavior.

Eventually, as the raw emotions come more into focus and the craving for the substance recedes, the addict begins to envision a life without the addiction. He may seek counseling to deal with personal issues which were caused or exacerbated by his dependence. As he works through the Twelve Steps or his chosen program of recovery, he will come to terms with unresolved matters from the past which have resurfaced. By talking with other recovering addicts, he will begin to see new possibilities for his life which he could not imagine while practicing his addiction. And as this vision matures, he will naturally move into action on that vision, recreating himself as he goes.

In terms of exploration of options, and vision and action steps, process addictions differ from substance addictions in that instead of complete withdrawal, it is usually necessary to experiment with varying models of how to use the process in a healthy way. For example, most of us must engage in gainful employment. If we are workaholics, however, our challenge is to determine whether we can work non-addictively in our current job by setting clear boundaries on our tasks and/or hours, or whether we must seek employment in another company, or even another field, to avoid practicing our addiction.

Evaluation of our recovery occurs any time we attend a meeting of recovering people. It continues during meetings with our "sponsor" (someone who has some experience with recovery and has volunteered to work with the new addict in his recovery program), and during personal reflection. As this process continues, and we have learned how to take action and experience feelings unaided by the addictive behavior, we enter what author Earnie Larsen calls "Stage II Recovery," in which we practice new, healthier living skills following the "drying out" of Stage I Recovery.

DEATH AND GRIEVING

When someone close to us dies, we confront one of the most demanding transitions of all: facing loss. Unlike other transitions, this type is not preceded by a Discontentment Phase. It begins with the Crisis generated by the phone call: "Jane passed away this morning . . ." What do we do first?

Step 1. Call people and ask for help. Bereavement counselor Kelly Osmont advises that our first step following the news of the death should be to "start calling people and letting them know that you need their help." After a while, we may get tired of asking them, so it is wise to tell them so in advance and to let them also know we may not always be certain of what we want. Encourage them to make specific offers, such as mowing the lawn or helping clean the house. Other friends or family members should be called to help make phone calls to notify others of the death, to coordinate food, and the like.

Step 2. Designate an advocate to go with you to see the funeral director. The second thing to do is to find someone to be an advocate for you when you go to the funeral director. Request that you be allowed to view the body, and to get a lock of hair from the deceased as a remembrance of them, as this will help with your transition process.

Step 3. Get an answering machine if you don't have one. Osmont strongly recommends that the grieving individual get an answering machine to avoid having to deal with difficult phone calls before they are ready.

Step 4. Care for yourself. As the funeral ends and the Sorting-out Phase begins, it is important to take good care of ourselves. As Osmont points out in her booklet, *More Than Surviving: Caring for Yourself While You Grieve,* it is common to feel like we don't want to live if the loved one isn't alive. Finding ways to affirm our own will to live can help motivate us to be self-nurturing. Talking to friends, family, support groups, and/or a counselor will also help, as will taking time off work. If that is not possible, we need to solicit the support of our boss and co-workers, and find a place to cry, rest if necessary, and otherwise care for ourselves during the workday. Massage, meditation, quiet walks in the park, or watching funny movies or television programs can all ease the pain—which seems to be never-ending in the early months of grief. And by paying close attention to our dreams, we can discover how we are processing the loved one's death. Finally, regular physical exercise and balanced nutrition are critical here, even though we may not feel like it. Both of those elements, along with sufficient sleep if we can get it, will make it easier to face the emotional upheaval of the grieving process.

Step 5. Use the Four Tasks of Grief. We should also review the Four Tasks of Grief discussed in Chapter 7. First, we must confront the reality that the loved one is gone. Second, we must face our pain and emotions. These two tasks are part of the Sorting-out Phase. As we begin to enter the Vision Phase, we embark on the third task: adjusting to an environment in which the deceased is missing. And fourth, we emotionally relocate the deceased (to heaven, to our heart, or anywhere besides "in the ground") and move on with our life. This latter task comprises the Action Phase of our transition.

Step 6. Evaluate our new lifestyle. The Evaluation Phase of a grief-driven transition examines how we feel about the quality of the life we are recreating without the loved one. Are we pursuing our dreams? Feeling more fulfilled? Are we accepting our feelings and allowing the pain to take its course, while opening the door to the emergence of happy memories? If so, we are integrating the loss of our loved one into a multi-dimensional life which honors his or her memory but also affirms the value of living fully.

COMPLEX TRANSITION

The process of transitioning is relatively simple when we face only one major event at a time, such as a divorce, a job change, or a health challenge. But the difficulty of transition multiplies when one of these transitions leads directly into another. Just as one transition reaches resolution, our feelings of depletion and our longing for stability escalate as the wave of another transition crashes down upon us. And most challenging of all is when we face all three changes simultaneously: we may be in the Sorting-out Phase as to our divorce, but in the Crisis Phase regarding our health problems, which puts our desired job change in abeyance pending surgery and a recovery period. Both of these situations—two or more sequential or simultaneous transitions—comprise the phenomenon I call *complex transition*.

The Thriver traits can provide significant assistance during such times, which may characterize most of our life in the New Zero. First and foremost, we must make the critical shift in thinking from "This transition time is temporary; it will be over soon and my life will return to normalcy," to "Being in transition is part of my everyday experience, and I embrace it and learn to thrive in it *without* expecting it to resolve into any sort of stability." Then, when complex transition occurs, we can anticipate it.

Even in times of change, we can create and maintain personal stability zones by asking ourselves, "What is *not* changing?"

Through utilizing our skills of attentiveness—particularly self-awareness—we constantly monitor our surroundings to detect the slightest hint of impending change. We can rely on our three-fold foundation of groundedness—spirituality, support network, and inner resilience—to provide support *regardless of external circumstances*. By trusting our process (even if it seems chaotic), refusing to insist on instantaneous resolution of ambiguous circumstances, embracing our feelings as they arise, and nurturing ourselves, we stay focused on our purpose even during times of flux.

Thrivers recognize when it is the right time to reevaluate their life and sort things out, because they understand the key principle of life change:

A clear life purpose provides the most effective anchor amidst the storm of complex transition.

In the midst of complex transition, Thrivers may take some personal time off to attend an in-depth seminar or get away for a personal retreat. They will reexamine their personal mission, journal about their feelings, and pay attention to the insights their dreams may supply concerning the changes they are experiencing. They may also perform a "worst case scenario" analysis to minimize any fears they may have about the process—or its outcome. And they may need to complete unfinished business from the past, particularly if the resonance effect has revealed patterns that are now ripe for resolution. By removing themselves from the turmoil of changing circumstances for a short time, they can reaffirm their vision and return to face their transitions with renewed commitment and energy.

Thrivers have enough optimism and confidence in themselves, as well as the ability to take risks when appropriate, to build an inner awareness that they can handle with grace and ease what life offers them. In addition, they understand the principle that life only evolves forward, and this generates an unflappable optimism. And throughout this process Thrivers keep a systems perspective and a sense of humor, as well as a finely tuned balance between their work, relationships, and self.

Another way of restating what I am suggesting is this:

Complex transition does not call for new skills, but for an even more diligent and consistent application of the Thriver skills we have already explored.

By staying "light on our feet," much as a boxer does, we can move *with* the shifts of our lives, rather than resisting them. That, after all, is what Thriving is all about.

NOTES

1. Welwood, John, *Journey of the Heart,* Harper 1990, p. 18.
2. Lonky, Edward, et al., "Life Experience and Mode of Coping: Relation to Moral Judgment in Adulthood," *Developmental Psychology* Vol. 20, No. 6. pp. 1159–67 (1984).
3. Gerzon, Mark, *Coming Into Our Own,* Delacorte 1992, p. 86.
4. Millman, Dan, *No Ordinary Moments,* Kramer 1992, pp. 32–33.
5. Prochaska, James, *Changing for Good,* William Morrow 1994, p. 15.

EPILOGUE:

THE PRACTICE
OF THRIVING

❧

*We are changing, we have got to change,
and we can no more help it than leaves can
help going yellow and coming loose in au-
tumn.*

—D. H. Lawrence

The practice of becoming a Thriver, and of effectively facing
ongoing transitions, is just that: a practice, not a lesson to learn
once and for all. As the athlete practices his sport, the musician
rehearses on his instrument, and the artist works on her craft,
we must cultivate the art of Thriving. We are like warriors
skilled in the martial arts, who learn to anticipate the movement and strategy of their opponent and incorporate that
movement into their own. In the words of Fritjof Capra:

> Such a state of awareness is not unlike the state of mind of a
> warrior who expects an attack in [a state of] extreme alertness,
> registering everything that goes on around him without being
> distracted by it for an instant.[1]

As Thrivers in the New Zero, we must learn to use our transitioning tools vigilantly, so that we view change much as a martial artist perceives his opponent. With the nimbleness of the t'ai chi master, and the concentration of the judo artist, we become keenly aware of our surroundings, and develop our flexible adaptivity to respond quickly to the transitions life brings. We then masterfully pass through them, learning their lessons and keeping our focus on our goal of personal growth and evolution.

Becoming a Thriver is thus much more than a temporary bandage on the open wound of constant change. As a daily practice, we apply ourselves moment by moment in an effort to expand our ability to stay calm, centered, and clear in the midst of the chaos around us. George Leonard, in an interview concerning his book *Mastery*, recommends that each of us perfect this ability through some kind of formal practice. For him it is the art of aikido. He points out that such activities take on a far more pivotal role in our lives than do hobbies:

"A hobby is something you do casually; a practice is something you do on a regular basis that really defines you. It's the path on which you walk."[2]

Our practice arena is the events of our daily life. As we start where we are, beginning to apply the Thriver skills in each new situation we face, we discern our own rhythm, our own pace. We design a lifestyle that fulfills our vision while simultaneously offering us fresh, new alternatives in scheduling our time, nurturing our family and ourselves, and providing us with financial, emotional, and spiritual support. We take risks, make change, and extend ourselves in ways we have never done before. We invent unconventional ways of fulfilling our responsibilities to honor our newfound priorities. And as we learn to trust our intuition, listening to the guidance of our Higher Power moment by moment, we see the positive results and we start to trust more and more.

Thriving bears many parallels to Dan Millman's concept of the "peaceful warrior," whom he describes in his book *No Ordinary Moments* as combining courage and love, the warrior's spirit with a peaceful heart.[3] Actual examples of such warriors include Mahatma Gandhi, Harriet Tubman, Albert Schweitzer, and Martin Luther King, Jr., among others. These individuals were committed to seeing the transformative power contained within the everyday events of their lives and dared to marshal that power toward inner healing and external change. The peaceful warrior's perspective recognizes that the external trappings of everyday living—working, going to school, raising a family, and the like—are not what is lasting in life. Rather, it is the evolutionary growth which we each experience during our lives that matters. Millman's teacher, whom he calls Socrates, explains:

> You are not only here to grow up and go to school and work and make money and marry and raise children and retire. These occupations only form the backdrop in the Theater of Life. They provide the wrapping, but they are not the gift—only the means of your education—important aspects of life, but not the purpose of it, not the whole of it.
>
> Life develops what it demands. The issues you face are the spiritual weights you lift to strengthen yourself. Your task is to shine *through* the petty details of your life, not to get preoccupied with them. And when life puts hurdles in your path, my friend, you had better become a hurdler.[4]

This approach takes Thriving to a higher level: from beyond merely developing the skills needed to manage life's circumstances successfully, to a deeper, more comprehensive perspective which views all of those transitional circumstances as ultimately transitory and fleeting. Thriving stretches us, enlightens us, and challenges us to put forth our best. As we improve in our practice of it, we will see our lives become happier, more peaceful and fulfilling places in which to live. And it will not be because we have fewer transitions to face, nor because anything else has materially changed in our external world. Rather, it will be due to our own courageous and consistent application of the skills of the Thriver to the increasingly complex circumstances of the New Zero—and to our own ever-changing individual lives.

THE DAILY PRACTICE OF THRIVING

1. Focus on and expect only good.
2. Be kind, courteous, and generous to everyone.
3. Eat lots of fresh vegetables and fruit each day, as part of a varied, balanced diet. Avoid alcohol, tobacco, and drugs.
4. Surround yourself with positive, supportive people for whom you feel mutual support and respect.
5. Exercise daily, as often as possible, outdoors.
6. Love what you do for your livelihood, but don't mistake it for your identity.
7. Take time to cultivate meaningful friendships.
8. Stay in regular contact with God as you understand It.
9. Forgive yourself for past mistakes; refuse to feel guilty— you did the best you could.
10. Forgive others who have "wronged" you, and refuse to hold resentments, knowing they did the best they could at the time. Live fully in the here and now!
11. Keep growing and trying new things.
12. Let love rule all of your dealings.
13. Acknowledge others for their specialness. When you feel bad, give of yourself to someone else. Don't be afraid to ask for help and support when you need it.
14. Handle money joyfully and wisely.
15. Let your true self shine—express your ideas and your creativity in all you do.
16. Continually challenge yourself to see the new, to live a higher quality of life today than in the past, and to rise to ever higher awareness of yourself, God, and others.
17. Realize that the circumstances in your life are your "training ground," and that they reflect your beliefs and thoughts. Be open to learning the lessons they present, and to accepting your part in creating what happens to you.

NOTES

1. Capra, Fritjof, *The Tao of Physics*, Shambhala 1991.
2. Whitten, Phillip, "The Joys of Mastery," *New Age* June 1990.
3. Millman, Dan, *No Ordinary Moments*, Kramer 1992.
4. *Ibid.*, p. 293.

Appendix A

RESOURCE LIST

Resources for Particular Kinds of Transitions

Addiction—see "Recovery"

Aging

Anderson, Barbara Gallatin, *The Aging Game*, McGraw-Hill 1979.

Chopra, Deepak, *Ageless Body, Timeless Mind*, Bantam 1994.

AIDS—see "Illness"

Alcoholism—see "Recovery"

Burnout

Pines, Ayala and Aronson, Elliot, *Career Burnout: Causes and Cures*, Macmillan 1988.

Cancer—see "Illness"

Career Change

Anderson, Nancy, *Work With Passion*, Carroll & Graf 1984.

Bolles, Richard Nelson, *What Color is Your Parachute?* Ten Speed Press, annual editions.

Dail, Hilda Lee, *The Lotus and the Pool*, Shambhala 1983.

Half, Robert, *The Robert Half Way to Get Hired in Today's Job Market*, Bantam 1983.

Jackson, Tom, *Guerrilla Tactics in the Job Market*, Bantam 1978.

Noer, David, *Healing the Wounds*, Jossey-Bass 1993.

Perkins-Reed, Marcia, *When 9 to 5 Isn't Enough: A Guide to Finding Fulfillment at Work*, Hay House 1990.

Sher, Barbara, *Wishcraft*, Ballantine 1979.

Sinetar, Marsha, *Do What You Love, The Money Will Follow*, Paulist Press 1987.

Tulku, Tarthang, *Skillful Means*, Dharma 1978.

Chronic Fatigue and Similar Conditions—see "Illness"

Death—see "Grief Work"

Divorce—see "Relationship Change"

Drug Addiction—see "Recovery"
Emotional Issues
  Whitfield, Charles L., *Healing the Child Within*, Health Communications 1989.
Grief Work
  Anderson, Patricia, *Affairs in Order*, Macmillan 1991.
  Carroll, David, *Living with Dying*, McGraw-Hill 1985.
  Nudel, Adele Rice, *Starting Over: Help for Young Widows & Widowers*, Dodd, Mead 1986.
  Osmont, Kelly and McFarlane, Marilyn, *Parting Is Not Goodbye*, Nobility Press 1986.
  Osmont, Kelly, and McFarlane, Marilyn, *What Can I Say?: How to Help Someone Who Is Grieving*, Nobility Press 1988.
  Osmont, Kelly, *More Than Surviving: Caring for Yourself While You Grieve*, Nobility Press 1990.
  Contact also: The Compassionate Friends, National Office, P.O. Box 3696, Oak Brook Illinois 60522-3696, (312) 990-0010.
Health Challenge—see "Illness"
Heart Attack—see "Illness"
Illness and Healing
  AIDS Project Los Angeles, *AIDS: A Self-Care Manual*, IBS Press 1987.
  Bell, David, *Curing Fatigue*, Rodale Press 1993.
  Bresler, David, *Free Yourself from Pain*, Simon & Schuster 1979.
  Chopra, Deepak, *Quantum Healing*, Bantam 1989.
  Chopra, Deepak, *Unconditional Life*, Bantam 1991.
  Hay, Louise, *You Can Heal Your Life*, Hay House 1984.
  Siegel, Bernie S., *Love, Medicine & Miracles*, Harper & Row 1986.
Inner Child Work—see "Emotional Issues"
Recovery
  Alcoholics Anonymous, 1976.
  Larsen, Earnie, *Stage II Recovery*, Harper & Row 1985.
  Twelve Steps and Twelve Traditions, Alcoholics Anonymous 1981.
  Contact also: Alcoholics Anonymous World Services Inc., Box 459, Grand Central Station, New York NY 10163.
Relationship Change
  Hendricks, Gay and Kathlyn, *Conscious Loving*, Bantam 1990.
  Kingma, Daphne Rose, *Coming Apart*, Fawcett 1987.
  Welwood, John, *Journey of the Heart*, HarperPerennial 1991.
Sexual Abuse—see "Emotional Issues" for recalled memories of childhood abuse

Workaholism

Fassel, Diane, *Working Ourselves to Death,* HarperCollins 1990.

Robinson, Bryan E., *Work Addiction,* Health Communications 1989.

Schaef, Anne Wilson and Fassel, Diane, *The Addictive Organization,* Harper & Row 1988.

Schor, Juliet, *The Overworked American,* Basic Books 1992.

RESOURCES CONCERNING OTHER ISSUES

Balanced Living

Eyre, Linda and Richard, *Lifebalance,* Ballantine 1987.

Ornstein, Robert and Sobel, David, *Healthy Pleasures,* Addison-Wesley 1989.

Eastern Philosophy and Religion

Dass, Ram, *Journey of Awakening,* Bantam 1978.

Dhiravamsa, *The Way of Non-Attachment,* Crucible 1984.

Levine, Stephen, *A Gradual Awakening,* Doubleday 1989.

Suzuki, Shunryu, *Zen Mind, Beginner's Mind,* Weatherhill 1980.

Life Purpose

Bennett, Hal Zina and Sparrow, Susan, *Follow Your Bliss,* Avon 1990.

Tieger, Paul and Barron-Tieger, Barbara, *Do What You Are,* Little, Brown 1992.

Millman, Dan, *The Life You Were Born to Live: A Guide to Finding Your Life Purpose,* Kramer 1993.

Perkins-Reed, Marcia, "Discovering Your Life's Purpose," Hay House Audio 1991.

Quantum Physics

Capra, Fritjof, *The Tao of Physics,* Shambhala 1991.

Prigogine, Ilya and Stengers, Isabelle, *Order Out of Chaos,* Bantam 1984.

Wolf, Fred Alan, *Star Wave,* Macmillan 1984.

Wolf, Fred Alan, *Taking the Quantum Leap,* Harper & Row 1981.

Wolf, Fred Alan, *The Dreaming Universe,* Simon & Schuster 1994.

Zohar, Danah, *The Quantum Self,* Quill/Wllliam Morrow 1990.

Ritual

Driver, Tom Faw, *The Magic of Ritual,* Harper 1991.

Paladin, Lynda S., *Ceremonies for Change: Creating Rituals to Heal Life's Hurts,* Stillpoint 1991.

Stress Management

Charlesworth, Edward, *Stress Management,* Ballantine 1984.

Pelletier, Kenneth, *Healthy People in Unhealthy Places,* Delacorte 1984.

Thriver Traits

Covey, Stephen, *The 7 Habits of Highly Effective People,* Simon & Schuster 1989.

Garfield, Charles, *Peak Performers: The New Heroes of American Business,* Avon 1986.

Moore, Thomas, *Care of the Soul,* HarperPerennial 1994.

Olesen, Erik, *Mastering the Winds of Change,* Rawson Associates 1993.

Siebert, Al, *The Survivor Personality,* Practical Psychology Press 1993.

Sinetar, Marsha, *Developing a 21st-Century Mind,* Ballantine 1991.

Transition

Barker, Joel, *Paradigms: The Business of Discovering the Future,* Harper Business 1992.

Bridges, William, *Managing Transitions,* Addison-Wesley 1991.

Bridges, William, *Transitions,* Addison-Wesley 1980.

Grof, Stanislav and Christina, *Spiritual Emergency,* Tarcher 1989.

Hyatt, Carole and Gottlieb, Linda, *When Smart People Fail,* Penguin 1987.

Schlossberg, Nancy, *Overwhelmed: Coping with Life's Ups and Downs,* Lexington 1989.

Vaillant, George, *Adaptation to Life,* Little, Brown 1977.

Viorst, Judith, *Necessary Losses,* Fawcett Columbine 1986.

Visioning

Fritz, Robert, *Creating,* Fawcett Columbine 1991.

Fritz, Robert, *The Path of Least Resistance,* Fawcett Columbine 1989.

Appendix B

EXERCISES FOR

BECOMING A

THRIVER

♈

*If we are willing to flow with the process
and shed our old ways, accepting life's challenges and the gifts of the Heart with
courage and a cavalier sense of adventure,
we will be reborn more quickly and easily.*

—Jacquelyn Small
Awakening in Time

Having completed the journey through transition and examined how the Thriver responds to it, it is now time to begin
our own excursion through the wilderness. The following exercises are designed to help you increasingly embody the Thriver
traits as you face current and future life transitions.

Part I: The Fundamentals

Exercise 1: Identifying Our Coper and Thriver Aspects

By now, you have probably identified yourself as primarily either a Coper or Thriver. We need ask for no more than that simple awareness. As the Eastern mystic Dhiravamsa advises us, "Always start from where you actually are, not from where you imagine yourself to be, or where you would like to be, or think you ought to be." We begin where we are, and we grow from that point.

To review our journey, here is a comparison of the Coper characteristics and the traits of the Thriver:

Coper Characteristics	Thriver Traits
Disconnection from feelings	Self-awareness
	Willingness to feel
Mistrust and suspicion	Receptivity
	Self-confidence
Victim thinking and blaming	Internal motivation
	Resilience
	Commitment to growth
	Proactive creation skills
	Interactive experimentation
No sense of purpose	Strong sense of purpose
Disconnection from spirituality	Spirituality is key component
Rigid thinking	Flexible adapting
	Comfort with ambiguity
	Systems thinking
Negative attitudes	Optimism
	Dreaming beyond the practical
No healthy support systems	Support from others
Need for control	Trusts the process
	Playful risk-taking

Lack of balance/achievement orientation	Self-nurturing
	Seeks balance
	Sense of humor
Mechanistic, Newtonian view	Organic, quantum physics view

Which list of characteristics best describes you? After reading the preceding pages, have you come to realize that cultivating the Thriver Traits will increase your ability to experience satisfaction and fulfillment in your life? If so, I am assuming you wish to make some movement from the left to the right side of the chart, and to begin progressing toward becoming a Thriver.

I have frequently been asked whether a person can be a Coper part of the time and a Thriver at other times. Certainly, we are all involved in the process of growth. However, I believe that using Coping behaviors is only advisable in two situations: (a) when you don't know better—i.e., you haven't yet learned that there is an alternative, or (b) when you lapse into Coping in a crisis because you can't think of anything else to do at the moment. To consciously choose Coping over Thriving for any other reasons is not in our best interest.

Exercise 2: Making the Commitment to Change

The evolution from Coper to Thriver begins with a *commitment to change,* which we each must decide to embrace before we can begin any transformation. Often, the decision point comes only when the pain of Coping becomes so great that we feel desperate: "I'll do *anything* not to feel this agony again!" At other times, our eyes are suddenly opened and the unproductive consequences of our approach becomes clear: "How could I have stayed in this job/marriage/city for this long, knowing how it deadens me inside?" Only then are we ready to sincerely re-examine our methodology.

Exercise 3: Trait Cluster Questioning

As we face our next transition—even if it is minor—we can keep the list of Thriver Traits before us, and ask ourselves questions such as the following to elicit those traits even in the midst of challenging times:

Attentiveness Cluster:
Am I allowing myself to be aware of my discontent?
Am I honestly open and receptive to new experiences?
Am I committed to my own growth?
Am I practicing Continuous Self-improvement?

Groundedness Cluster:
Are my spiritual beliefs intact?
Am I utilizing my support network?
How can I bounce back from this apparent adversity?

Trust Cluster:
Am I willing to feel *all* of my feelings?
How can I nurture myself in this process?
How can I let go of the need to control, and be comfortable even though things are ambiguous?
How can I let myself trust the process?

Proactive Purpose Cluster:
How can my life purpose statement help me sort out my options?
Am I using the eight principles of proactive creation?
What do I really want? (Dream big!)
Am I thinking in terms of "both and"?

Optimistic Confidence Cluster:
How is my self-confidence being enhanced now?
How can I build on past experiences to succeed in this transition?
In what ways am I being called upon to be flexible?
What is the positive side of this situation?
How can I make playing the game of life more fun?
What risks is my soul calling me to take?

Systems Thinking Cluster:
What is the meaning of this situation in the context of the macrocosm [bigger picture] of my life?
What systems or structures are changing now?
How can I make this simpler?
How can I learn to laugh at myself, or to develop my joy of living in the midst of this situation?
How can I better balance my life among my work, personal time, and personal relationships?

Most of these questions are open-ended, and require more than a simple "yes" or "no" answer. I have discovered through research, personal experience, and working with clients that one of the keys to our transformation is the kinds of questions we ask ourselves. If we challenge ourselves to think beyond our apparent situation (using inquiries such as those listed above), we can tap creative depths in ourselves of which we were unaware. New possibilities emerge, as do simple solutions to what seemed to be complex problems.

Exercise 4: Some Hypothetical Scenarios

Following are three vignettes involving transitional situations for which you have the chance to explain how each person would respond as a Coper, and as a Thriver. Let's see what you've learned. Some suggested answers are given following the vignettes.

1. Jean, age thirty-five, married John fifteen years ago. Jean moved directly from her parents' home to her husband's home, and they began a family right away. She didn't work in the early years, when the children were young, but now that they're beginning high school, she feels that she would like to go back to school and prepare for a career. Despite objections from John, she began classes two nights a week six months ago. John has done nothing but complain since then, and is not willing to help with the housework, shuttling the children to their various events, and meal preparation. "That's my wife's job," he claims. What would Jean's response to the situation be if she were a Coper? If she were a Thriver?

2. Bob, now age forty-seven, was laid off last week from his job as a systems analyst with ComputerWhiz with no prior notice. He has been with ComputerWhiz for eighteen years, in progressively more responsible positions. His first career was as a fifth-grade math teacher, after which he received his master's degree and began work at ComputerWhiz. He doesn't want to teach math anymore, and has no other job or career plans (other than a little savings toward his retirement) since he enjoyed his systems analyst job tremendously. However, he is an avid sport fisherman and has developed a series of rather unique lures that all of his friends rave about. What would Bob's response to the situation be if he were a Coper? If he were a Thriver?

3. Diane's husband, Dave, died in a freak car crash two years ago, leaving her with two young children, ages eight and ten, to care for. Diane was devastated by her loss, and has gained twenty-five pounds since it happened. Thankfully, she had training to work as a legal secretary, and she went to work soon after Dave's death, as a secretary to three trial attorneys in a medium-sized firm. Just last month, she discovered a lump in her breast, and it has been determined to be malignant. She will undergo surgery next week to remove the lump, and will need to take at least two months off work to recover. Her firm will not compensate her for more than two weeks' leave, although 80 percent of her medical expenses will be paid by her employer's medical benefits. How would Diane respond to the situation if she were a Coper? If she were a Thriver?

SUGGESTED ANSWERS TO THREE VIGNETTES
COPER RESPONSE

1. *Jean:* Say to herself, "That's how it is"; try to do it all; blame herself, turn anger inside; blame her husband; blow up; seek divorce; fall victim to substance abuse; become an alcoholic; withhold sex; make threats.
2. *Bob:* Draw unemployment; sue his company; fall victim to substance abuse; hold on to blame; get in one relationship after another.
3. *Diane:* Get depressed and wallow in self-pity; gain more

weight; get addicted to something; become bitter (which would work against her own recovery from over-stress); become more controlling of her family and co-workers.

THRIVER RESPONSE

1. *Jean:* Restructure her school schedule; discuss with husband plans to balance school and home; discuss all transitions with family and ask for support; invite husband to go to class with her; get a housekeeper; lower her housekeeping standards; get the kids more involved.
2. *Bob:* Use unemployment benefits to fund time for rethinking; combine his skills into a fishing lure job or business which also uses the computer; see the opportunity and take the time to enjoy life; take a "time out"; find a new job as a systems analyst.
3. *Diane:* Rely on her support network; get public assistance; seek spiritual guidance; look for opportunities to work part-time while recovering, maybe in her same job; use her sense of humor and positive attitude; journal about her experiences; get counseling to deal with her husband's death.

PART II: TEN TOOLS FOR SORTING OUT YOUR PURPOSE AND PRIORITIES

The following ten exercises will help you determine your purpose and priorities. They follow Diagram 8-1, "Life Purpose as an Organizing Principle." Actively using our purpose and priorities in making decisions, coupled with application of the Thriver traits, will greatly ease the transition process.

Exercise No. 1: Your Life's Purpose

A. Look back at the ten clues to your life's purpose in Chapter 8. Take a piece of paper and a pen and, after putting yourself into a non-judgmental mindset (as though you were brainstorming), spend at least five minutes on each clue, writing constantly and responding to them in the order presented.

B. As you ponder the answers to the questions in Part A (take any length of time you deem necessary), be open to any unusual ideas or thoughts which come to you in unexpected times. It is also critical not to draw too narrow and precise a definition around your life's purpose. You may only have a feeling, a visual symbol, or a sense about what it is. Eventually, it will materialize into a form you can verbalize. But meanwhile, follow the subtle urgings of your soul to pick up a new hobby, visit a part of town you have never been to, or to spend quiet time in nature. As countless people have discovered, when the time for action comes, you will know it. Before that, wait and be patient.

C. Finally, as your life purpose becomes clearer, you will want to articulate it clearly. Our life purpose statement has a permanent component, called the "essence," and a changeable aspect, called the "expression." It is usually stated like this:

> "My life's purpose is to [essence] through [expression]." For example:
> "My life's purpose is to <u>increase harmony in the world</u> through <u>working as a mediator, creating lovely surroundings in my home, spending time in nature, and facilitating a harmonious family life.</u>"

The essence is the hardest to identify for most people. It is the core of us, the primary motivator for our choices in life. It is often so obvious that we overlook it. The expression—which changes over time as we go through different periods in our lives—reflects the many ways in which the essence expresses itself in the various aspects of living. Ideally, our work, our home, our family life, our health, our hobbies, our finances, and every other dimension of our life experience will reflect our essential life purpose.

Write your life purpose, as you now understand it, below:

My life purpose is to _____

_____

through _____

_____.

Exercise 2: Assessing My Balance

A. Take about twenty or thirty minutes to respond to the following series of questions, which are designed to measure your balance, or lack thereof, in your life:

BALANCE SELF-ASSESSMENT

1. What are the primary strengths which you bring to a primary relationship?
2. How many times in the past week did you sit and do nothing, just enjoying life and/or nature?
3. What skills do you have that make (or would make) you a good parent?
4. What goals do you and your spouse and/or family have during the next five years?
5. What was the last book you read for pure relaxation and entertainment?
6. Name two times in the past week when you followed intuition.
7. What are two examples of your expressing your creativity during the past month?
8. When was the last time someone sought your advice or confided in you?
9. Name three goals you have for your career during the next ten years.
10. What was the last work-related book you read?
11. Name three recent accomplishments in your work of which you feel proud.
12. When did you last use your analytical skills to solve a problem?
13. What are your five strongest traits or skills that make you good at what you do?
14. What work-related goals must you achieve for your life to feel complete?
15. Which of your job duties give you the most satisfaction?
16. When was the last time you chose a work-related commitment over a conflicting family commitment?

As you look over the quiz, did you find it easier to answer questions 1 through 8 (which deal with your relationships, intuition, and creative self) or questions 9 through 16 (which deal with work and achievements)? The area which you find easiest to respond to is the area in which you have developed a level of skill and comfort. Your challenge will be to develop a similar level of expertise in dealing with the other areas of your life.

B. Think about the various roles you play in life. You are a parent, a student, an employee, a spouse, a church member, etc. On the diagram below, write your name in the center. Then, on each of the rays of the sun, write each role you are expected to fulfill, as well as any important goals which you want to begin spending more time doing (e.g., taking a night class, learning to play tennis, etc.)

Diagram B-1
ROLES ASSESSMENT

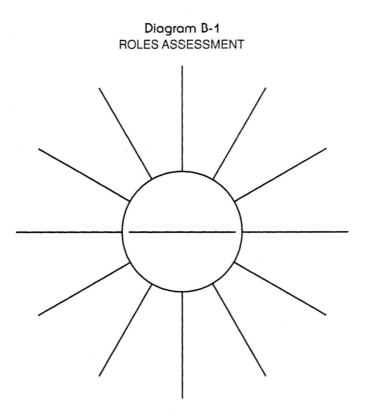

Now look carefully at the diagram. Do you feel over-whelmed? Are you trying to fulfill more roles than there is time in the day? If so, are there roles that others are expecting you to fulfill that you would like to discard? Put an X through those. Would you like to see a reordering of time so that time spent on some roles increases, while others decrease? Use an *I* for in-crease, and a *D* for decrease, noting those roles accordingly. Among those that have not been X'ed out, you will now need to set some priorities.

Exercise 3: Priorities versus Time/Energy Investment

A. We each have to do some juggling of time among various priorities. Looking at the following list of competing demands, order them first by how important they are to you, then by how much thought and time you spend on each.

THE PRIORITIES:
Work/Career
Spouse/Family
Close Friends
Hobbies and Other Activities
Personal Growth

IMPORTANCE OF EACH:

1.
2.
3.
4.
5.

TIME SPENT ON EACH:

1.
2.
3.
4.
5.

Now, look at your responses. Do you see any misalignment between the two sections? Are you spending the majority of your time on priorities which are less important to you than others? This in itself causes stress, resentment, and frustration. By increasing our awareness of the source of the stress, we can then begin to realign our time allotment to better balance our lives.

Diagram B-2

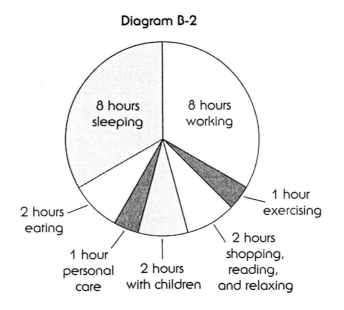

B. Diagram B-3 contains two circles. The left circle is a pie chart on which you may indicate the percentage of your twenty-four-hour day taken up by each of the roles you have listed above, as well as other routine activities such as sleeping, eating, showering, dressing, exercising, and the like. An example follows:

Now, put your *actual* time allocation on the left below, and your *ideal* or *desired* time allocation on the right:

Diagram B-3

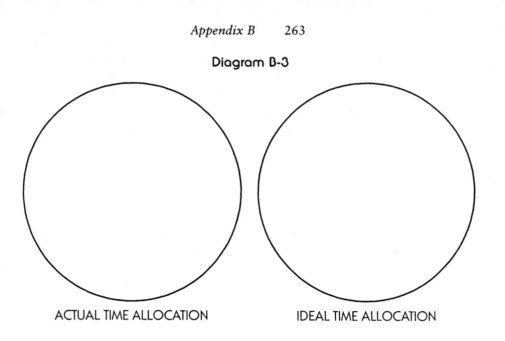

ACTUAL TIME ALLOCATION   IDEAL TIME ALLOCATION

What do you need to do to begin moving from your actual to your ideal time allocation? List three changes you would like to make below:

1.
2.
3.

Exercise 4: Transition Assessment

The following questions are designed to assess the transitions you are currently facing. Identifying them, particularly if you are in a time of complex transition, can be quite revealing as the source of your feelings of being overwhelmed and frustrated become clear.

1. In which of the following areas of your life are you currently in transition:
   _____job/career (promotion, change, layoff, etc.)
   _____medical or health issue (recent disease diagnosis, accident, etc.)

____relationship change (new relationship, marriage, divorce, breakup, new child, etc.)

____finances (pay increase, buying a home, bankruptcy, excess debt, etc.)

____geographic location (recent or impending move)

____spiritual crisis

____emotional issues (regardless of being in therapy)

____addiction treatment (recent intervention, recovery, or awareness)

2. In how many of the life areas in Part 1 have you faced transition during the past year?
3. At what phase is each of your current transitions:
   a) Discontentment
   b) Crisis/Decision
   c) Sorting-out Phase part 1: completion/feeling feelings
   d) Sorting-out Phase part 2: exploring options
   e) Vision
   f) Action
   g) Evaluation
4. What has been your style or pattern in facing past transitions?
5. How do you want that to be different in confronting the transitions you now face?
6. What gifts or opportunities can you already see in your current transitions?
7. What disowned and/or shadow parts of yourself are you becoming more aware of in these transitions?
8. What is the highest and best possible outcome you can imagine for these transitions?

Exercise 5: Developing a Vision

Drawing on question 8 from the previous exercise, write out a vision statement for your desired resolution of each transition. Remember the characteristics of an effective vision statement listed in Chapter 8: It is written in the present tense, open-ended, and sufficiently specific so that you can recognize it when you see it; it stretches your rational mind's beliefs about what is possible for you; and it focuses on the feelings you will experience as the transition resolves itself.

Exercise 6: Current Objectives/Subgoals

Objectives follow from the formulation of a clear vision. They are the more manageable pieces of our vision. Realizing our dreams relies on the following sequence:

PURPOSE ——> VISION/GOAL ——> OBJECTIVES/SUBGOALS ——>
ACTION PLANS

On which competing priorities and visions will you focus most of your attention on in the coming months? List them below:

MY CURRENT OBJECTIVES

1.
2.
3.
4.
5.

You should plan to reassess these objectives at the conclusion of the time period to which they apply, and establish new objectives (if necessary) at that time.

Exercise 7: Action Plans

The next step in realizing your vision is to brainstorm one or more possible action plans through which it could manifest itself. If your vision centers around a new job, your action plan may include a meeting with one or more managers in your company concerning upcoming openings, updating your résumé, conducting a job search through networking interviews or responding to advertised openings. If your vision relates to healing past hurts, your action plan may include designing and executing appropriate rituals to complete the grieving process, joining a grief-support group, seeking counseling, or learning ways to form new relationships that are more satisfying.

For each of your current objectives, visions, or important

goals, formulate an action plan which could serve as a series of steps which will begin moving you toward your desired result. The plans should not be viewed as the *only* way it could happen, so as to lock you in.

Exercise 8: Daily Planning

As you begin your day, spend at least fifteen minutes in silence, reflecting on nature and/or upon your inner being. You may use this time for your chosen meditation practice, by which you connect with the God of your understanding. Or you may prefer to do as we discussed in Chapter 7, just staring out the window and gently pushing all thoughts and concerns to one side for that fifteen-minute period.

Then, to prevent your vision from becoming merely a paper and pencil exercise, you must have a routine which carries it throughout each day. One of the best ways to do this is to set, each morning, *one goal in each of the three key life areas: work, family/personal relationships, and self.* Put these three goals at the top of your day's pocket or desk calendar. This ensures two things: (a) that you will set out to accomplish at least one important goal in each of the key life areas during your day, and (b) that you will avoid setting goals only in the work aspect of your life rather than for yourself or your personal relationships. While one goal in each area per day may sound like a minimal accomplishment, the cumulative effect of over 300 goals in one year's time is striking.

Exercise 9: Weekly Evaluation and Check-In

Just as taking action during a transition is meaningless without subsequent evaluation to see whether it is moving us toward our vision, so too is our daily and other short-term planning. We must set aside a designated block of time each week to evaluate our previous week's progress and to set our vision for the following week. Many Thrivers find that Sunday is the ideal time to do this "saw-sharpening" activity, as Stephen Covey and Linda and Richard Eyre call it. Whether you use a tool such as Jack Boland's Master Mind Journal, a Daytimer,

Dayrunner, Franklin planner, or another device, it should allow you to easily review your previous seven days and evaluate the results of your "experiments." Ask yourself the following questions as you do so:

1. How many of my daily goals did I achieve?
2. For those I didn't achieve, is there a theme or pattern? A particular issue or activity I seem to be avoiding? This is not to be used as a process of self-criticism, but to develop enhanced self-awareness so that we can look deeper within ourselves and discover what deep-seated issues are blocking us. If I am achieving all of my work goals and none of my relationship goals, do I need additional assistance to help me do so?
3. Did I take at least one action each day that furthered my life's purpose?
4. [If you are pursuing a longer-term vision or goal]: Did I take at least one action each day that furthered this important vision/goal?
5. What can I learn from last week's actions and results that will help next week go more smoothly?
6. What feelings do I want to create through my visioning and goal-setting for next week?

Exercise 10: Repetition

Finally, any time you begin to feel unclear about your direction, become confused by changes in circumstances, or sense that you are losing your focus, repeat any or all of the above exercises to reorient yourself. They should be done at least once a year in any event, as part of an annual "life-cleaning." But they are available for use at any time along your path toward becoming a Thriver.

INDEX

ABOUT THE AUTHOR

MARCIA PERKINS-REED has studied emerging trends in the workplace and personal lifestyles for the past seventeen years. A respected consultant, seminar leader, and lecturer, she is the author of several books, including *When 9 to 5 Isn't Enough: A Guide to Finding Fulfillment at Work*. She has become a recognized expert on the transition process, and her articles are regularly published in national magazines. Her interest in transition and personal growth was developed during her undergraduate studies in psychology. She later became an attorney, selling her practice after four years to pursue writing and speaking on a full-time basis. Over 23,000 individuals have been personally affected by her work.

She is currently CEO of Marcia Perkins-Reed and Associates, a ten-year-old career- and business-consulting firm. She is frequently featured as a keynote speaker and seminar presenter. She lives with her husband in Portland, Oregon.